Germany:

A New History

Germany:

A New History

Hagen Schulze

Translated by
Deborah Lucas Schneider

Harvard   Cambridge, Massachusetts
University   London, England
Press   1998

Originally published as Hagen Schulze, *Kleine Deutsche Geschichte,*
© C. H. Beck'sche Verlagsbuchhandlung, München 1996.
Illustrations from the German Museum of History. Publication
of this work has been subsidized by Inter Nationes, Bonn.

Library of Congress Cataloging-in-Publication Data

Schulze, Hagen.

[Kleine deutsche Geschichte.   English]

Germany : a new history / Hagen Schultze ;

translated by Deborah Lucas Schneider.

p.   cm.

Includes bibliographical references and index.

ISBN 0-674-80688-3

1. Germany—History.   I. Schneider, Deborah Lucas.

II. Title. DD89.S39613   1998

943—dc21   98-23629

Contents

Preface

Earlier generations of Germans were in no doubt about what their history was. It began with Hermann of the Cherusci, who defeated the legions of Quinctilius Varus in battle in the Teutoburg Forest in the year A.D. 9 and was unquestionably a hero. The sword at the monument to him near Detmold still bears an inscription in gold letters: "Germany's unity—my strength, my strength—Germany's might." From Hermann and his battle German history swept in a great, clearly defined arc down to their day. There was Theoderic, king of the Goths, celebrated in German sagas and legends as "Dietrich of Bern"; then came Charlemagne—*Karl der Große*—who became Roman emperor and transformed the Romans' empire into a German one. There followed the Staufen emperor Frederick Barbarossa and his grandson Frederick II, who, in a mysterious amalgamation, slumber in the Kyffhäuser, the magic mountain, awaiting the day when they will return to rescue Germany in its hour of greatest need.

Next came Martin Luther, the "German nightingale," and Emperor Charles V, on whose dominions the sun never set; Frederick the Great and Maria Theresa, who battled one another when disunity among the German tribes reached its tragic climax; Baron vom Stein and Blücher, nicknamed "Marshal Forward," and finally Bismarck, the "Iron Chancellor," who forged the new German *Reich,* a direct descendant of the Holy Roman Empire of the German Nation. It made for an imposing gallery of ancestral portraits, in which Germans took pride.

But then came what the historian Friedrich Meinecke called the "German catastrophe," Hitler's *Reich* and the Second World War, which left the German nation state shamed, occupied, and divided. The Swiss historian Jacob Burckhardt had earlier referred tartly to German historians' tendency to "paint their country's history in the colors of victory"; these colors had now cracked and peeled, simultaneously rupturing the context in which German history had been interpreted. The shining legend of the unbroken ascent of Germany from empire to empire was replaced by the black legend of evil and its ruinous divergent path *(Sonderweg),* in which the only true Germany consisted of the Third Reich and its crimes, except when some declared it was pointless to write national history at all or mourned the "loss of history" with Alfred Heuss.

For a time the inhabitants of West Germany were quite content to repress all thoughts of their history and simply enjoy the present, with its high rates of industrial growth and increasing mass prosperity; they observed with mild astonishment the rest of the world, where the principle of national identity still held unbroken sway and offered daily proof of its political effectiveness. Although West Germans occupied an extremely exposed position in world affairs, they seemed to express only one wish in all their political decisions—a desire to be left alone and not required to make any decisions. In the German Democratic Republic, on the other hand, people were served up their history by the politburo of the Communist party; it was dictated by party ideologists, adapted to fit changing political circumstances, and not open to discussion.

However, the state of comfortable domestic prosperity and blessed lack of responsibility for foreign affairs vanished overnight when the Wall came down and a new German nation state came into being, one whose mere existence has changed Europe. This has created a need for Germany to explain, to both its own citizens and the rest of the world, what kind of country it sees itself as being. If Germany is to have a future in the center of Europe, we must know the past on which the German present rests. One can never begin anew but only pick up the threads of the past and continue. People who believe they have undertaken something completely new in fact do not really know what they are doing.

In order to answer the "German question" for Germans themselves, for their neighbors in Europe, and for the rest of the world, we must explain what Germany is, and what it can and should be. This in turn requires a retelling of German history. And since not everyone has the time or patience to plough through volumes of scholarly treatises, it is my aim here to present this history in brief summary, with an eye to its most essential aspects.

Even a short survey of German history cannot be accomplished without assistance from many quarters. Ina Ulrike Paul, Uwe Puschner, and my wife, Ingrid, read the manuscript with care and made corrections. The first chapter benefitted from a critical reading by Joachim Ehlers, and Detlef Felken edited the book with great commitment and a wealth of knowledge. To Christoph Stölzl, director of the German Museum of History in Berlin, I owe not only the illustrations but the idea and encouragement to write this book. My thanks go to all of them.

Germany:

A New History

1

The Roman Empire and

German Lands (to 1400)

The origins of German history lie not in the primeval forests of the north but in Rome, the unique city-state that at its height ruled the entire Mediterranean basin and all of Europe to the Rhine, the Danube, and the *limes,* the wall at the empire's northern boundary. Roman civilization, while taking on many local forms, acted as a unifying force; for the people of ancient times it provided a world with clearly defined outlines under an ecumenical roof. There was no higher status than being a Roman citizen; the apostle Paul was just as proud of it as Hermann, tribal chief of the Cherusci, despite their differences with Rome. The poet Virgil, who in the *Aeneid* conceived and related the legend of how the Roman state was founded, declared that it was Rome's task to rule the world and to bring law

The Battle in the Teutoburg Forest
(print, ca. 1903)

In the year A.D. 9 a Roman army suffered a devastating defeat against allied German tribes under the leadership of Arminius, prince of the Cherusci. The Battle in the Teutoburg Forest—which in reality probably took place near Osnabrück—has been considered a historical turning point ever since. After it the Romans did in fact give up the attempt to extend their rule to the regions east of the Rhine. In the view of nineteenth-century German nationalists, this battle liberated German tribes from Rome and marks the beginning of German history. Seen in this light, Hermann, as Arminius came to be called, was the first hero of German liberation. In the view of other observers—and not only western Europeans—this event represents Roman failure to extend its civilization to central Europe; it was the starting point for a separate development of German culture and politics that extends down to the present day. In fact nothing that could accurately be called "German" history existed until many centuries later.

and civilization in times of peace, sparing the conquered and punishing the rebellious.

In modern times the *Imperium Romanum* is the "distant mirror" (in Barbara Tuchman's phrase) in which all the nations of Europe, and certainly Germany, have continued to recognize their own reflection up to the present day. The foundations of national statehood and law, the customs of urban life, our languages and ways of thinking, our alphabet and books, our architecture—in short, the whole basis of the modern world in the West is unimaginable without the contributions of Roman civilization and the two older civilizations interwoven with it, those of Greece and the Hellenistic Orient.

But while "eternal Rome" endured, it also experienced great changes. In the course of the fourth century A.D. two profound upheavals occurred. During the reign of Constantine the Great (306–337), an oriental religion based on belief in human redemption—Christianity—was adopted as the official state creed. And during this same epoch the empire, which had grown too vast to be ruled from one center, split into two parts, a Latin-speaking western empire based in Rome, and a Greek-speaking eastern empire ruled from Byzantium. The break-up of the empire affected the Christian Church as well: eastern orthodoxy split off from the Latin Christianity of the west, adding a religious dimension to the political partition of Europe. This was the starting point of the long-lasting political, religious, and ideological division of the Western world. Two distinctly different civilizations arose on European soil, experiencing friction in their repeated contacts without one ever succeeding in permanently absorbing the other: Rome and Byzantium, Roman Catholicism and the Eastern Orthodox Church, the liberal West and the Slavophile East, ultimately the culture of democracy and human rights versus the Bolshevist system of the Soviet Union. Only now, before our very eyes, it appears, has this millennial gap dividing Europe begun to close, a fact we may have failed fully to grasp as yet.

While Byzantium continued to flourish in the east for fully a thou-

Charlemagne
(stained glass window of Strasbourg Cathedral, ca. 1180)

Seated on a gold throne encrusted with jewels, the Emperor Charlemagne is shown as an idealized Christian ruler with a scepter and the imperial orb; his crowned head is surrounded by a saintly halo. In 1165 Emperor Frederick Barbarossa arranged for Charlemagne, whom he regarded as his ancestor, to be canonized, in order to secure the throne for his family and emphasize the exalted position of the emperor compared to that of the pope. It was an era in which kings throughout Europe emerged as national saints, but while the canonized founder kings of Hungary, Bohemia, Norway, and other countries became highly effective symbols of national unity, the cult of Charlemagne remained limited to the Rhineland. In addition, the French royal family disputed the right of the Holy Roman Empire to claim Charlemagne's traditions and preeminence in the Christian world for itself.

sand years, losing power gradually and falling only with the capture of Constantinople by the Turks in 1453, the western Roman Empire did not survive for long. It was swamped by ever more frequent waves of invading barbarians from the foggy and amorphous North, in flight from the harsh climate and the consequences of overpopulation, and other migrating peoples. These Nordic barbarians, who wished to settle within the Roman Empire and participate in its defense, were known in Rome as "Germans," a name Caesar had borrowed from the Gauls. The Gauls used this term for the savage peoples who tried to penetrate Gaul from across the Rhine, and from the name of these tribes Caesar also derived the term for the region beyond the Rhine and the Danube: Germania. The word "German" was not much more than a designation of origin for someone who came from the little-known regions east of the Rhine; the degree of ethnic and linguistic homogeneity prevailing among these peoples is still a matter of debate among scholars.

In any case the hordes sweeping down from the north were such fierce warriors that they made ideal candidates for military employment. Soon the majority of the emperors' Praetorian guards were recruited from German troops, and Germanic peoples were granted permission to settle within the empire in territories adjacent to the borders and to take on Roman citizenship. Protection of this sort could easily become a threat when the objects to be protected—the emperor, his institutions, and the empire—were themselves weak. As the empire grew dependent on the barbarian military experts, German commanders and military units decided who was to be emperor with increasing frequency, until finally Odoacer, a commander of German mercenaries, deposed the last western Roman emperor, Romulus Augustulus, in 476 and had himself proclaimed king by the army.

Although it represented another decline, this event was not the end of the Roman Empire but only the beginning of a further transformation. The Germanic peoples of the migratory era—Goths and Lombards in Italy, West Goths in Spain and southern France, Anglo-Saxons in Britain, Burgundians and Franks in Gaul—sought to become Romans themselves by taking up residence in the empty shells of the crumbling empire and adapting the Roman and Near Eastern civilization of late antiquity, which was enormously complex and refined, to their simpler cultures. They took over the traditional Roman administration, although in simplified form; they reshaped the Germanic kingdoms into Roman monarchies; and Roman law served as a model as they transformed Germanic traditions into fixed written legal codes. Though the title of Roman emperor may have disappeared in the west, none of the Germanic kings had any doubt that the Roman Empire still existed.

While the city on the banks of the Tiber decayed and its population level dropped rapidly, Rome lived on in yet another sense. As urban life died out and cattle grazed on the Forum, the Bishop of Rome in his capacity as successor to the Apostle Peter acquired the status of Pope, thereby becoming head of the western church. Not only did Rome develop into the spiritual center of Catholic Christendom, to which the Germanic tribes gradually converted, but in certain respects the church also absorbed the structure of the empire, and the old imperial administration lived on in the church hierarchy. The chasubles present-day Catholic priests wear to celebrate the Mass are derived from the uniforms of Roman officials, and the adoption of Latin as the language of the church, politics, and literature assured that western Europe remained culturally unified; in its monasteries, the manuscripts over which monks sat bowed still included the works of Cicero and Virgil. The Roman Empire continued to exist— as an idea and in scaled-down institutions, but above all in the church triumphant.

The twin ideas of empire and church proved so long-lived that more than three hundred years after the overthrow of Romulus Augustulus a new emperor appeared in the city of Rome: Charles, King of the Franks, later called "the Great," or (in the French form that has passed into English) Charlemagne. Having made himself the most powerful ruler in western Europe by his victories over the Saxons and the Lombards, he wished to cement his power through a lasting alliance with the Roman pope. He confirmed the donation his father, Pépin III, had made to the pope, which laid the territorial foundations of the later Papal States, and Pope Leo III repaid the favor

Emperor Otto III on His Throne
(Reichenau Gospels, late tenth century)

A beautiful scene from an illuminated gospel, depicting the transfer of rule from the Roman emperors of antiquity to Charlemagne and his East Frankish successor. Otto III is shown seated on the imperial throne, holding the insignia; flanking him, two dukes represent the empire, and two bishops the church. In symbolism borrowed from classical art, the four women depicted approaching the emperor to pay homage represent the lands he rules: Roma, Gallia, Germania, and Sclavinia (the Slavic lands).

on Christmas Day, in the year 800, by crowning Charles emperor at St. Peter's Basilica in Rome. The porphyry slab on which he knelt is still on view in St. Peter's today. Einhard of Fulda, who chronicled Charlemagne's reign, reports that his king was sunk in prayer and made emperor against his will, so to speak, as Pope Leo crept up be-

hind him and placed the crown on his head before he knew what was happening. Charles was well aware that the step would inevitably lead to conflict with the only legitimate emperor in Christendom, the one in Byzantium. Nonetheless, he took up the succession of Caesar and Constantine, calling himself *augustus imperator,* and henceforth his seal bore the motto *Renovatio Imperii Romani,* "renewal of the Roman Empire." The claim was justified: From that date, Roman emperors would rule almost uninterruptedly for another thousand years. The last in the line, Franz II of the house of Hapsburg, renounced the title and crown in 1806, a step largely ignored by the public.

Comparisons between the ancient Roman Empire and that of

Charlemagne were not far-fetched, insofar as Charles had united almost all the Germanic kingdoms and duchies of Europe under his rule, except for Scandinavia and Britain. His realm stretched from the Eider River near the present-day German-Danish border to the Tiber, from the Elbe to the Ebro in northeastern Spain, and from the English Channel to Lake Balaton. Charlemagne introduced reforms in political and ecclesiastical administration, transportation, the reckoning of the calendar, art and literature, and—as the foundation for all the rest—the spoken and written language, taking up surviving elements of Roman civilization whenever possible. He invited an Anglo-Saxon, Alcuin of York, to serve as his chief adviser on cultural matters, and he also consulted scholars from Italy and Spain. The Carolingian Renaissance found sources of inspiration throughout Europe.

All these efforts were placed in the service of creating an *aurea Roma iterum renovata,* a renewed "golden Rome." We owe our ability to read the classical Latin authors today largely to the enthusiasm and diligence of Carolingian scribes, who also wrote poetry themselves. Their verses in classical meters, some of them excellent, fill four large volumes of the *Monumenta Germaniae Historica,* the great collection of medieval sources.

In western France, Gaul, and Italy, some parts of the old Roman administration continued to function; the German regions east of the Rhine had their own rudimentary administrative network, since they were organized not only as *Gaue* (tribal districts) but also as parishes, dioceses, religious communities such as monasteries, and manors, both church-owned and secular. Charlemagne established administrative districts called *ducati* (duchies), each headed by a *dux,* a title derived from the administrative reform of Emperor Constantine the Great. The *dux* was no longer a tribal chieftain but a high official recruited from the Frankish aristocracy. Charlemagne dispatched envoys, known as *missi dominici,* to supervise the empire's administration; the imperial Frankish church, whose bishops he appointed, provided further administrative links and oversight.

Despite all these efforts, his empire could not last. Even if Charlemagne's heirs had not fallen out among themselves, how was an empire to be held together when instructions sent to Rome by the emperor in Aachen, on the north Rhine, took two months to reach their destination? Local and regional authorities could—and indeed had to—act as they saw fit most of the time. Eventually, Charlemagne's three grandsons divided the empire among themselves, Louis taking the eastern and Charles the western part, while Lothar took the land in the middle. This region, called *Lotharingien* after its king, stretched from the mouth of the Rhine all the way to Italy. When Lothar's line died out in 870, Louis added it to his eastern domains.

The ensuing family dispute divided the continent of Europe down the middle for the next twelve hundred years. As the brothers' western and eastern kingdoms drifted apart, they evolved into France and Germany; both countries inherited the legacy of Rome and Charlemagne, and both claimed the territory of the former middle kingdom, called Lorraine by the French and Lothringen by the Germans.

In school we were taught that this division marked the beginning of German history. And soon after came Henry, Duke of Saxony, who was out trying to catch birds one day, according to a hearty nineteenth-century folk ballad, when emissaries of an unnamed assembly burst upon him shouting, "Long live Emperor Henry! Long live the bright star of Saxony!" Henry I (ruled 919–936), elected by the Saxons and Franks, went down in history as founder of the Saxon or Ottonian dynasty, but he ruled as king, not emperor. After compromises and threats of military force, the Swabians and Bavarians accepted his rule; he brought the Lotharingians, Bohemians, and Slavs of the Elbe region under his sway and was recognized as king of all this territory by the West Franks of the Carolingian era.

The unanimous election of Henry's son Otto (ruled 936–973) as his successor contributed to the permanence of the East Frankish realm; it would not be fought over and partitioned by quarreling heirs, as Charlemagne's empire had been earlier. In 955 Otto I defeated the Hungarians at Lechfeld and acquired the epithet "the Great." Seven years later he had himself crowned Roman emperor by Pope John XII in Rome and once more placed the city under imperial protection. Otto persuaded Byzantium to recognize him as emperor and arranged for the marriage of his son and heir, the future Otto II (ruled 961–983), to a Byzantine princess. From then on the two titles of king and Roman emperor were almost always held jointly. Following the tradition of Charlemagne, Otto the Great's grandson, Otto III

The Pope, the Emperor, and Rome
(fresco in the Church of the Four Crowned Saints, Rome, ca. 1250)

Rome was the center of western Christendom, from which both the emperor and the pope derived their power. But whereas the emperor could enforce his claims with the sword, the pope could only appeal to ancient rights, and thus in the Middle Ages it was not uncommon for the papacy to bolster such claims when the pope was sure his cause was just. This is the case in the "Gift of Constantine," a document in which Emperor Constantine the Great transferred supreme authority over Rome and the western Roman Empire to the pope. This provided the crucial legal basis for the pope's claims to supremacy over the emperor, depicted here in a fresco from the thirteenth century. The emperor is shown leading the pope's horse by the reins, a gesture of submission. Not until the fifteenth century did humanist scholars prove what emperors had been claiming since the reign of Otto III, namely, that the "Gift of Constantine" was a forgery.

(ruled 983–1002), aspired to renew the Roman Empire; he died near Rome at the age of twenty-one and was buried in Aachen.

The century of the Salian emperors (1024–1125) is known to us today mainly as the period in which the dramatic struggle between the emperors and the papacy had its origins. Until the early eleventh century, the kings and emperors of Europe had exercised the right to fill high church offices with men of their own choosing. But as a reform movement spread from the Benedictine Abbey of Cluny in Burgundy during the tenth century, the view prevailed among ecclesiastical leaders that it was the task of the church to mediate between God and fallible human rulers. They concluded from this that a higher divine law gave the church ascendancy over secular government; accordingly, they demanded the elimination of all secular influences on the appointment of church officials.

On the other hand, since the reign of Otto the Great the church had become an important institution for maintaining and controlling

the empire, and both the Ottonian and Salian emperors had exerted a strong influence on the choice of popes and the way in which they governed the Papal States. For these reasons open conflict broke out between pope and emperor beginning in 1075. Pope Gregory VII (1073–1085) issued a formal proclamation forbidding King Henry IV to invest bishops and abbots, to which the king responded by openly flouting its demands and deposing Gregory.

The controversy escalated; its repercussions carried far beyond the original participants and continued after their deaths, for at bottom it was a dispute about the fundamental order of the world, the relationship in which spiritual and secular authority, *sacerdotium* and *regnum*, ought to stand to one another. After a long struggle that seesawed back and forth and ultimately left both the emperor and the pope defeated, church and state drew apart. This was a decisive step for the emergence of the modern nation state and the development of two principles fundamental to political culture in modern Europe: freedom of religion without secular control, and political freedom without domination by the church.

The summit and decline of German emperors' power in the Middle Ages are connected, in the currently accepted view, with the Hohenstaufen dynasty (1152–1254). Frederick I (1152–1190), whose reddish-blond beard led his Italian contemporaries to nickname him "Barbarossa," epitomized the German medieval emperor. Beloved by his people, he lived on in the memory of later times as a heroic figure. The splendor of his court days, his marriage to Beatrice of Burgundy, the ups and downs of his Italian campaigns, his triumph over the rebel leader Henry the Lion, and finally the unusual circumstances of his death in Asia Minor during the Third Crusade, surrounded with an aura of mystery—all this offered fertile ground for the growth of myths. No other emperor has so gripped the imagination of later generations, down to the nineteenth-century romantic poet Friedrich Rückert, who retold in verse the legend that the emperor was not dead but only asleep inside his magic mountain, the Kyffhäuser, until the time should come for his return:

> Er hat hinabgenommen
> Des Reiches Herrlichkeit,
> Und wird einst wiederkommen
> Mit ihr zu seiner Zeit.
>
> He took empire's fame and power
> Down with him to the deep,
> And now they both await the hour
> To waken from their sleep.

Barbarossa became a symbol, in the early nineteenth century, of the German people's longing for a nation, although their dream of the fulfillment of German destiny in the form of a renewed empire had more to do with romantic imaginings than the actual Hohenstaufens. The original legend of the emperor in the mountain concerned not Barbarossa but his grandson, the oddly un-Germanic Hohenstaufen Frederick II (1212–1250), who inherited the Norman kingdom of Sicily from his mother, Constance, and developed a system of government there based on combined Roman, Byzantine, Norman, and Arabic foundations. Frederick II's reign represented a grandiose attempt, quite out of keeping with the spirit of the times, to design a state from top to bottom according to rational principles, conceived by a single mind as if on a drawing board: the state as a work of art.

Frederick, whose enormous abilities and versatility make him appear the precursor of the great Renaissance princes, aspired to be a new Constantine and usher in a golden reign of peace. He delighted and appalled his contemporaries; his inevitable opposition to the papacy led to power struggles and a propaganda war the likes of which had never been seen before in Christendom. The favorable propaganda described him in messianic terms as the ultimate emperor, the culmination of world history, while the pro-papal reaction portrayed him as the beast of the Apocalypse, the Antichrist. After his death in 1250, pious legend relegated him to Aetna, the hellish, fire-spewing volcano; but late medieval yearnings for the coming of the prince of peace—the emperor who would reign at the end of time—transported Frederick II, the *stupor mundi,* to the Kyffhäuser, where over the centuries he became fused with the figure of Barbarossa.

The glory of the Hohenstaufen empire died out with Frederick II, and his design for a rational empire came to naught. The pope gave the fief of Sicily to Charles of Anjou, brother of the French king. Frederick's son, Conrad IV (1237–1254), died four years later in Italy without being crowned as emperor, and his son, Conradin (1252–1268), who led a campaign in Italy to reclaim his Sicilian inheritance, was defeated and captured by Charles at Tagliacozzo and executed in Naples when only sixteen years old.

Emperor Frederick Barbarossa in the Kyffhäuser
(copper engraving after a drawing by Wilhelm von Kaulbach, 1841)

In German history, the myth of the hero who will come to the rescue of his country in time of need is concentrated in the figure of the Staufen emperor Frederick Barbarossa. In the original legend the emperor asleep inside the magic mountain was Frederick II, but over the course of time Barbarossa's popularity as a folk hero and his mysterious death far away in the Holy Land led to his being substituted for his grandson. Impassioned champions of German nationalism in the nineteenth century saw him as a symbol of the sleeping nation, and thus it was only logical that propagandists for the German Empire of 1871 would see a parallel between Barbarossa and "Barbablanca," the white-bearded Emperor William I, and between the medieval empire of the Hohenstaufens and that of the Prussian Hohenzollerns.

Thus began the interregnum (1254–1273), "the dreadful days of no emperor," which saw a rapid weakening of central authority in the empire, until the election of Rudolf of Hapsburg (1273–1291) brought about a partial reconsolidation of royal power. There followed an epoch in which political and administrative links within the empire grew looser, although the continued existence of the empire was never seriously threatened. The period is characterized by relatively open elections for king that brought a whole range of rulers from the houses of Hapsburg, Nassau, Wittelsbach, and Luxembourg to the German throne in mixed succession; beginning with Henry VII of Luxembourg (1308–1313), they also assumed the title of emperor.

The period just covered is usually presented in textbooks as the epoch of the medieval German empire. We should pause here, however, and ask how German these kings and emperors, from Henry I and Otto the Great on, actually were. The word "Germany" would come to exist only at a much later date: It was not coined until the fifteenth century and did not come into general use for another hundred years or so after that. For many centuries the people living east of the Rhine had no inkling that they were Germans; in contrast with the Franks or Anglo-Saxons, for example, a single "German people" did not exist. Instead, after the Carolingian empire disintegrated during the ninth century, the area east of the Rhine became a collection of duchies, inhabited by different groups—Thuringians, Bavarians, Alemanni, Saxons—who did not correspond at all to the various tribes of the migratory era. These "peoples" were not real ethnic groups but products of the administrative divisions of Charlemagne's empire.

Political cohesion east of the Rhine—a territory that had been designated as Germania from Roman times—was provided not by "German tribes" but by an aristocracy of Frankish origins. It was this aristocratic class that accepted the rule of Charlemagne's grandson Louis after 833 in the eastern sector of the Frankish empire; Louis thus became *rex Germaniae,* king of the lands east of the Rhine, a far cry from

Ludwig der Deutsche (Louis the German), as nationalistically-minded historians began calling him in the nineteenth century. The realm created east of the Rhine would continue to consider itself a Frankish empire until well into the eleventh century; that is, the East Franks traced their origins back through the Carolingians and Merovingians to Rome and Troy, just as the West Franks did in their part of Charlemagne's former empire.

The kings of the East Franks avoided adding any narrower ethnic label to their royal title, calling themselves simply *rex* and not *rex Francorum,* for example, much less *rex Teutonicorum,* "king of the Germans." After Henry I attained the crown for the Saxon dynasty in 919, the Saxons replaced the Franks as the most prominent group in the region. The monk Widukind of Corvey (ca. 925–973), who wrote a history of the Saxons devoted mainly to the reign of Otto I, understood the empire to be *omnis Francia Saxoniaque,* or all of the Franks' and Saxons' land; he did not know of any place called "Germany."

After Pope John XII crowned Otto I emperor in 962, the Ottonian-Saxon dynasty was elevated to new status. As perpetuators of the traditions of Charlemagne and the Roman Empire, they possessed the highest legitimation known to the Middle Ages for secular affairs. Saint Augustine had established the importance of the Roman Empire in world history, which was at the same time the history of humankind's progression toward salvation: it was the last of the great monarchies on earth. According to Augustine, the Roman Empire was a universal power, derived directly from God for the purpose of earthly rule; this is why, from 1157 on, imperial decrees referred to the "Holy Roman Empire." Such a conception opened up perspectives far beyond the kingship of the East Franks or, later, of Germany; the unifying idea of the empire was therefore Roman, not German.

The word *deutsch* comes from *thiutisk* or the Latin *theodiscus,* a term meaning simply "vernacular." It thus referred not to one particular language but to any language spoken by the people distinct from the learned Latin of the church, as well as from the Romance and

Slavic languages; *theodiscus* included Alemannish, for example, or Old Saxon, Bavarian, or East Frankish. *Thiutisk* or *theodiscus* appears in the historical sources only rarely. *Theodiscus* crops up for the first time in a Carolingian bishop's report to the pope on a synod held in 786 in Mercia, in Britain. On this occasion the motions adopted by the synod were read aloud "both in Latin and the vernacular *(theodisce)* . . . which all could understand"—in this particular instance Old English.

Significant works of literature were written in some of these popular tongues; the language known today as Old High German developed chiefly from the dialect spoken along the Rhine, which was the language of the Carolingian court. It disappeared in the course of the tenth century, however, when power in Germania had passed to the Ottonian dynasty of Saxony. The poetry of the High Middle Ages, beginning in about 1150, was composed in various forms of Middle High German based on different regional dialects; the variant from the area of Limburg near the Rhine and Alemannish from the south west were particularly successful. A "German" language, however, in the sense of a common tongue understood by everyone in the various regions east of the Rhine, did not exist at all. For a long time, if a Saxon wanted to converse with one of the *Alemanni* and could not speak Latin, he would have to fall back on West Frankish, the *lingua franca* of western and middle Europe, out of which modern French later developed.

The Middle High German variant *diutsch* turns up in about 1080 in the *Annolied,* a text containing a reference to *diutsche lant,* "German lands" in the plural: not a single land but the lands of the Swabians, Bavarians, Saxons, and Franks, regions linked by the fact that similar vernacular languages were spoken there. *Deutsch* was a purely linguistic term and remained so for a long time to come.

Teutonicus, the Latin translation used from the middle of the ninth century onward, is also misleading. There was in fact no connection between the spoken tongues and the Germanic Teutons, who suffered a devastating defeat at Aquae Sextiae in 102 B.C. at the hands of

Marius and disappeared from history thereafter. The memory of the fear inspired by the first attacks of the Germanic tribes lived on in northern Italy, however, and Italians continued to refer to the people who came from Germania and claimed that the title of Roman emperor had passed to one of them as "Teutons." The term was condescending, with more than a hint of mockery at their crude and barbaric appearance. In 1076 the term took on a political connotation as well when, at the height of the investiture controversy, Pope Gregory VII referred to the future emperor Henry IV as a *rex Teutonicorum*. The pontiff meant to imply by this that the emperor ought to be stripped of his preeminent rank in the history of salvation and reduced to the status of an ordinary Christian monarch, like the kings of the Hungarians or the Danes.

Originally, then, the word *teutonicus* had unfriendly undertones; the Italians, French, and English used it when they wished to express derision and disdain for the people of Germania and their rulers, as John of Salisbury, the Bishop of Chartres, did in 1160 when annoyed by Barbarossa's attempt to have a candidate for pope elected without the support of the English and French: "Who made the Germans judges over nations? Who gave these rough and violent people the authority to set a prince of their own choosing over the heads of the earth's children?"

The empire continued to be called "Roman"—from 1157 on, the "Holy Roman Empire"—but *thiutisk* and *teutonicus* gradually came into use as well, since the conglomeration of tribes known as the East Franks, ruled by the "Roman" emperor in his capacity as East Frankish king, needed a separate name of its own. The term "Franks" had established itself among their neighbors to the west; the peoples to the east desired to distinguish themselves not only from this group but also from the Italians and the Curia in Rome. Thus, over the course of the eleventh and twelfth centuries the terms *regnum* ("kingdom") and *teutonicum* gradually came to be linked together. Still, the notion of a "German nation" remained murky since, following the decline of the

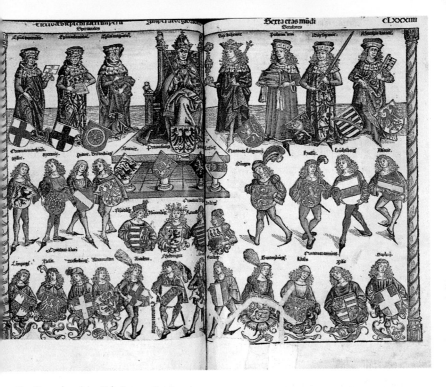

The Hierarchy of the Holy Roman Empire
(Hartmann Schedel, *Weltchronik*, "Chronicle of the World," Nuremberg, 1493)
The Empire is depicted as a human body: the Emperor is the head, flanked by the seven prince electors, while the estates, each represented by four figures, form the limbs.

Hohenstaufens, centuries passed without any one dynasty succeeding in attaining and holding the German crown. Unlike in England, France, and Denmark, where single dynasties established themselves in the thirteenth century as strong nuclei around which nation building forces could coalesce, kings in Germany remained weak. The German nation existed in the shadow of the Holy Roman Empire and its powerful mythical associations, and the important political symbols—the holy lance, the crown, Charlemagne's throne in the Aachen cathedral—were all connected with the empire, not the kingdom. In his 1927 biography of the Hohenstaufen emperor Frederick II (1196–1250), the historian Ernst Kantorowicz observed about the thirteenth century: "On some auspicious occasion, in solemn moments of enthusiasm, when they assembled for crusade or pilgrimage, they felt with a thrill of pride that they—Saxons and Franks, Swabians and Bavarians—were one. But they did not even then feel 'German.' At most they felt that they stood together as heirs of the Empire of the Caesars, they prided themselves on being descendants of the Trojans, or styled themselves 'Roman' citizens." Only gradually did the Germans grow accustomed to being called "Deutsche" or Germans, and when they adopted the term themselves, they attached no particular importance to it.

In sum, then, the period we are dealing with cannot be called the German Middle Ages or the noonday of "German" emperors; we cannot even speak of the beginnings of German history, for the people in question had as yet no notion of being Germans. What we have instead is a prehistory of Germany, the prologue to a play whose leading actors have not yet come on stage. Familiarity with it is essential, however, if one is to follow the developing plot, for the Holy Roman Empire survived in a number of transformations down to the threshold of the modern era, with a strange, distorted echo perceivable even in Bismarck's German Empire of 1871, which finally perished in 1945. The area of German settlement, Germany's geographical position, decisive aspects of the German constitution, the linguistic foundations of German culture—all these developed during the period we customarily refer to as the Middle Ages, in which there is little trace either of Germany or the Germans.

The East Frankish kings, who came to be referred to as German kings more and more often over the course of the eleventh and twelfth centuries, ruled over areas settled by Franconians along the banks of the Main River, and other areas populated by Saxons, Frisians, Thuringians, Bavarians, Swabians, and also west of the Rhine by Lotharingians and Burgundians, who for the most part spoke not Germanic but Romance languages. Beginning in the tenth century these kings extended their rule eastward, across the Elbe River. This expansion, generally called the colonization of the east, had far-reaching consequences. In competition with Denmark, Poland, and

Bohemia, the empire subjugated the lesser dominions and tribal communities of western Slavs between the Baltic and the eastern spurs of the Alps—asserting political and religious hegemony to start with, and later imposing their language and culture as well by means of an influx of settlers from Flanders and Thuringia. But whereas the regions west of the Rhine retained their links to the Romance languages, apart from a small German-speaking belt along the western bank, the Slavic and German elements east of the Elbe gradually merged. The Slavic populations were assimilated, becoming part of new German tribes and language zones, with the exception of small islands of Slavic-language speakers in Lausitz and Carinthia. Present-day Germans and Austrians thus have Slavic ancestors as well as Germanic and Celtic ones. The population represents the crossing of northern with southern, and western with eastern, Europe; it is a mixture of most European ethnic groups of ancient times and the Middle Ages, reflecting its location in the middle of the continent.

The polity that developed here lacked clear definition at first. Throughout the Middle Ages the Holy Roman Empire—with its foundations in the kingdoms of Germany, Burgundy, Lombardy, and Bohemia—was far removed from what we would today call a state. A medieval ruler had direct political relations with a relatively small number of people. His power derived from land owned by him and his relatives, and from the fact that other landowners recognized him as the most powerful among them and were willing to submit to his authority. Personal relationships arose out of these circumstances and were solidified in the form of contracts. The feudal lord swore an oath to protect his vassals, while the vassals swore loyalty to their lord. Over the course of time it became customary for feudal lords also to convey certain rights to their vassals in exchange for the oath, such as land or entitlement to an office. The vassal could be lord in his turn and dispense certain of his privileges to still less powerful men, giving rise to a branching and complicated system of legal and purely personal ties.

Rule in virtually all of Europe rested on such feudal foundations. Medieval Europeans knew no states based on a specific territory but only associations of people created by individual oaths of fealty. Nation states of the kind with which we are familiar are founded to outlast individuals; they are tied to institutions rather than to single persons. The medieval collective, by contrast, was limited to the lifetimes of its members and had to be recreated over and over again by the oaths of new lords and vassals as the old ones died.

How such a feudal relationship could work in practice is suggested by the case of Henry the Lion (1129–1195). The Guelph duke, although a vassal of the king and emperor Frederick I "Barbarossa," ruled over his large dominions of Saxony and Bavaria almost like a king, and in 1176 even refused to raise an army and join the emperor's campaign against the cities of Lombardy. For this disloyalty Henry was formally tried in Würzburg at a court assembly of the imperial princes presided over by the emperor, and deprived of his Saxon and Bavarian fiefs. His familial territorial possessions around Braunschweig and Lüneburg were left intact, however, with the result that the duchy and later kingdom of Hanover continued under Guelph rule until Prussia annexed it in 1866, while Braunschweig survived as a distinct territory until 1946.

It is significant that Barbarossa did not absorb into his own immediate dominions the imperial fiefs he took from Henry, although he could have strengthened the position of the Hohenstaufens decisively had he done so. In comparable situations the kings of England and France usually appropriated such territories; the beginnings of the modern nation state in western Europe were directly connected with such expansion and consolidation of royal possessions. Barbarossa refrained from this step, however, and awarded the free fiefs to other princes of the realm, because even then, at the height of his power, his own position was dependent upon their support. It may be that some historians are correct in seeing in Barbarossa's decision not to impose direct dynastic rule on these territories a decisive turning point, when the course of German history took a crucial turn away from western European developments. But presumably Barbarossa had no choice. The emperor was too weak to assert his rule over the opposition of the most powerful men in the realm.

And so the attempt of the Hohenstaufens to consolidate the power of the emperor over the princes and other nobles ended in failure. The sheer extent of the empire made unified rule extraordinarily difficult, and imperial power was further weakened by Barbarossa's death on the crusade in 1190, Henry VI's untimely end in 1198, and his son Frederick II's concentration on his Italian territories. The ongoing dispute with the papacy, the energy absorbed by the campaigns in Italy, numerous rival powers, and lagging cultural development in comparison with western Europe—all these factors contributed to the empire's maintaining its traditional, outdated character. While its neighbors to the west acquired relatively fixed frontiers and developed centers that served as capital cities, royal residences, and hubs of culture and trade, the Holy Roman Empire's boundaries remained unclear, and until its end in 1806 the empire never possessed a permanent capital comparable to London or Paris. Instead of concentrating power in its center, the empire was dominated by territorial authorities—powerful noble families in large regions, and independent governments in the free "imperial cities" (meaning that they were ruled by the emperor directly) and the cities of Italy, the latter pulling further and further away from imperial control.

Thus in the center of Europe two levels of politics developed simultaneously: first the empire itself, whose head, the emperor, exercised more symbolic than actual power, and second the imperial estates, headed by spiritual and temporal princes who early on established firm positions that the emperor was compelled to respect. The *Kurfürsten,* or prince electors, who had the right to elect the king, enjoyed special status, but the group also included imperial cities and imperial counts and knights who held their titles as the emperor's immediate vassals. They met at court assemblies, and in the twelfth cen-

tury established the principle that the emperor must consult them and gain their approval on all important matters of policy. By the fifteenth century the court assemblies had developed into a permanent institution known as the Imperial Diet, which played an important role in decision-making.

How, one might ask, could such a weak structure, with an elected leader dependent on the support of the prince electors and imperial

Hanseatic Ships of the Fifteenth Century
(miniature from an illustrated manuscript,
Hamburg, 1487)

The Hansa, originally a mercantile association of the thirteenth century, evolved into a
powerful alliance of about a hundred cities
located mostly in northern Germany, of
which the most important were Lübeck, Hamburg, and Cologne. The league dominated
trade in the Baltic region and owned great
warehouses in cities from Novgorod in Russia to Bergen in Norway, London, and Venice. Goods were moved mainly by ship, the
only economical mode of transportation for
cargos such as grain, salted fish, wood, and
building stone. The rounded hulls of Hansa
ships could hold considerable quantities,
while the large amounts of sail they carried
and their deep keels made them faster than
earlier ships. The Hansa reached the peak
of its power in 1370 with the Treaty of
Stralsund, in which the king of Denmark was
forced to accept its conditions for trade in
the western Baltic. As territorial states grew
more powerful and trade routes shifted, the
league gradually lost importance and broke
up during the Thirty Years' War.

estates, survive in the heart of Europe until the early nineteenth century without disintegrating or being carved up? The answer is complicated, with one reason being the development of a community of surrounding nations that needed a weak, internally fragmented center in which they could adjust the shifting balances of their own interests and fight their wars. Another reason was the emperor's very weakness, which tended to make him an effective peacemaker and a sovereign who ruled through fixed laws instead of as a despot. A further reason for the surprising longevity of the Holy Roman Empire was the principle of elective kingship. The higher ranks of the aristocracy participated in the institutions and were disposed to support and cooperate with the sovereign they chose. Every vote they cast in a royal election was a renewed vote for the continuation of the empire, and thus it was precisely the prince electors who came to serve as guarantors of its cohesion and permanence.

On the other hand the territorial states of which the empire was composed—and which acquired more and more power and independence as time went by—were a veritable zoo of political life forms. There were electoral principalities, ordinary principalities, duchies, bishoprics, counties, imperial cities, abbey lands, and districts controlled by military religious orders such as the Knights of the Teutonic Order. And the principle of dual power applied in all these, too: The ruler's power was balanced by that of the regional diet or parliament, in which the estates were represented. Given that boundaries in central Europe were constantly shifting as wars were won and lost or dynasties died out or intermarried, these diets acted as a force for order and continuity in their lands. They performed the same stabilizing function in dangerous times, for example when a ruler died leaving a minor as his successor. The powers in the hands of the estates—the parliaments and diets—also contributed to the stability of the empire, not only the princes.

The Germany of the nineteenth century has been described as a "delayed nation." In fact, this holds true for German history as a whole. The political institutions of the empire appeared on the scene only very late, as Europe was emerging into the modern era. In terms of creating constitutional, legal, and administrative systems and developing techniques for governing and strengthening royal power, realms such as France, England, Naples, Sicily, Aragon, Castile, and Portugal were far ahead of the empire, while the lands on the northern and eastern periphery of Europe—Scotland, Denmark, Norway, Sweden, or Hungary, for example—were far behind. Where power and culture were concerned, Europe consisted of two clearly differentiated regions, one more modern and with an older tradition of organized rule that corresponded quite closely to the territory of the ancient Roman Empire, and a more backward, newer region made up of the lands north of Hadrian's Wall in Britain, and north and east of the Rhine, the *limes,* and the Danube on the Continent. In the latter, royal power was exercised not from the court chancellery, with the pen, but from the saddle, with the sword.

The center of this divided continent was occupied by the Holy Roman Empire, some of which belonged to the older Europe, but most to the younger, reflecting the duality of the whole on a smaller scale. In many respects the empire could keep pace with the western regions of the continent. This was true particularly for the growth of trade, transportation, and crafts; it was also true for the development of cities, which slowly emerged from the shadow of great feudal estates and produced their own culture, with specific privileges, new

Pope Gregory Celebrating Mass
(Thomas Burgkmair, 1496)

Like most highly developed cultures in human history, European civilization was permeated by religion. This was the case until well into the modern period, otherwise the bitterness of the struggles to reform the church, which lasted hundreds of years, would be inexplicable. Christ, the saints, and the devil were real beings who intervened in every person's life and might appear at any time; the modern separation between the now and the hereafter was foreign to earlier Europeans. This painting shows Pope Gregory I (590–604) celebrating the Mass at which Christ appeared bodily on the altar, demonstrating visibly how the bread and wine have been transformed. Judas and his pieces of silver are depicted behind the altar to the left; to the right are the instruments with which Christ was scourged.

social gradations, and a new style and rhythm in daily life. Most German cities arose between the early twelfth and the early fourteenth centuries, from Freiburg im Breisgau near the French and Swiss borders, to Munich and Nuremberg, all the way to Lübeck on the Baltic Sea, but also cities in the east such as Berlin, Königsberg, and Elbing.

It is striking, however, that the great trade centers of the empire never coincided with the centers of imperial might. The former lay for the most part on the northern and southern peripheries, either on the North Sea and the Baltic (such as Lübeck, Bremen, Hamburg, and Rostock), or near the main passes through the Alps (such as Augsburg or Regensburg). The kings and emperors, on the other hand, tended to move eastward with the expansion of their empire, building their castles and dynastic burial monuments in places like Goslar, Magdeburg, Nuremberg, and Prague. The lack of a capital city, a fixed and permanent administrative center that could at the same time serve as a focus for culture, higher learning, and trade, symbolized a notable weakness of the empire at least from the thirteenth century, if not earlier. The low concentration of centralized power and the archaic administrative structures resulted chiefly from the dependence of the German king and Holy Roman Emperor on the great nobles of their realm. An elective monarchy is weak by nature and therefore backward in its development into a modern state.

In cultural terms, too, the midcontinent failed to keep pace with the west. The jurists and administrators needed by a modern ruler were trained at universities; around the year 1300 France had five of them, northern Italy three, England and Castile two, and Portugal one. Yet in the entire Holy Roman Empire, and indeed all of the "younger" east, there was not a single university at that time. Emperor Carl IV, in his role as ruler of Bohemia, founded the University of Prague in 1348, some two hundred years after the founding of its model, the University of Paris. In the thirteenth century, the cultivation of letters and learning was limited largely to the Latin countries and England. This does not mean that culture languished altogether in

Germany; there were flourishing centers of learning in the prosperous cities, at rulers' courts, in cathedral schools and monasteries. And the "German lands"—a term that might also include England, Denmark, or Poland—sent the largest contingents to the universities of Paris, Bologna, and Salamanca, ensuring that their intellectual elite shared in the developments under way in Italy, France, and Spain and was decisively shaped by them.

German culture was shaped in still other respects by taking over and reworking western models; this is true for the courtly love poetry of the High Middle Ages, the lyric poetry of Wolfram von Eschenbach and Neidhart von Reuenthal, but also for the verse tales based on the western European legends of King Arthur and his Knights of the Round Table, such as Wolfram's *Parsifal* and Hartmann von Aue's *Erec*. Politically, intellectually, and culturally, Germany remained a land of the center, into which European cultural movements streamed from the south and west. The Germans took them up, transformed them, and passed them on to their own neighbors. In the centuries to come, Latin models would be followed by others from France, Spain, and England.

2 Transitions
(1400–1648)

In 1400, on the threshold of the modern era, the center of the continent of Europe was occupied by the Holy Roman Empire. Its borders stretched eastward along the Baltic from Holstein on the Jutland peninsula roughly as far as present-day Słupsk (Stolp) in Poland, where the sovereign territory governed by the Teutonic Knights began. From here the frontier ran south following almost exactly the same path as the border drawn between Germany and Poland after the First World War, continuing on to include Bohemia, Moravia, and the Duchy of Austria within the empire, and reaching the Adriatic Sea near the Istrian Peninsula. The southern frontier ran across Italy, excluding Venice and its territories and dividing Tuscany, which formed part of the empire, from the Papal States to the south. It reached the Tyrrhenian Sea north of Rome, near Civitavecchia, and ran along the coast of the Mediterranean as far as Nice. There the frontier turned north again to enclose Savoy, Burgundy, Lorraine, Luxemburg, and the county of Hennegau, and ran along the western arm of the River Schelde, reaching the North Sea between Ghent and Antwerp.

Some regions, such as northern Italy, Savoy, Burgundy, and also the rebellious Swiss Confederation, belonged to the empire in name only, and a number of others definitely lay outside the core territories

Martin Luther
(Lucas Cranach the Elder, 1529)

31

known at that time as "the German lands." The inhabitants of Brabant and parts of the duchies of Lorraine and Luxemburg spoke French, while in the territories united under the crown of Wenceslaus—Bohemia, Moravia, and Silesia—German was essentially the language of the towns. People in the rural areas, but also some town dwellers, spoke Czech, and some inhabitants of Silesia spoke Polish.

This empire was still far from being a nation state; it lacked both prerequisites, being neither of one nationality nor organized as one state. To be sure, the emperor and the empire were in the process of shedding their sacred and universal character. With the enactment of Emperor Charles IV's Golden Bull in 1356—which derived its name from the gold seal affixed to it—the empire acquired its first constitution; this document made the German king dependent on the chief nobles of the realm, and not only the king, for the rank of emperor went hand in hand with possession of the German crown. The king reigned at their discretion and pleasure; he was *imperator electus,* an elected emperor. The bull made no mention of the pope at all. The group who voted, known as the prince electors, was now clearly defined; it consisted of the archbishops of Mainz, Cologne, and Trier; the King of Bohemia; the Duke of Saxony; the Margrave of Brandenburg; and the Count Palatine of the Rhine.

The emperor inherited sovereign authority only in his family lands; for the Luxemburg emperors Henry VII (reigned 1308–1313), Charles IV (1346–1378), and Sigismund (1410–1437), this was Bohemia. In the case of the Hapsburgs, who were to possess the imperial crown almost without interruption from the reign of Frederick III (reigned 1440–1493) to the dissolution of the empire in 1806, it was Austria. To this original realm the Hapsburgs succeeded in adding Bohemia, Hungary, and Burgundy without fighting a single battle, acquiring them either through marriage or inheritance. Their good fortune gave rise to the byword: "Others must fight wars; you, O fortunate Austria, simply wed."

But the home territories where these emperors reigned directly—

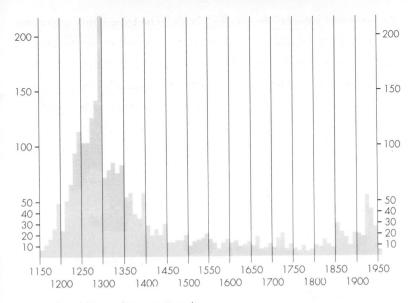

The Founding of Cities and Towns in Central Europe: Development from 1150 to 1950

Towns inhabited by a middle-class population barely existed north of the Alps before the tenth century; the towns arising from then on had no direct links with communities founded in ancient times. Towns and cities were centers of power, but also sites of markets that attracted traders and settlers. In the course of the thirteenth century the number of cities within the empire rose dramatically as a result of population growth, territorial expansion, and settlement of the east, and rulers vied with one another in founding new towns. More towns existed in central Europe between 1200 and 1300 than ever before or since.

and in which they could levy taxes and raise armies—lay on the periphery of the empire or, in the case of Hungary, even outside it. As a consequence the emperor might not show his face in the interior of the empire for years on end; Frederick III, for example, did not visit for a stretch of twenty-seven years. Meanwhile, the empire itself remained a jumble of some 1,600 separate member territories and cities, some of which made advances toward real statehood far ahead of the empire, although in very different ways. On the one hand there were principalities ranging from small to tiny, where the ruler could survey his whole realm from the battlements of his castle, along with rich and powerful free cities such as Nuremberg and Lübeck, but also absurdly inefficient "free imperial" villages and hamlets. On the other hand there were large member states governed by imperial

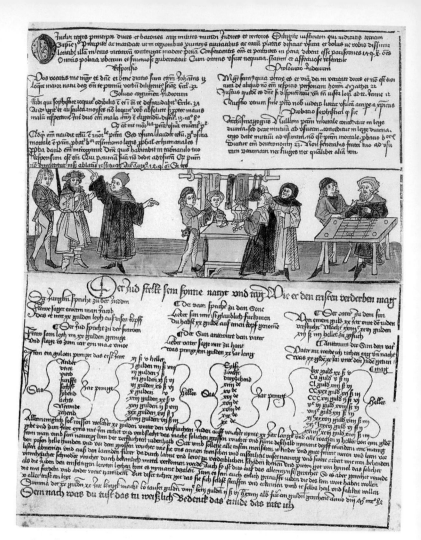

Jewish Moneylenders

(woodcut, probably from Nuremberg, ca. 1484)

Jews throughout Europe possessed few rights in the late Middle Ages; they could turn only to the king directly or the church for protection and were barred from practicing all trades. Money lending and financial transactions remained one of the few ways of earning a living. The leaflet protests against the practice of charging interest to lend money; the illustration depicts a pawn shop with drinking cups and articles of clothing; to the right a Jewish moneylender calculates interest at a counting table, and to the left a scholar raises a finger in warning. The intent is to equate the terms "Jew" and "usurer," a term of abuse that demagogues still employed effectively in the anti-Semitic propaganda campaigns of the recent past.

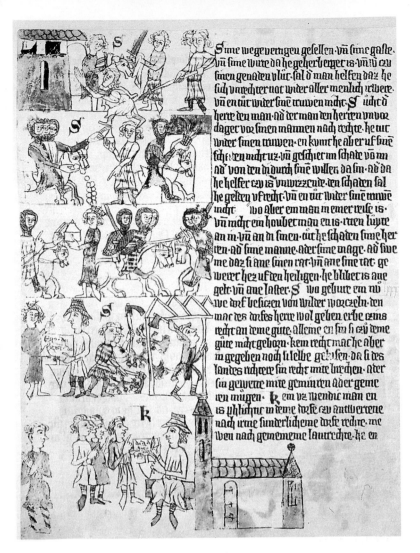

Sinne wegevingen gesellen · vn sine gaste.
vn sine lute da he geherbenget is · vn iu cu
sinen genaden ulit · sal d man helfen daz he
sich unrechter not under aller menlich erwere ·
vn entwic under sine truwen macht · Suhtet d
herre den man · nd der man den herren vn vor
dage vor sinen mannen nach rechte · he wic
under sinen truwen · en kumt he aber uf sine
scheden nicht uz · vn geschiet un schade vo m
nd von den dienst sine willen da sin · nd da
he helfer czu is vnwizzende · den schaden sal
he gelten uf recht · vn en wic under sine truwe
nicht. Wo aber em man in emer wise is ·
vn nicht em houbet man en is · twen lute
an in · vn an di sinen · durch schaden sine her
ten · nd sine manne · oder sine mage · nd swe
me daz si ane sinen rat · vn ane sine tat · ge
weret herz uf den heiligen · he blibet is ane
gelt · vn ane laster · S Wo gebure em nu
awe dorf besiczen von walder worczeln · den
mac des dorfes herre wol geben erbe czins
recht an deme gute · alleme en sin si czu deme
gute nicht geboren · kem recht mache aber
in gegeben noch si selbe geschen · da si des
landes richtere sin recht mite brechen · oder
sin gewere mite geminren oder geme
ren mugen · k em vr wendic man en
is phlichtic in deme dorfe czu antwertene
nach irme sunderlichene dorfe redire · we
den nach gemeinene lantrechte · he en

A Village Is Founded

(Heidelberg copy of the *Sachsenspiegel*, illustrated manuscript, early fourteenth century).

The undertaking that later came to be called the "colonization of the east" was for the most part, although not always, a peaceful process. In the course of general expansion between the eleventh and thirteenth centuries, hundreds of towns and thousands of villages were founded east of the Elbe River, inhabited by peasants attracted by promises of liberal rights from the great landowners. In this illustration a landowner is shown granting the newcomers their rights of settlement; land is being cleared, and the first houses are under construction. At the bottom the village court is shown in session. The native Slavic people were not driven out; they participated in the colonization process but over time gave up their language, with few exceptions, becoming absorbed into the mixed, largely German population of the region.

princes, with highly developed central administrations and their own diets, such as the duchies of Bavaria, Württemberg, Lorraine, Luxemburg, and Savoy. Next in size came the principalities of Saxony and Brandenburg, the Palatinate, and Hesse, and the territories of the spiritual rulers, the archbishop-electors of Cologne, Mainz, and Trier, to name only some of the most important. This motley collection of territories was distinctly old-fashioned in comparison with the modern state systems arising in western Europe. Centralized political institutions, on which an evolving German nation could have depended for support, were lacking altogether in central Europe.

The inhabitants of these regions continued to live as their forebears

Chronicle of the Council of Constance (Augsburg, 1483)
The two pages show John XXIII (1415–1419), antipope to the popes in Avignon, and King (later Emperor) Sigismund (ruled 1410–1437), who invited him to the Council of Constance (1414–1418). Both John XXIII and his rival in Avignon were deposed, ending the Great Schism of the church: a late echo of the struggles lasting many centuries between emperor and pope, who for all their conflict could not do without each other.

A Later Edition of the Chronicle of the Council of Constance
(Augsburg, 1536)

The Bohemian reformer Jan Hus (ca. 1370–1415) came to Constance to defend his teachings, because King Sigismund had promised him safe conduct. He was arrested nevertheless, condemned as a heretic, and burned. The illustrations depict him being stripped of his priestly rank by two archbishops; then clad in the black robe of a heretic, he is led through the city and burned at the stake in the presence of Duke Ludwig of Bavaria. The last picture shows two hangman's apprentices shoveling his ashes into the Rhine.

had in a world dominated almost entirely by agriculture. Four out of five of them lived on farms or in rural villages, although the number of villages had risen significantly during the thirteenth and fourteenth centuries. West of the Elbe River the last primeval forests had been cleared; even sites with poor soil were now ploughed for fields, and landowners were forced to issue edicts forbidding further felling of trees in order to protect the remaining forests. East of the Elbe the number of agricultural settlements grew, too, so that population density began to approach that of the west.

At the same time the prevalence of serfdom in many places declined, and more people joined the ranks of free peasants. Property

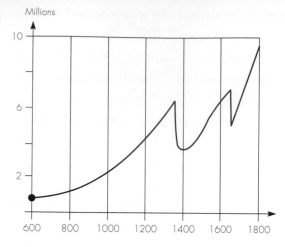

The Population of Germany West of the Elbe River from 600 to 1800

There are no precise population figures available for the period before 1800, as censuses were extremely rare. We must rely on estimates, which often diverge widely. (This table excludes the region east of the Elbe, because we know little about it, and the overall picture would be distorted by the settlements founded east of the Elbe in the High Middle Ages.) The population in western Germany was very low about 600 and grew slowly until the middle of the eleventh century; then, under favorable climatic conditions, it began to grow more rapidly, reaching a peak in the mid-fourteenth century. The steep drop thereafter was caused by epidemic diseases and famines, and further growth was hindered considerably by the Thirty Years' War. After the mid-eighteenth century the rate of population growth increased rapidly.

rights in villages remained in the hands of a few, usually aristocratic owners, but peasants had rights to the use of the land. Inhabitants of rural areas were now typically tenant farmers whose rents provided landowners with a secure income—at least in the regions west of the Elbe. East of this boundary farmers had been less successful in establishing legal rights when the area was colonized in the High Middle Ages, and the nobility exploited the weakness of their feudal overlords to claim extensive rights over the peasants living on their land. These became the basis for hereditary serfdom. On the estates east of the Elbe peasants fell completely under the sway of their manorial lords, the Junkers, in oppressive conditions of servitude that left them with virtually no rights at all. This situation would remain essentially unchanged until the peasants' emancipation in the nineteenth century.

About 20 percent of the inhabitants of the empire lived in towns and cities; there were some 4,000 such population centers, which decreased in density as one moved east. Two-thirds of these towns were very small, ranging from a few hundred to 2,000 inhabitants. Among the few cities with populations above 10,000, Cologne ranked first with about 40,000 inhabitants, followed by Prague and Lübeck. Other major centers included Augsburg, Nuremberg, Bremen, and Hamburg, followed by Frankfurt, Magdeburg, Strasbourg, and Ulm. None of them, however, even approached the size of the great European metropolises such as Paris, Florence, Venice, Genoa, and Milan, which by 1340 all had populations of about 100,000.

Most towns and cities of the empire belonged to the territory of one principality or another and were governed by its ruler. Others fell into the category of imperial cities, which were ruled by the emperor without any intervening authority. The imperial register of 1521 listed 85 of them. This category included a few "free" cities, such as Cologne and Regensburg, that had originally been ruled by bishops but had succeeded in winning their independence from the church.

Only a portion of the residents of a city possessed the rights of citizens. In addition to old established families and local patricians, this "honorable estate" included merchants and members of craft guilds. Typically excluded from citizenship were such groups as domestic servants, tradesmen's assistants, journeymen and apprentices, invalids, beggars, knackers, and hangmen, but also members of the nobility and the clergy, civil servants, and Jews.

It is difficult to give an accurate estimate of the total population of the Holy Roman Empire in those times, for no censuses were taken. Various conjectures by historians proceed from different assumptions that lead to widely diverging results, so all numbers should be viewed with appropriate caution. The population within the whole territory of the empire may have numbered about 5 million in the year 1000, rising to 15 million by 1340 and falling to around 10 million by 1450.

From these figures it is evident at first glance that on the threshold of the modern era, during a period of about a hundred years, some extraordinary catastrophe or catastrophes must have occurred. These were not limited to the empire, since the population estimates for western Europe and central Europe as a whole, including territories outside the empire's borders, show comparable fluctuations. In the year 1000 the total population of both areas was about 12 million; it rose to 36 million in 1340 but plunged to only about 23 million by 1450. What had happened?

Around the middle of the fourteenth century, Europe was over-

Pilgrimage to the Church of Mary the Beautiful

(broadsheet, after a woodcut by Michael Ostendorfer, 1490–1553; Germany, 1610)

Anti-Semitic violence could break out on the slightest pretext. In Regensburg the city council exploited the interim between the death of Emperor Maximilian and the election of his successor, Charles V, in 1519 to drive the Jews, who stood under the emperor's protection, out of the city and tear down the Jewish quarter. On the site of the synagogue a church was built to house an image of the Virgin Mary that worked miracles. The leaflet shows the new church, behind it ruins of the Jewish quarter, and ecstatic pilgrims in the foreground. The tone of the leaflet is unusually sharp; written from a Lutheran point of view, it directs accusations of fraud and extortion not against Jews, as was common, but against the Catholic Church instead.

populated. Traditional methods of agriculture no longer sufficed to feed everyone adequately. People suffered from malnutrition, and as a result were vulnerable to the waves of epidemics that swept across Europe regularly, bringing death and destruction. In the course of the fourteenth century about a third of the population was mowed down by the bubonic plague, the terrible Black Death, yet this did not lead to substantially improved nutrition, since without anyone to cultivate the fields, large stretches of fertile land very quickly reverted to wilderness. The horrors of the times were reflected in the old litany, *a peste, fame et bello, libera nos, domine:* "From pestilence, famine, and war, deliver us, O Lord." The three scourges in fact hung together, as the devastations of war created food shortages, and the resulting famines weakened people, making them vulnerable to epidemic diseases. The cycle appeared inescapable.

Shortages of food everywhere led to the most profound social upheavals ever seen in Europe. Rebellions became commonplace in urban centers; between 1350 and 1500 scarcely any city escaped uprisings and violent struggles over control of the municipal government. The town of Braunschweig, for example, experienced civil insurrections in 1293, 1294, 1374, 1380, 1445, and 1487. In the countryside, order was shattered by peasants' revolts—from the farmers of Appenzell in the south, who successfully opposed their ruler in 1405, to the rebellion led by the "Piper of Niklashausen" in 1476 and the *Bundschuh* uprisings (named after the peasants' type of footwear) along the upper Rhine. Bands of impoverished aristocrats, the so-called robber barons, roamed the countryside terrorizing the population with their

Emperor Maximilian I
(Bernhard Striegel, 1495)

raids, while gangs of unemployed
mercenaries could threaten the order of even good-sized towns when
they rampaged and plundered. "The people could not perceive their
own fates and the events of their time other than as a continuous succession of economic mishandling, exploitation, war and robbery,
inflation, want and pestilence," writes the Dutch historian Johan
Huizinga. "The chronic form that war tended to take, the constant
threats to the town and the country from all kinds of dangerous riff-
raff, the eternal threat from a harsh and unreliable administration of
justice, and on top of all this, the pressure of the fear of hell and the

anxiety about devils and witches, nourished a feeling of general insecurity."

In a crisis of such dimensions, even the two pillars of social order could no longer fill the roles they had played for so long. The church and the empire, although often enough at odds with one another, had nevertheless maintained a precarious balance of interdependence and mutual support for as long as anyone could remember; now, however, their prestige began to wane. In 1309 the pope was forced to leave Rome for Avignon, where pressure from France kept him largely under the control of the French crown. This "Babylonian Captivity" of the church was followed by the "Great Schism of the West": Between 1378 and 1415 there were two popes, one in Rome and another in Avignon. Their conflicting claims divided western Christianity and left the reputation of the papacy badly tarnished. The schism was ended through the great councils of Constance (1414–1418) and Basel (1431–1449), but at the cost of a permanent weakening of the institution's authority.

This was accompanied, in the popes of the Renaissance, by a considerable increase in worldliness. The lavish style of life deemed necessary for the papal court and the highest officials of the church cost enormous sums, which were raised by demanding heavy taxes from the faithful without regard for their circumstances. The popes' extravagance, the church's greed, the conflict between popes, counter-popes, and councils—all these contributed to a significant loss of trust in pope, church, and clergy. The Roman Catholic Church had no satisfactory responses to the collective spiritual crisis brought about by famines and plagues during the "autumn of the Middle Ages."

Heresies sprouted on all sides along with opposition movements fueled by antichurch sentiment. Both were driven by fears that the Apocalypse was imminent, by turmoil inside and outside the church, but most of all by longings for a new sense of wholeness and security. The Lollards sprang up in England, the Hussites in Bohemia, the Anabaptists in the Netherlands and northern Germany. Calls for reform of the church at all levels grew more insistent, and the rulers of the empire faced similar pressures.

From the middle of the fifteenth century on, the inhabitants of the empire grew painfully and increasingly aware of how backward their state and its rulers were, compared with states such as France, England, and Spain, which had modernized and strengthened their institutions of government. A general clamor arose for reform of the empire, and in the view prevailing at the time political reform was inseparable from ecclesiastical reform. The empire and the church were interdependent, after all, and together constituted the basis of God's plan for salvation.

The term "Holy Roman Empire of the German Nation," which came into use after proclamation of the Imperial Decree of Cologne in 1512, merely reflected how rapidly the empire's real might and claims to universality were diminishing. As the earlier sanctity of the imperial crown was eroded by the growing influences of humanism and the Renaissance, and as its claims to be descended from the Caesars of Rome sank to the level of outworn tradition, it seemed more and more natural to fall back on the words "German Nation" as the operative part of the empire's full name. People tend to seek clearly defined boundaries and categories for themselves and for whatever group they perceive as foreign or alien, particularly in times of crisis. And had leadership of the empire not in fact passed to the Germans? At the close of the thirteenth century, a cleric in Cologne by the name of Alexander von Roes had written a treatise entitled "On Preeminence in the Roman Empire," in which he stated that "Charles the Great, the Holy Emperor, did determine and command, with the approval and by the authority of the Pope in Rome . . . that the power to elect the Roman emperor should remain with the German princes in perpetuity." This treatise was rediscovered in the early sixteenth century and widely circulated in numerous editions.

The German nation did not consist of all German-speaking people within the borders of the empire, however; rather, it denoted the select group of princes who were empowered to make political decisions and represented the emperor's subjects in all dealings with him. In the language of the times, the "nation" meant the aristocracy, the only estate able to take political action. The attempts to reform the imperial bureaucracy were designed to create institutions that would have given the empire the character of a modern state. Had these attempts succeeded, the German nation would have had a chance to establish itself as a nation state, following the same path as France and England.

The reform efforts of Emperor Maximilian I (reigned 1486–1519) demonstrated that the empire had not yet been reduced to a purely theoretical entity by any means. Maximilian intended his establishment of an imperial court of law in 1495, in combination with a proclaimed state of "lasting law and order" throughout the empire, to be just the beginning. Similarly, he thought of his division of the entire empire into ten administrative districts as only a first step. His plan was to create a representative body for the estates of the realm and to acquire the wherewithal to cement his effective power and sovereign authority by imposing taxes. But Maximilian died in 1519, and the reforms he had envisioned died with him.

His grandson and successor, Carl V (reigned 1519–1556), had his own plans for stabilizing and modernizing the realm, within the framework of an even grander vision—a "universal monarchy" encompassing Spain and its transatlantic possessions as well as Germany, Bohemia, Burgundy, and Milan. Such a perspective pushed the notion of distinct "German lands" far into the background.

Nonetheless, the welfare of the German nation remained a strong argument in the debate over reform of the empire. At the "Turkish diet" of 1454 in Regensburg, for instance, when the head of the emperor's delegation, Enea Silvio Piccolomini, called for a crusade to recapture Constantinople from the Turks, the German prince electors replied that the emperor ought to see to matters closer to home first, since "the most worthy and noble land of the German tongue . . . and also the Holy Empire, so laudably handed down to those who speak the German tongue," were in "great disorder." In short, their message to the emperor ran: No war against the Turks without reform of the empire. East or west, home was best to the princes, and nearer and dearer to them even than the empire was the land of the "German tongue" or the "German nation," meaning the German-speaking estates within the empire.

The degree to which political reform was tied up with ecclesiastical reform is indicated by the ever-increasing frequency of official protests entitled "Remonstrances of the German Nation," dispatched by the imperial estates to the papal curia. The complaint that Rome had invented a thousand ways to part Germans from their money was only one of many included in a compilation of such protests; as a result, the "once celebrated nation" that had won control of the empire through its "blood and valor" was now reduced to poverty and the condition of servitude. In political terms, therefore, the German nation at the beginning of the modern era was a concept used by opponents of the universal institutions of empire and papacy; but neither they nor their idea had enough strength or broad support to create a lasting state.

The conception of a German nation had cultural as well as political undertones, however, and in this respect the "nation" gained considerably after the Italian humanist Poggio Bracciolini rediscovered the lost text of Tacitus' *Germania* and published it in Italy in 1455. In the era of humanism and the Renaissance, the old notion that the early tribes of Europe were descended from illustrious legendary forebears led to a search of classical Greek and Latin sources for proof. Humanist scholars of the sixteenth and seventeenth centuries wrote studies designed to confirm and strengthen the identity of each contemporaneous nation on foundations from classical antiquity, an era whose thinking and experience were considered exemplary. As a result, the strivings for national individuality had their roots in a cosmopolitan, shared European culture.

The White King and Artillery

(woodcut by Hans Burckmair, Vienna, 1775)

The *Weisskunig* (White King) is the autobiography of Emperor Maximilian I, printed for the first time in the eighteenth century. The illustration documents Maximilian's interest in firearms. Cannons came into use around the middle of the thirteenth century and could destroy every castle; hand guns, which could pierce all suits of armor, appeared on battlefields about the beginning of the fourteenth century. With this development, the participation of the aristocracy—previously indispensable in military campaigns—was no longer necessary to conduct a war. This is one more reason why Maximilian could consider himself "the last knight."

The discovery of the *Germania*, written for the Emperor Trajan about 100 B.C., created a furor for just this reason: No less an authority than one of the great and revered classical writers, it was now learned, had shown that the Germans were a distinct people even in ancient times, and one worthy of interest. Prior to discovery of this manuscript, German scholars had fallen far behind in the international competition for national glory, since a German tribe from which a German nation had developed did not exist in the same way the Franks had given rise to France. "German" had been a collective term for a variety of popular dialects—a purely artificial construct. But now a simple translation was possible: Tacitus' *Germānī* were the ancestors of present-day Germans, and the *Germania* of the Romans

Emperor Charles V
(after Titian from the school of Rubens, first quarter of the seventeenth century)

Charles V ruled over an empire composed of numerous territories with very diverse historical antecedents and legal structures. The empire was founded solely on the law of dynastic inheritance and held together by one person, the ruler who inherited on the basis of this law. The empire's structure is reflected in the following formula, which appeared at the head of all imperial decrees and laws from 1521 on: "We Charles the Fifth, by the grace of God Roman Emperor, at all times Increaser of the Empire, King in Germany, in Castile, Aragon, Leon, in both Sicilies, Jerusalem, Hungary, Dalmatia, Croatia, Navarre, Granada, Toledo, Valencia, Galicia, Majorca, Seville, Sardinia, Cordoba, Corsica, Murcia, Guyenne, Algarve, Algeciras, Gibraltar, the Canary and Indian Islands and the *terra firma* of the Oceanic Sea, etc., Archduke of Austria, Duke of Burgundy, Lorraine, Brabant, Styria, Carinthia, Carniola, Limburg, Lüzenburg, Geldern, Calabria, Athens, Neopatria, and Württemberg, etc."

was equivalent to a contemporary "Germany." Not until about 1500 did this word come into use in the singular, replacing the earlier phrase "German lands."

With the aid of Tacitus' authority, German humanists finally had some ammunition to use against the many derogatory descriptions of their countrymen in circulation among foreigners. The popular topos of crude, alcohol-sodden barbarians was now countered by the literary idealization of uncorrupted, loyal, brave, and plain-living Germānī —without it occurring to anyone that Tacitus might have invented or stylized his Germanic paragons as a way of confronting his Roman contemporaries with their own decadence. This is precisely what the German humanists of the sixteenth century did, however. They began presenting Germans as the representatives of a natural, unaffected culture they saw as destined to succeed the jaded, worn-out civilization of the Italians and French, and they took pleasure in contrasting German probity with the moral corruption of the Roman curia.

Their French neighbors also came in for their share of attacks from newly confident German scholars. In his *Epitome Germanorum* of 1505 Jacob Wimpfeling dismissed as ridiculous the cornerstone of the current Capetian dynasty's legitimation, namely that its right to the French crown descended from Charlemagne. The Emperor Karl had in fact been a German who ruled over the French, whereas no Gaul or Frenchman had ever been Roman emperor—sufficient proof, in the author's eyes, to demonstrate German superiority. For Wimpfeling, who like many German humanists came from Alsace, it was equally certain that since the time of Augustus the inhabitants of Alsace had been Germans, and for that reason Strasbourg and the whole province must never fall under French sovereignty.

In this way—around 1500, within a single generation—the foundation was laid for a conscious awareness of German nationality that amounted to more than a vague sense of "us" as opposed to "them." This consciousness was based on a myth of national origins, one of many being developed all over Europe at that time in similar processes. Erasmus of Rotterdam, who refused to participate in the construction of national myths, observed with sorrow that nature had implanted a sense of self-regard not only in individuals but also in nations. In the case of Germany, however, this national myth lacked both the political framework that could give it permanence and a linguistic basis: With very few exceptions, the German humanists wrote in Latin. As humanists they remained first and foremost citizens of the world, with close ties to the European community of scholars. Their national mission—to lead Germany out of barbarism—took the route through classical learning and culture. It was in this manner, at the turn of the fifteenth to the sixteenth century, that the first clear and lasting outlines of a German nation took shape. If we want to be precise, this is the earliest point at which one can speak of "German history," or at least a "history of the Germans." But from the very beginning it was a history deeply rooted in humanism and the cosmopolitan soil of Europe.

Yet what stamped Germany for succeeding centuries was neither the learned efforts of the humanists nor the failed political reform of the empire but rather the reforms of Martin Luther. They would not have been possible, of course, without numerous forerunners; from the thirteenth century on, there had been many attempts to renew the church, to return it to the ideals of Christian poverty and humility, and to bridge the chasm between the clergy and the children of God. The church was able to absorb the early reformers, Saints Francis and Dominic, the founders of the mendicant orders. Later advocates of reform such as John Wyclif in England (1320–1384) and Jan Hus in Bohemia (1370–1415) pressed for more radical measures, including abolishing the papacy and the veneration of saints, establishing the unconditional authority of Holy Scripture and individual conscience, and permitting priest and congregation to share the cup at Holy Communion. They remained outside the church and were condemned and persecuted—Hus was burned at the stake at the Council

Crucifixion with Turkish Soldiers
(Ruprecht Heller, ca. 1560)

After the conquest of Constantinople in 1453, Turks came to be regarded as the archenemies of Christendom. The Turks' siege of Vienna in 1528 brought the threat as far as central Europe, and among the most difficult tasks Emperor Charles V faced was warding off their attack. His preoccupation with it was one of the reasons Protestantism could spread relatively unhindered. Small wonder that in this crucifixion scene Turkish soldiers appear under their standard with three crescent moons next to the Roman soldier.

of Constance and Wyclif's remains were burned after his death—but it was impossible to eradicate all their followers.

Martin Luther, a monk in Wittenberg, was equally unwilling to concede that divine mercy could be purchased with earthly goods to the benefit of the church. In his theses of October 31, 1517, he rejected the church's answer to the question, "How do I find mercy with God?" and replaced it with *sola fide,* "through faith alone," and *sola scriptura,* "through the Scriptures alone." With this stroke he dismissed not only the theological foundation for the sale of indulgences, the traffic in human souls, and the established church's abuse of its authority but also the clerical monopoly on mediation between God and humankind.

The rebellious monk from Wittenberg, who had broken with the pope and hoped to rebuild the true church of Christ from the community of the faithful, was summoned to appear before the Imperial Diet at Worms in 1521—the first time a secular body had presumed to pronounce on questions of church dogmatics. The mood in the Diet was sharply critical of the widespread corruption in the church and papacy, and the councillors of Emperor Charles V were inclined to make use of Luther as a means to exert pressure on the pope. But Luther could not be prevailed upon to make diplomatic concessions, and his refusal to recant even a part of his doctrine was too radical for the emperor.

Luther would have shared the fate of the Bohemian reformer Jan Hus had he not been protected by several princes of the realm. No doubt they did so partly—or even primarily—for religious reasons. The papal legate reported to Rome that "nine-tenths of Germany has taken up the battle cry of Luther, and the other tenth is shouting 'Death to the Roman court!'" Not least, however, Luther's Reformation also proved a helpful tool in resisting the emperor's claims of authority over the imperial estates and in consolidating the power of these same princes.

At the Imperial Diet of Speyer in 1526 a compromise was reached

Martin Luther's Open Letter to the Christian Nobility of the German Nation: On the Improvement of the Christian Estate (Wittenberg, 1520)

"It is an invention that the Pope, bishops, priests, and the inhabitants of monasteries are called the spiritual estate, and princes, lords, craftsmen, and tillers of fields the secular estate, which is a fine commentary and hypocrisy. But no one should be intimidated by this, and for this reason: All Christians are truly of the spiritual estate, and no difference exists between them on the basis of their office."

that allowed Lutheran rulers and city officials to regulate church matters in their own territories independently. The Protestant leaders willingly stepped in to head their respective ecclesiastical organizations as "emergency bishops." Luther had envisioned this as a temporary solution, but the princes would not hear of relinquishing control over the church once they had it in their grip, especially since in the meantime almost all church property had been seized. Some of it had been sold again, but in fact most of it had ended up in the possession of the princes themselves. Their assumption of control over the church was made easier by Luther's doctrine, based on the teachings of the Apostle Paul,

which delegated to secular rulers the task of protecting the community of Christians from evil: "For there is no authority, except from God; but where there is authority, it is ordained by God." Thus the Protestant ruler of a German principality, like the king of England, became *summus episcopus* and head of a rigidly organized ecclesiastical hierarchy. By the same means the religious sphere was completely absorbed into the machinery of the state.

The rulers of principalities that remained loyal to the old faith also attempted to subject the church to state controls, as in the case of the dukes of Bavaria, who forged an alliance with the University of Ingolstadt in order to reduce the bishops' official powers and establish the right of civil authorities to oversee church doctrine. In this instance,

Frederick the Wise
(from the workshop of Lucas Cranach the Elder, ca. 1525)

Martin Luther's Reformation would most likely have perished as a heretical movement if powerful imperial princes had not adopted his teachings. Their decision was affected at least as much by the goals of cementing their rule and increasing state revenues as by religious convictions. Frederick III, Prince Elector of Saxony (ruled 1486–1525), protected Luther, a professor at the University of Wittenberg, but tried to steer a middle course both politically and doctrinally, for which efforts he earned the sobriquet "the Wise." He is reported to have studiously avoided ever meeting Luther in person and formally confessed his adherence to Lutheran doctrine only on his deathbed.

however, they had renewal of the Catholic Church in mind, for there were all too many clerics whose view of their responsibilities did not measure up to the new, stricter standards of Catholic morality or who had proved overly receptive to Luther's teachings. It should be noted, incidentally, that the "Counter-Reformation" was not merely the Roman Catholic Church's response to the Reformation. The upheavals set in motion by Hus, Luther, and Calvin had also strengthened pro-reform forces that had long existed within the church itself; these now set about fighting corruption, improving the training of the clergy, and trying to win members lost through the Reformation back to the true faith. In any event, both the Reformation and Catholic renewal movement placed themselves in the service of the various principalities and their rulers. As these territories struggled to patch together functioning wholes from a myriad outdated feudal rights and privileges, they needed religion as a cohesive force for political reasons, and given the importance of religion, which penetrated into all areas of life, this cohesion could only be provided by denominational unity.

Consequently the Peace of Augsburg of 1555, which finally established the Lutheran estates of the empire on an equal footing with the Catholics, granted the *ius reformandi*, the right of reformation, to all territorial rulers. This meant that the "soul's eternal life" was in the hands of the ruler and not of the individual believer—in other words, the populace had to adopt the denomination of their overlord. For those unwilling to do so, there remained at least the *ius emigrandi,* the right to emigrate to a territory where their denomination was established. The internal unification of the German principalities and imperial cities was thereby taken a considerable step forward, a decisive prerequisite for their growing identity as separate states and for inner and outward independence. Simultaneously the Holy Roman Empire suffered another setback, for the tendency of the constituent territories to splinter was increased by the denominational divisions. In the ensuing period, as the empire's official status as a unified state lost more and more substance, the emperors retreated increasingly to their hereditary lands in Austria. The gradual decoupling of Austria from German history began in the Reformation.

Luther's theology was a theology of the word, which took as its starting point the opening verse of the Gospel according to St. John: "In the beginning was the Word, and the Word was with God, and the Word was God." For Christians of the Protestant faith the Bible therefore represented the sole authority, and since for Luther the church was the entire community of believers, the Word of God had to be proclaimed in the language they understood. Thus Luther's translation of the Bible into his own robust Meissen-Saxon German became the primer for a nation of readers, and the same applied to his tracts and open letters. His sermon on "Indulgence and Grace" published in the spring of 1518, for example, went through twenty-five editions and reprintings by 1520; 4,000 copies of his *Open Letter to the Christian Nobility of the German Nation* were sold within 18 days after publication, and the second edition appeared a week after the first. Further Protestant authors sprang up in large numbers alongside the great reformer—fellow theologians, members of spiritual orders, educated members of the middle class, and laborer-poets.

The stream of works in German, mainly theological in content, reflected a rapidly growing reading public. In the regions where the Reformation had established itself on a solid footing, education of the laity and literacy rates made enormous gains. The Protestant parts of Germany, at least, were culturally united through Luther's language; from then on "German" was more than a collective term for a large variety of dialects and local idioms. Nevertheless, when Luther issued

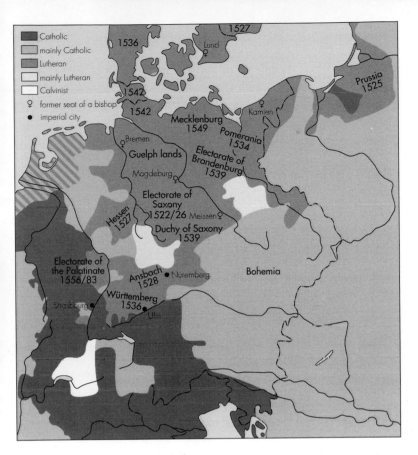

Catholic
mainly Catholic
Lutheran
mainly Lutheran
Calvinist
♀ former seat of a bishop
● imperial city

1527
1536
Lund ♀
1542
1542
Mecklenburg 1549
Bremen ♀
Guelph lands
Magdeburg ♀
Electorate of Saxony 1522/26
Hessen 1527
Duchy of Saxony 1539
Electorate of the Palatinate 1556/83
Ansbach 1528
Strasbourg ●
Württemberg 1536
Ulm
Nuremberg ●
Prussia 1525
Kamien ♀
Pomerania 1534
Electorate of Brandenburg 1539
Meissen ♀
Bohemia

Denominational Divisions in Germany and Central Europe in 1555

The dates indicate the year in which the Reformation was introduced in a given region. The majority of imperial cities joined the Reformation between 1522 and 1530.

his call to the "Christian nobility of the German Nation" in 1520, he was using the term "German nation" entirely in its traditional sense of the German aristocracy, meaning the ecclesiastical and secular rulers. His aim was not to bring about cultural unity or stimulate political action but to foster "improvement of the Christian estate" and reform of the Roman pope's church.

Martin Luther was celebrated by the humanist scholars of his time as a "German Hercules," the "German nightingale." His appearance on the scene evoked feelings of emerging national identity. It is an extraordinary example of historical irony that Luther's Reformation dealt a decisive setback to the development of a culturally—and perhaps also politically—unified country. Because the Reformation did not prevail in all parts of the empire, and Protestantism was taken over by Lutheran rulers and their established church hierarchies, the interdenominational struggle in Germany remained unresolved, and hardened into the principle based on territorial sovereignty: *cuius regio, eius religio* (the ruler of the region determines its religion). As a consequence, the territorial division of the empire was paralleled and intensified by the denominational split.

People who used the word *patria,* the fatherland, were not referring to the empire, for it was and remained remote; it existed as a tangible institution for the inhabitants of imperial cities and the upper echelons of the nobility, perhaps, but no one else. *Patria* did not mean "Germany" either, for that was a vague notion at best, related more to cultural than political experience. And *patria* certainly did not refer to the German nation, for that denoted quite precisely the members of the Imperial Diet who represented the estates in negotiations with the emperor and not the people who lived within the borders of the empire and spoke German. "The fatherland" was the city where you lived, or the principality in which you had to be loyal to the ruling house and belong to its denomination.

And it was not only in the political and denominational sense that paths diverged in Germany; culturally there was also a parting of the ways. The regions of the empire that remained Catholic—mainly the west and south with the exception of most larger cities—came under the influence of the Counter-Reformation culture of southern Europe. This meant a broadening of perspective and openness toward the culture of the rest of Catholic Europe, but at the same time ties with the Protestant north were cut off. From then on, under French and Italian influence, Catholic Germany experienced a flowering of painting, sculpture, theater, and architecture. Splendid churches and

Title Page of Luther's Bible
(Augsburg, 1535)

No fewer than 4,000 Biblical manuscripts in German were in circulation during the Middle Ages, including 43 complete Bibles, but none of them succeeded in gaining general recognition. Martin Luther's translation enjoyed success not only because he borrowed the colorful idiom of popular speech but also because as a university-trained scholar and humanist he was concerned with producing an accurate text. Luther finished his translation in 1534, and only a year later a luxury edition for princes, patrons, and officials was printed in Augsburg, with large woodcuts by artists of the stature of Holbein and Cranach. The first owner of the copy shown, Count Casimir of Ortenburg, was a strict Calvinist and therefore rubbed out God's countenance above the words *Gottes wort bleibt ewig*, "the word of God endures forever."

The Seasons in Augsburg
(after Jörg Breu the Elder, Augsburg, sixteenth century)

The wealthy mercantile city of Augsburg is shown in fall and early winter, around the year 1530. October is the month of slaughtering; as pigs are driven across the market square to be slaughtered, vendors offer poultry for sale in the foreground. In November the ground is already covered with snow, inviting citizens to take a sleigh ride. In December the city councillors leave the city hall in a solemn procession. All in all, the atmosphere is peaceful and festive; there is not the slightest trace of unrest or rebellion, and the countryside is always very close.

palaces were built in these regions, whereas the Protestants, in addition to their cultivation of church music, focused on language and works of literature. The consequences of this cultural divergence are still recognizable in Germany today.

In this respect, too, Germany straddled a dividing line that ran across the whole continent. While the compromise negotiated by the Imperial Diet at Augsburg in 1555 between the Catholic and Lutheran estates brought peace to the empire, vehement religious conflicts erupted throughout the rest of Europe. The source of this contention was not Luther's teachings, but the more radical doctrine of Calvinism, whose followers rejected Luther's obedience to authority and insisted on acceptance of their faith as the true one, no matter what the cost. According to the teaching of

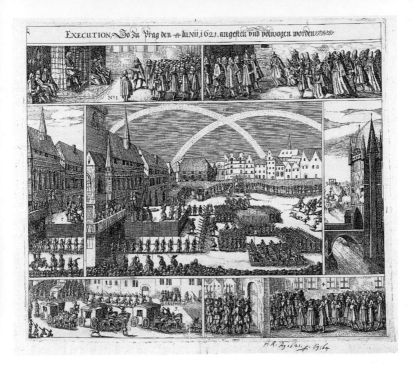

EXECUTION, So zu Prag den 4 Iunii, 1621. angestelt vnd volnzogen worden

Broadsheet on the Prague Executions
(Germany, 1621)

The rebellion of the Protestant estates in Bohemia, which set off the Thirty Years' War, was put down by the troops of the emperor and the Catholic League at the battle of the White Mountain outside Prague on November 8, 1620. The revenge exacted by Emperor Ferdinand II, King of Bohemia, was intended to set an example. He revoked freedom of religion in Bohemia, abolished the electoral monarchy, and had almost all the leaders of the uprising sentenced to death. The broadsheet depicts the proclamation of the death sentences, relatives' vain appeals for clemency, the transport of the prisoners into the city, their torture and execution, and the display of their severed heads on a bridge tower—all scenes that left a deep impression on the Czech national consciousness and have continued to affect Czech–German relations up to the present day.

John Calvin (1509–1564), if a ruler proscribed the beliefs of his subjects, each individual was duty-bound to offer active resistance. That meant a willingness to go as far as civil war, and in 1562 just such a civil war broke out in France. The Calvinists, called Huguenots in France, took up arms all over the country, and until 1598 France was wracked by a series of bloody conflicts, in which inflamed religious passions led to the commission of atrocious crimes by both sides.

France was finally saved from being torn apart by the conversion of the Huguenot leader Henry of Navarre to Catholicism, and his coronation as king. But the French civil war was only one episode of a prolonged bloodbath that threatened to submerge most of the nations in Europe. In the seven northern provinces of the Spanish Netherlands the Reformed aristocracy rebelled against the Counter-Reformation policies of Madrid. The armed conflict that erupted in 1567 was part war of liberation, part civil war; it dragged on long past the turn of the century and was not truly ended until Dutch independence was recognized in the Peace of Westphalia in 1648. At that time the English Civil War—which had begun in 1642—was still raging between two factions, one loyal to the king and one to parliament. In England, as in the Netherlands, the political power struggle was overlaid by denominational discord. But there the unthinkable actually happened: The defeated monarch was sentenced to death by the House of Commons as a tyrant and enemy of the people, and publicly executed.

Germany, on the other hand, was experiencing the longest peacetime era of its whole history, from 1555 (the Peace of Augsburg) until 1618. It ended mainly because over the course of this time ambitious leaders had formed alliances along denominational lines and were only waiting for the right moment to strike. The opportunity presented itself when the simmering tensions between the Protestant majority of the Bohemian estates and the provincial administration of the Catholic, Counter-Reformation Hapsburg dynasty came to a boil. On May 23, 1618, the Bohemian estates rebelled. Following an old custom of theirs in cases of political protest, they threw several of the emperor's officials out of a window in Prague Castle, then formed a provisional Bohemian government, expelled the Jesuits, and raised an army. Emperor Ferdinand II (reigned 1619–1637) suppressed the uprising with force, supported by the states of the Catholic League under the leadership of Bavaria, while the member states of the Protestant Union took the side of their Bohemian co-religionists.

Albrecht Wenzel von Wallenstein, Duke of Friedland

(copper engraving, middle of the seventeenth century)

The Thirty Years' War shook the empire to its foundations and made a reordering appear possible. Wallenstein (1583–1634), commander of mercenary troops for the emperor, was a great general with autocratic tendencies. Supported by the army he had assembled, which came to feel increasingly more loyal to him than the emperor, Wallenstein wanted to concentrate imperial rule and make it absolute, perhaps for the emperor, but perhaps also for himself. Emperor Frederick II began to fear his commander's revolutionary zeal for power and had him murdered on February 25, 1634, in Eger.

Out of this conflict developed a war that spread far beyond the borders of the empire, led by great generals whose names came to symbolize the diametrical oppositions of the times: Wallenstein, Tilly, Mansfeld. The aim of this Thirty Years' War—actually a succession of several wars—was to restore the Catholic unity of Europe with the aid of the mighty Hapsburg and Wittelsbach dynasties. When King Gustavus II Adolphus of Sweden (reigned 1611–1632) entered the conflict, he was welcomed by the Protestant estates as a virtual Protestant counter-emperor, and his intervention might well have resulted in a division of the empire into a Catholic and a Protestant Germany had he not been killed at the Battle of Lützen in 1632.

In addition, however, the Hapsburgs and France were engaged in a power struggle for hegemony in Europe, and Catholic France, despite its own internal turmoil, took up the Protestant cause outside its borders under the leadership of its great statesmen Richelieu and Mazarin. And last but not least, the territorial rulers within the empire hoped to quash the emperor's designs to consolidate his power over them, and used the issue of Protestantism as their justification.

The Peace of Westphalia, negotiated at Münster and Osnabrück, put an end to the looting and pillaging by mercenary troops in 1648. Large areas of Germany had been laid waste; the casualties, besides the direct combatants and civilians murdered by marauding soldiers, included the victims of famines and the plague, carried across great distances by roving bands of mercenaries and streams of refugees. By 1648 the German population had dropped from 17 million to 10 million; it took a century and a half for it to regain the levels existing prior to the blood-letting of the Thirty Years' War.

The peace treaties of Münster and Osnabrück, which ended a conflict that in the end had drawn in most of Europe, were therefore a European accord. It had taken the devastating, all-encompassing war to convince the nations of Europe that in the long run the only way to prevent ongoing universal strife was a political order that included everyone. What emerged from the Thirty Years' War was the European community of nations, and the Peace of Westphalia became in effect a European constitution. This became the starting point for the development of a *ius publicum europeum,* a prevailing international law on the continent, although a series of later treaties and conventions was necessary to ensure the stability of the European nation-state system. Henceforth the coexistence of European states would be regulated by binding legal norms that transcended day-to-day politics and remained valid even in wartime, regarding the special status of diplomats, conventions for declaring and ending hostilities, the legitimacy of war, and ways to maintain peace.

Above all else, however, they established the inviolability of na-

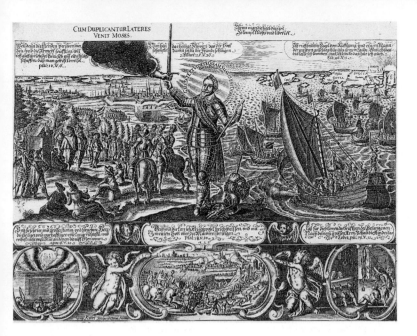

Gustav Adolf Landing in Germany
(broadside, Cologne, 1632)

On July 6, 1632, King Gustavus II Adolphus of Sweden (ruled 1611–1632) landed on the island of Usedom on the Baltic coast at the head of a peasant army. German Protestants, under pressure in the Thirty Years' War, flocked to the rescuer from the north as if he were a Protestant emperor. The broadside depicts him as a Moses liberating the Chosen People; crowned with laurels, he stands on a rise near the coast, accepting a sword from the hand of God. The Biblical quotations place him among the redeemers and prophets of Israel, creating a perspective in which the war appears as a struggle between good and evil in the spirit of the Old Testament.

tional sovereignty. From that time on the existence and sovereign rights of every European state were recognized by every other state. But to ensure that this system of nation states would remain in balance for the foreseeable future, the center had to be weak and fragmented, as a means of separating the powerful nations on the periphery: Sweden, Denmark, the Netherlands, Great Britain, France, the Ottoman Empire, and Russia. If hostilities broke out, this central region would serve as their theater of war; in peacetime, it would offer strategic and diplomatic maneuvering room. Thus the Holy Roman

Soldiers Plundering a Farmhouse
(Sebastian Vrancx, ca. 1600)

Robbery, murder, rape, arson—that was war from the perspective of the civilian population, as in the case of the Dutch peasants depicted here under attack from a band of pillaging soldiers. This picture was in fact painted before the outbreak of the Thirty Years' War, but precisely where the atrocities were committed, or by which party, is of little significance. The wealth of detail included by the artist gives a powerful impression of the suffering inflicted by war throughout the calamitous seventeenth century.

Empire, weak and exhausted after a long, devastating war, became the soft center of the European nation-state system. The Peace of Westphalia was not only a comprehensive treaty of baroque complexity; it was also the basic law of the empire. Simultaneously it granted independence to Switzerland and United Provinces in the northern Netherlands, which had in any event been part of the empire in name only for some time.

The old imperial constitution, consisting of the Golden Bull and the Peace of Augsburg that had resolved the denominational question in 1555, was expanded and made more detailed. The new treaty declared that Protestants and Catholics were to have equal representation in all institutions of the empire, and granted the denominations themselves official status under the constitution. Formally organized as the *corpus evangelicorum* and *corpus catholicorum,* they met as a separate chamber of the Imperial Diet and debated questions of religion, without running the risk that one party might achieve a majority over the other. By granting official recognition to Calvinism as well, the new law ensured that the empire would remain multidenominational. At the same time the imperial princes were granted full authority over all spiritual and temporal matters within their territories. Henceforth they had the right to raise armies and also conclude treaties with one another and with foreign powers. This provision made each and every one of the German princes an independent party under international law; their sovereignty was limited only by the allegiance they owed to the empire and its main institutions, the Imperial Diet, the Imperial Cameral Tribunal (Reichskammergericht), and the Imperial Council.

The new balance, in which the empire was fragmented and considerably weakened in favor of greater rights of independence for the German principalities and imperial cities, was guaranteed by two powers on its flanks, France and Sweden. The French took over the bishoprics of Metz, Toul, and Verdun, replaced the Hapsburgs as rulers of Alsace, and simultaneously sought to increase their influence in the empire through an extremely active policy of alliances with the German princes. The Swedes acquired West Pomerania and two former bishoprics, Verden and Bremen; this gave them strategically important possessions at the mouths of the Oder, Elbe, and Weser rivers and simultaneously made Sweden one of the imperial estates. Later, after Sweden lost the Great Northern War and its power went into decline, Russia stepped in as the guarantor of the empire on its eastern flank and allied itself with France to suppress change there as far as possible. The empire's constitution had now passed into the hands of the European powers.

3

Twilight of the Empire

(1648–1806)

In later times Germans tended to view the peace treaties of Münster and Osnabrück as a misfortune, a low point in German history. And indeed, from a perspective that saw the establishment of a nation state as the goal of all German history, these treaties could not appear as anything but a grave setback. "Imperial power and national morale had dropped to zero," lamented the historian Heinrich von Sybel in 1889. "Particularism had taken over completely on German soil and in the Germans' minds." Yet while this assessment was not entirely wrong, neither was it altogether true. It is an astonishing but little-noted fact that the Holy Roman Empire continued to exist—not only through the guarantees of the European powers but also legally, through feudal privileges and obligations handed down since the Middle Ages, on which relations between the princes and the emperor, their feudal overlord, continued to

Frederick Augustus I, Prince Elector of Saxony, as King Augustus II of Poland
(Louis de Silvestre the Younger, ca. 1728)

Augustus the Strong (ruled Saxony 1694–1733) was one of the most glittering rulers of the German baroque, yet he also had a popular touch. Thanks to a flourishing economy, he could afford to emulate the splendor of the Viennese imperial court at his own court in Saxony. Frederick Augustus enjoyed political success as well; by converting to Catholicism he attained the Polish crown in 1697. In this portrait by Louis de Silvestre he is depicted as king of Poland: Over his armor he wears the blue ribbon of the Polish Order of the White Eagle, and the sash around his waist is red and white, the Polish colors. The crown and other royal insignia behind his left arm are an invention of the artist.

be based. The emperor and his subjects carried on under the old cumbersome and inflexible code of laws, a tangled thicket of virtually impenetrable complexity. Nonetheless, it provided for peace and stability by protecting and balancing the rights and claims of the vest-pocket territories against the giants, and by providing a framework, respected by all, for the heterogeneous collection of principalities that had grown up over the centuries. The legal foundations of the empire constituted a minor peace accord within the general harmony now reached by the major powers of Europe.

Even at the time, however, its structure was regarded as old-fashioned, backward, and too complex for the ordinary person to grasp. In a famous 1667 critique of the empire's constitution, the legal scholar Samuel von Pufendorf claimed that the empire had become a monster; although the imperial censors immediately banned his book, his complaint was taken up and repeated on all sides. And indeed many factors contributed to the tradition-bound backwardness of the empire compared with its neighbors to the west. The drastic decline in population and general poverty following the end of the Thirty Years' War were matched by widespread economic stagnation, as the territories of the empire were cut off from the growing transatlantic trade and the fruits of colonial conquests abroad. One exception is the attempts of Prince Frederick William of Brandenburg, the "Great Elector" (ruled 1640–1688), to found colonies on the coast of West Africa. His determination foundered on lack of funds, however, and in the end he was forced to sell his colonies to the Dutch. Besides the lack of capital, problems of trade were exacerbated by the small size of most principalities, which did not permit the growth of sizable economic markets, and a density of customs barriers that bordered on the ludicrous. A merchant trying to transport his wares down the Rhine from Basel to Cologne, for example, had to tie up at a toll house and pay customs duties every six or seven miles on the average. The numerous principalities ranging from small to minuscule, which gave the empire its dominant character, possessed neither the financial means nor the will to mold themselves into new-style states with modern administrations.

This drove many of the lesser princelings to invest all the more energy in copying the splendor of the courts of Versailles and Vienna, as a demonstration of their political sovereignty. They celebrated their rank in elaborate displays and court ceremony, laid stress on their divine right to rule, and kept court circles remote from ordinary people—all to further their image as absolute monarchs, in the style of their model who resided at Versailles: King Louis XIV. For their subjects this often resulted in a somewhat claustrophobic form of absolutism, for in contrast to spacious countries such as France, Spain, or Austria, there was no easy way to avoid notice: His Highness was always just down the street. "Don't seek out your ruler's halls, / Keep out of sight until he calls," ran the popular rhyme, a sensible recommendation perhaps, but hardly conducive to the development of a liberal, self-confident outlook among the bourgeoisie.

To the outside world the empire appeared weak and unimpressive. Under Louis XIV (reigned 1643–1715) France, which had succeeded Spain as the dominant power in Europe, reached out to seize territories far to the north and east, with the aim of interrupting the strategic march route from Hapsburg controlled northern Italy through the Upper Rhine valley and Alsace to the Netherlands, controlled first by Spain and later by Austria. This would destroy the link between the two territories that had previously held France in a pincer's grip. The Sun King had a further interest: to gain the Rhine as a natural frontier and establish bridgeheads on its eastern banks, in order to control as much terrain as he could between Paris and potential staging areas for hostile armies.

Imperial troops offered only feeble resistance to the French forces that advanced into Alsace and the Palatinate and caused terrible devastation. In Vienna the French envoy delivered offensive and threatening speeches, to which Emperor Leopold I (reigned 1658–1705) did not dare object. Powerful German princes such as the electors in the

A Water Hunt in the Grounds of Schwetzingen Palace
(Jacobus Schlachter [?], ca. 1730)

An artificial pond has been created in the palace grounds, and the game to be killed has been driven into the water, where the festive aristocratic company has no trouble dispatching it. The mood is heightened by a painted backdrop behind the basin. Hunting was a privilege reserved for aristocrats and court circles; it was considered a form of knightly exercise, and poaching by a ruler's ordinary subjects was viewed as an infringement of these privileges and punished with extreme severity. Large-scale hunts with beaters driving the game into an enclosure went out of fashion in the eighteenth century, and hunting became just one of the many pastimes available to the nobility. The privilege was defended fiercely well into the nineteenth century, arousing bitter and lasting resentment in the rural population.

Rhineland, but above all the "Great Elector" Frederick William of Brandenburg, had no scruples about entering into periodical alliances with France against the emperor. After the imperial city of Strasbourg fell to French troops, the emperor signed a humiliating truce in Regensburg in 1684 that allowed France to keep all the territory and towns it had conquered. This outcome was formally confirmed in the Treaty of Rijswijk in 1697. The empire had no alternative; a more dangerous enemy was threatening its borders in the east, with French consent.

In 1683 the archenemy of Christendom was encamped outside

The Siege of Vienna Is Lifted, 1683
(ca. 1700)

In July 1683 the Turkish Grand Vizier Kara Mustafa Pasha attacked Vienna with an army of 250,000 men. After a nine-week siege the city was in imminent danger of falling but was rescued in the nick of time by the Christian troops of King John III Sobieski of Poland and Charles of Lorraine, the emperor's field marshal. The defeat put an end to Turkish expansion, but the Turkish wars that followed turned Austria's attention toward southeastern Europe, an area of influence that became a lasting preoccupation.

the gates of Vienna in the form of a Turkish army under Grand Vizier Kara Mustafa Pasha. The city's rescue at the last minute by imperial and Polish troops under Charles, Duke of Lorraine, and John III Sobieski seemed like a miracle. And it also seemed miraculous that after stumbling along from one truce to the next, the lethargic emperor Leopold I managed to pull himself together

Allegory on the Coronation of King
Frederick I of Prussia on January 18, 1701
(copper engraving, first half of the eighteenth
century)

Frederick I was the grandfather of King Frederick II "the Great," who summed up his forebear's reign as follows: "Frederick I acquired some new territories, but they were too insignificant to attract the attention of the rest of Europe. Even his weaknesses worked to the advantage of his house: His vanity prompted him to seek the rank of king, which at first seemed entirely lacking in foundation; later, however, this title acquired a firm footing."

for a decisive confrontation with the Ottoman foe. The Turkish War (1683–1699) was a resounding success, unlike the attempts to defend the Rhine against Louis XIV. The imperial propaganda machine cranked away, and the fame of commanders such as Prince Eugene of Savoy, Prince Elector Max Emanuel of Bavaria, and Margrave Ludwig of Baden—"Turkish Louie"—swelled to legendary proportions; their exploits provided the basis for appalling rumors, sensational broadsides, and folk songs. Germany was swept by a wave of enthusiasm for the emperor and the imperial cause.

Strangely enough, however, while the public held the empire responsible for the losses to the French, it gave credit for the victories over the armies of Süleyman II and Achmed II to Austria. While this should be ascribed in part to the effectiveness of Hapsburg propaganda, it also shows the extent to which Austria was beginning to loosen its ties with the empire and to become a major power in its own right.

The emperor, residing in Vienna, was simultaneously head of the royal house of Austria, a "country" that actually consisted of a number of territories united under the crown with widely differing law codes and separate representative bodies for their estates. The hereditary German lands included the archduchy of Austria, the duchies of Styria, Carinthia, Carniola, and the county of Tyrol; then there was the kingdom of Bohemia with the margravate of Moravia and the duchy of Silesia, and finally, outside the borders of the empire, the kingdom of Hungary. Since the Peace of Westphalia, the emperor's power had been strictly limited, and thus the Hapsburg rulers concentrated all the more on consolidating and strengthening their power base in their hereditary lands, which formed a colorful world of their own. All the different parts met in Vienna, the capital that grew into one of the great metropolises of Europe during this period. Here the cultures of southern Germany, Bohemia, and Hungary mingled with those of other Catholic countries like Italy, France, and Spain. A baroque, cosmopolitan splendor unfolded, utterly unlike anything ever seen in the stodgy provincial backwaters where the other German princes resided.

The Austrians were unable to project a sense of their might much beyond the denominational divide between Catholic and Protestant to their north, however. The empire's reduced influence in northern Germany was matched by the decline of Sweden and Poland, its

**Grenadier James Kirkland, a Soldier in [the]
Royal Guard of King Frederick William [of]
Prussia**
(Johann Christof Merk, ca. 1714)

Prussia's rise to the status of a major European power was accompanied by a mi[litary]
build-up of vast proportions that was ma[in]-
tained, prompting Count Mirabeau's fam[ous]
observation, "Prussia is not a country wi[th an]
army, but an army with a country it app[ears]
to be occupying." King Frederick Willia[m]
(ruled 1713–1740) had the largest arm[y in]
Europe in proportion to total population, [yet]
he never fought a war. Instead, he comb[ed]
Europe for the tallest soldiers he could fi[nd]
and hired them for his personal guard a[t]
great expense—one of the few areas in
which he overcame his habitual stingine[ss.]
All over Europe people laughed at the "[big]
boys" of the Potsdam Guards, dismissing
them as a foolish affectation of the king's[;]
at that date no one took the Prussian arm[y]
seriously.

King Frederick II "the Great" of Prussia in the Uniform of a Field Marshal
(Antoine Pesne, ca. 1745)

neighbors to the north and east. The resulting power vacuum in central Europe was filled by the rise of Brandenburg-Prussia. The territorial conglomerate centered here was a largely artificial construction that had come into being through the sheer willpower and organizational talent of its ruling family, the Hohenzollerns, but managed to outlast them. It consisted of Brandenburg, long governed by prince electors, the minuscule territories of Cleve, Mark, and Ravensberg on the Lower Rhine, and Prussia—later known as east Prussia—located just within the northeastern limit of traditionally German-speaking areas but already outside the borders of the Holy Roman Empire.

When Prince Elector Frederick III (ruled 1688–1713) crowned himself "King in Prussia" at Königsberg in 1701 and desired to be addressed henceforth as King Frederick I, people in Vienna just laughed and dismissed him as a crank; his act changed nothing whatsoever in the states he ruled. He had no contiguous territory comparable to France or Bavaria, for instance, or even to the hereditary Hapsburg lands of Austria. There were several such states in Europe, created by the fortunes of war and dynastic inheritance and made up of scattered bits and pieces, but as a rule they collapsed within a few decades after their founding. Prussia was the great exception, thanks to its success in finding an answer to the main problem confronting it.

This problem consisted of an apparently insoluble paradox: Prussia's location in the center of Europe demanded a foreign policy that did not make any of its neighbors feel threatened. At the same time, however, as long as its borders lay open, inviting the armies of neighboring powers to walk in, its continued existence remained precarious. Historical precedent offered two different avenues of escape from this dilemma. The first was for Prussia to follow the example of the empire as a whole—to open itself up to political influence from the outside and allow its neighbors to dictate its policy. This was the path chosen by Poland, the other sizable nation in central Europe. As a consequence, Polish sovereignty was undermined, the country fell into anarchy, and it was finally divided up among its neighbors. The second strategy was for Prussia to organize and arm itself to the point where it could repel an attack on any of its borders—which offered no natural protection and were widely distant from one another—and win the ensuing war even against a coalition of several enemy states.

And winning was essential. If any of the major European powers lost a war, they had to reckon with being forced to pay reparations or cede a bit of territory here or there, but they knew their core would survive. For an upstart nation like Prussia, however, its very survival was at stake in every conflict. In addition there was the question of finances: Prussia was dirt poor. It had practically no natural resources and a relatively small number of inhabitants. Around 1700 the Prussian states had a population of 3.1 million, whereas Poland had 6 million people, the Hapsburg states 8.8 million, Russia approximately 17 million, and France, the most populous country in Europe, 20 million.

By 1740 Prussia ranked tenth among the nations of Europe in terms of area, thirteenth in population, but third or fourth in military might. Prussia had chosen the second strategy. This decision accounts for the disproportionate emphasis on the military in the Prussian state and its bureaucratic organization of all aspects of life so that every last resource could be mobilized in case of need; it also explains much in the Prussian—and later the German—character that made that nation so unpopular with its European neighbors: the heavy earnestness, the strained rigidity, the lack of urbanity and *joie de vivre*. All of this was necessary if Brandenburg-Prussia was to survive and, it should be added, if the new king Frederick II's well-calculated grab for the Austrian territory of Silesia in December 1740 was to succeed.

This coup by the young king just after ascending the throne caused a sensation throughout Europe. With the death of Emperor Charles VI on October 20, 1740, clouds of war had gathered on the horizon. The Austrian emperor had no male heirs, and although he had been

Empress Maria Theresa as Queen of Hungary
(Marin van Meytens the Younger, second half of the eighteenth century)

trying for decades to persuade the European powers to agree to the terms of the "Pragmatic Sanction," which would allow his daughter Maria Theresa to inherit the throne of an undivided Austria, naturally the temptation to exploit the Hapsburgs' weakness was great. Even before the emperor's death, members of the cabinets of France,

Spain, Bavaria, and Saxony had begun planning how they would divide up the assets of the Hapsburg monarchy which, they assumed, would soon be bankrupt. But Frederick II pre-empted them all. His daring wager that he could succeed in seizing Silesia staked everything on one card, for he knew that in all likelihood his throne and the state of Prussia would cease to exist if he were defeated.

The shifting of national boundaries was certainly no great rarity in the eighteenth century; in the aftermath of major wars, whole provinces and even empires changed hands. Thus Austria had wrested the greater part of Hungary from the Turks, along with the region of Banat, Serbia, and a portion of Wallachia (part of modern Romania). France secured Lorraine in 1766, and Naples, together with Sicily, even changed hands twice. Russia won Estonia and Livonia from Sweden, and the southern Netherlands passed from Spanish to Austrian rule. But unlike even Louis XIV in his predatory campaigns for territorial aggrandizement, Frederick II made not the slightest pretense of having right on his side. He risked everything, as he wrote to Voltaire, from a wish "to read his name in the newspapers and later in the history books," and for reasons of state: He wanted to see Prussia as a great power in Europe, instead of a place "neither fish nor fowl, more like an electoral principality than a kingdom."

Frederick profited from the factor of surprise, from the well-trained and well-equipped army his father had left him, and from the greed of the other European powers, who sought alliances with the unscrupulous aggressor in the hope of sharing in the Hapsburg spoils. Supported by Saxony, Bavaria, France, and Spain, Frederick was able to hold on to most of Silesia in the first Silesian War (1740–1742). He began the second Silesian War (1744–1745) out of concern that the Austrians might try to recoup their losses, but he was lucky to achieve a draw against the allied forces of Austria, England, and Saxony. Austria ceded the greater part of Silesia in return for Prussian recognition of Maria Theresa as the Hapsburg heir and her consort, Francis Stephen of Lorraine-Tuscany, as Holy Roman Emperor.

Recruiting Poster for the Infantry Regiment of Anhalt

(Germany, 1762–1763)

Although every region of Prussia supplied a regiment to the army, the population was not large enough to supply the number of soldiers demanded by the king. Prussian recruiters thus traveled throughout Europe looking for promising men, resorting to criminal tactics and impressment if necessary. This recruiting poster suggests that a pleasant life awaits those willing to sign up; although soldiers will have to drill, the advertisement promises instruction in French, dancing, and fencing as well as reading and writing, "a goodly cash allowance," and plentiful wine in barrels.

From the central European perspective a tremendous upheaval had occurred. Germany was now split into two camps, divided by the Main River. The empire in the south faced an opponent of nearly equal strength in the north, and the Catholic emperor was confronted by a virtual Protestant counter-emperor in the shape of the Hohenzollern king. Now Protestant Germany had a defender within the empire itself, and no longer needed to turn to foreign powers for protection. Austria neither could nor would accept the loss of Silesia as permanent, however; it was too important. The Hapsburg monarchy derived 18 percent of its revenues from this one rich province, and its strategic location as the northeastern bastion of hereditary Austrian lands made it seem indispensable to the state chancellor, Count Kaunitz. And so fourteen years later yet another struggle over Silesia and supremacy in German-speaking territories took place, the Seven Years' War (1756–1763), and this time Prussia, a troublemaker apparently thoroughly determined to upset the balance of power in Europe, was opposed by a daunting coalition of Austria, France, Russia, and the majority of imperial princes.

It was in this war against overwhelming numbers and odds that Frederick earned his epithet "the Great." While he was certainly helped by subsidies from Britain and the unexpected death of Empress Elizabeth of Russia in 1762, it was his tactical genius in the field that won the day, in combination with almost suicidal determination and phenomenal good luck. At the same time all this was only a minor episode in the epochal battle between France and Britain over supremacy on the seas and the great colonial empires in North America and Asia. In the eyes of the British, Prussia was merely a "Continental hussar" with no purpose other than to tie up French forces and prevent their being deployed in India and North America. The peace treaty of Hubertusburg, signed by the exhausted parties on February 15, 1763, and guaranteeing both Prussia's status as a great power and its possession of Silesia, came only five days after the Treaty of Paris, in which France ceded most of its overseas colonies to Britain. The conquest of America, observed former Prime Minister William Pitt (1708–1778), had taken place in Germany.

After the Seven Years' War, it might have appeared as if the world of German states had broken free from the empire to a large degree and caught up with their neighbors in the European system as sovereign powers capable of political action. Austria, Prussia, Bavaria, Saxony, and Württemberg were all independent states in the same sense as France or Poland. And the empire? It was more a fading myth than a political reality, a lawyers' construction that existed largely on paper, apart from a few institutions such as the Imperial Council in Vienna, the Imperial Cameral Tribunal in Wetzlar, or the "permanent diet" in Regensburg. To Johann Wolfgang von Goethe, growing up in the old imperial city of Frankfurt, the coronation in 1764 of the German king who later became Emperor Joseph II seemed an exotic spectacle—an interminable, complex, antiquated ritual full of arcane symbolism that nonetheless touched him, since it made "the Empire, nearly buried under so many parchments, papers, and books, come alive for a moment."

This does not imply that the empire had drifted off to an existence on a purely metaphysical plane. For the small German estates, the ecclesiastical principalities, free cities, and imperial knights, who would otherwise have been utterly defenseless against the rapacious appetites of the great powers, the emperor and empire still meant a great deal in terms of protection and support. Yet it was also true that imperial troops—contingents supplied by the German states allied with the Hapsburgs—had played only a marginal role over the course of the long Silesian wars; satirical popular songs portraying the imperial

Estate	Percentage of the population			
	Germany		Europe	
	1500	1800	1500	1800
Nobility (ruling estate)	1–2	1	1–2	1
Bourgeoisie (town dwellers)	20	24	20	21
Peasants (rural population)	78	75	78	78
Landed farmers	58	35	53	43
Agricultural laborers (with little or no land)	20	40	25	35
Population in millions	12	24	55	190

Percentage of the Estates in the Total Population of Germany and Europe in 1500 and 1800

In the Middle Ages and the early modern period, Europeans understood their social order as a pyramid formed by the estates. Generally speaking the nobility and clergy formed the ruling estate, with the bourgeoisie and peasantry following in order. The percentages of the population making up each estate remained more or less stable for centuries, and the figures for Germany do not deviate significantly from the rest of Europe. The picture that results is of an extremely static society, in which the only alterations occur in the rural population: The numbers of peasants with little or no land of their own rise, as a result of overall population growth and the constant division of farms among heirs.

army as taking to its heels every time Frederick sneezed hardly showed the empire and its present sad condition in a good light. In the years of peace after 1763 a discussion thus sprang up over ways to renew and reform it.

The idea of forming a third Germany—that is to say, a new federation of the small and midsized German territories alongside the two great powers of Austria and Prussia, now only loosely attached to the empire—gained adherents; so, too, did plans to revive the obligations owed to the empire by the princes, in their role as vassals and one of the estates, and to strengthen the ties between the emperor and his realm. The empire had transformed and rejuvenated itself so many times since the days of Caesar, of Charlemagne, of Maximilian I—why should the old shell not be able to take on new life once more? At the end of the eighteenth century the future of central Europe seemed open. In the many small territories, the newly kindled patriotic feelings for the empire that could protect them contrasted sharply with the more limited Austrian or Prussian national sentiment that the Silesian wars had awakened in the subjects of the Hapsburgs and Hohenzollerns.

Given the realities of the empire and its constituent states, the actual significance of the term "Germany" remained elusive. In 1656 Ludwig von Seckendorff (1626–1692), a civil servant and political philosopher in Saxony, had declared in his *Teutscher Fürstenstaat* ("The German Principality") that a "German nation" existed in the political sense, but conceded that it was difficult to describe and that many other nations existed within it on lower levels. The more than three hundred German principalities were based on the idea of "nationhood," too, from the kingdom of Württemberg to tiny Anhalt-Zerbst, from Brandenburg to minuscule Braunschweig-Calenberg.

In the seventeenth and eighteenth centuries "German" still referred only to a language, nothing more, and at times even the prospects for its future were murky. Here and there learned societies sprang up such as the Fruitful Circle in Weimar or the Pegnitz Shepherds of Nuremberg, which devoted themselves to the cultivation of a pure German language in a rather touching imitation of the Académie Française. Their rigidly puristic tendencies amused other Germans, who made them the target of many jokes. It is a striking fact that such efforts on behalf of the German language were largely restricted to Protestant areas—and small wonder, for the literary standard of Protestant Germany was Martin Luther's translation of the Bible into his own Saxon-Meissen idiom. As late as the nineteenth century, Jacob Grimm expounded in the preface to his *German Grammar* that it was in fact legitimate "to describe Modern High German as the Protestant dialect."

Never more than in the last third of the eighteenth century did the Germans match the description of them given in 1766 by Friedrich Carl von Moser, a member of the Imperial Council: "a constitutional enigma, booty for our neighbors, the butt of their ridicule, divided

Family Group Making Music
(Germany, mid-eighteenth century)

In this scene the family has finished drinking coffee and the parents have begun to play on the clavichord and lute, while the children follow in their songbooks and wait for their entrance. *Hausmusik,* chamber music played at home, was more than just a family pastime; it was a declaration of independence from aristocratic music—operas and concerts at court—by a middle class that had found an inexpensive means of producing its own performances and created its own cultural domain.

Duchess Luise Dorothea of Saxe-Gotha-Altenburg in Her Study
(S. Hellmund, 1754)

The Enlightenment was not so much a distinct and defined philosophy as a cultural climate that prevailed throughout Europe in the eighteenth century and created an intellectual community. This community knew no national boundaries—and included a considerable number of women. Duchess Luise Dorothea of Saxe-Gotha-Altenburg (1710–1767) was a friend of Frederick the Great and corresponded with Voltaire, Diderot, Rousseau, and Empress Catherine the Great of Russia. She founded factories in the principality ruled by her husband and took an active interest in exports. This portrait shows her at her desk, which is piled with books and letters. The door to her study is ajar, giving a glimpse of the adjoining library. The painting contains a globe on the left, and on the right a statue of Minerva, goddess of wisdom and technical arts.

among ourselves, weakened by our partition, strong enough to harm ourselves, powerless to save ourselves, insensitive to the honor of our name, lacking unity on principles but violent in asserting them nevertheless, a great and yet despised people, fortunate in theory but in fact most pitiable." Yet at the same time the Germans were further along the road to seeing themselves as a nation than ever before.

The nation grew, in fact, precisely because of its fragmented identity and the practical requirements of a multitude of small states and governments. The absolute monarchs and rulers insisted on knowing what was going on in every corner of their territories and on being able to intervene in every area of their subjects' lives. These demands increased the size and scope of their administrations and required highly trained officials, who understood as much about markets and trade as about law and public finance. Aristocratic birth no longer sufficed; what was needed were ability and qualifications, and to assure a supply of capable civil servants, every prince did what he could to support secondary schools, universities, and academies. Consequently the second half of the eighteenth century saw the growth of an educated elite in Germany, composed of civil servants, clergymen, academics, jurists, teachers, doctors, book-dealers, and other professional men, recruited from the ranks of both the lesser aristocracy and the middle classes. All of them had one thing in common: They held their positions not on the basis of their inherited station in life but as a result of their training and ability.

As this new educated class grew, its existence contributed in turn to the development of a standard German language out of the myriad regional dialects and local idioms. Pan-German literature, drama, and opera created a unified opinion and taste that extended across the borders of the German territorial states. Writers who published in German in the second half of the eighteenth century did so not only because the market demanded it; they also identified themselves with a modern spirit being embraced by middle-class Germans throughout many regions, which consciously set itself apart from the French spoken at German courts and the aristocratic French culture favored there. It was in the sphere of a language distinct from the hegemony of French culture throughout Europe at this period that the educated German elite experienced a sense of national identity.

The political journalist and historian Justus Möser encouraged the

Germans in 1785 to stop being "apers of foreign trends," and the poet Klopstock included in his patriotic ode the verses:

> Nie war, gegen das Ausland,
> Ein anderes Land gerecht, wie du!
> Sei nicht allzu gerecht. Sie denken nicht edel genug
> Zu sehen, wie schön dein Fehler ist!

> Never was another country
> As just toward foreigners as you!
> Be not all too just. Their minds are not noble enough
> To see the beauty of your mistake!

Klopstock was addressing the German nation—one that existed only in the heads of its educated class, however. As long as four out of five Germans were rooted in peasant traditions, and experienced their only connection with the larger realm of politics when they prayed for the ruling family on Sundays or suffered the miseries of war, billeting of troops in their village, or plundering (the last just as likely to be committed by their own soldiers as those of the enemy)—as long as the younger generation in the cities, like Goethe as a young man, had no national hero except for the far-off Prussian, King Frederick the Great, who had defeated the French and Russian armies—as long as all this was the case, there was no soil able to nourish a real nation of active citizens.

According to the estimate of the Berlin book-dealer Friedrich Nicolai (1733–1811), there were only about 20,000 people in all of Germany participating in the national discourse in 1770—not a large enough number to have even the slightest effect on politics. For the time being, the German nation existed solely on the plane of language and culture; the growing degree of communication among educated people in all the various territories, an enormous outpouring of books in larger editions, a significant increase in the number of newspapers and journals, and a blossoming of reading circles in even the small towns resulted in a sophisticated public capable of rational thought, but one with definite limitations. As the French author Madame de Staël (1766–1817) observed in the early years of the nineteenth century, "Educated Germans debate one another with the greatest vigor in the theoretical sphere and will tolerate no restrictions in this area, but they seem quite content to leave all of real life to their earthly rulers."

In short, the German nation was born in the minds of the intelligentsia, as a cultural entity without direct ties to politics. It was therefore only logical that its great heroes were not princes and military leaders as in France and England but rather a collection of poets and philosophers, with the exception of Frederick the Great, himself renowned as "the philosopher of Sanssouci." For the Germans, Goethe and Weimar became the center of the nation, just as the king and London were for the English, or Napoleon and Paris for the French. Their political partition was not felt as a particular burden: Even though it had often been deplored since the days of the humanists, the remedy was by no means seen as the creation of a single nation state along the lines of France or England but rather an increase in solidarity among the princes and more committed support for the emperor. The problem was thought to lie not in the empire's territorial fragmentation but in the egotism of its rulers.

People considered the multitude of ruling families, capitals, and constitutions as an advantage; the poet and professor Christoph Martin Wieland summed up public opinion when he wrote that such diversity set limits for the despotic exercise of power, just as the natural diversity not only of habits and customs but also theaters and universities fostered culture and tolerance. Furthermore, he noted, wealth was more equally distributed than in countries whose riches were all concentrated in a single place. Germany's extraordinary cultural flowering made it the new Greece, said both Friedrich Schiller and Wilhelm von Humboldt—powerless but intellectually supreme. The new Rome, on the other hand—politically dominant, centrally or-

Cover of *Der Gesellige* ("The Socializer"), a Moral Weekly

(Germany, eighteenth century)

The ideas of the Enlightenment were spread to a mass audience of avid middle-class readers by an enormously expanded book and journal market. The existence of about four thousand different periodicals has been documented in German-speaking areas of Europe for the eighteenth century. One popular type was the "moral weekly," which dealt with middle-class mores and attitudes. The themes and concepts that defined German cultural horizons were developed and discussed in such journals; they created an intellectual domain that united the educated bourgeoisie across political frontiers and provided the foundations for a national German culture.

ganized, and civilized, but lacking the kind of culture in which Germans took such great pride—the new Rome was France.

In the last third of the eighteenth century unrest flared up all over Europe; these urban and rural rebellions were usually quickly put down but created a climate of general uncertainty. Crises of this kind, brought about by bad harvests and the resulting fluctuations in food prices, had been known since the Middle Ages, but no one had thought to argue that for this reason the political and social order was in need of reform. All this changed now. The trappings of absolute monarchy and old established privilege had come to seem threadbare and flimsy in the strong glare of the Enlightenment, which was not so much an elitist philosophy as an intellectual and cultural climate affecting all areas of life. The spirit of the Enlightenment filled people with the optimistic belief that it lay within their own power to achieve happiness in accord with the laws of nature and the human intellect. Human felicity no longer lay in heaven but on earth, and all it took to attain it, it seemed, was the exercise of reason and a bit of determination.

In America the people had already risen up against the tyranny of the British crown, and their rebellion had an effect on Europeans everywhere. Thus the ground had been prepared when the news arrived from Paris in June 1789 that the third estate had transformed itself into a National Assembly, declared that it alone represented the French people, and was drawing up a constitution based on popular sovereignty and the rights of man.

In the German intellectual world there was only one response: "This revolution," Immanuel Kant observed, "arouses in the hearts of all onlookers a wish to participate that approaches fervor." But the delight of the educated bourgeoisie that the spirit of the Enlightenment had now spread to politics did not remain unclouded for long. The revolution slid out of control and turned blood-thirsty, and the Terror of 1793 and 1794—the first mass murder in modern history and one committed in the name of all the virtues of Enlightenment—was regarded by horrified German citizens as the downfall of reason. They retreated to their inner "theoretical sphere," far from politics: Germany's most brilliant poets such as Novalis, Ludwig Tieck, Achim von Arnim, and Clemens Brentano set off in search of the blue flower of romanticism, while Europe was engulfed by wars and revolutions.

From April 1792 on, a state of war existed between revolutionary France and the other powers of Europe. The French revolutionaries thought war posed no threat to them, for they believed the Hapsburgs to be weak and preoccupied with overcoming internal divisions. In Paris the idea of Prussia and Austria forming an alliance appeared inconceivable. The military commanders of the European countries that joined a coalition against France believed for their part that their armies, steeled by the experiences of the Seven Years' War, were invincible; they were sure they could mop up the rag-tag insurgents in Paris in short order. Thus this war, like so many others, began because each side misjudged the other. It proved that the armies of the absolutist states were no match for the highly motivated French citizen-soldiers, who employed new tactics and also outnumbered them.

Within a few years, revolutionary France had put even the achievements of the mighty Sun King in the shade and was dictating the future of the Continent. Wars and the aims envisaged by those who waged them took on gigantic new dimensions; it was no longer a matter of frontiers shifting a little within a generally stable system of checks and balances, but of a revolutionary new order for Germany, Europe, even the world, and all the great powers were involved. France's goal was to annex all the territory west of its "natural" border, the Rhine, and to create a broad band of satellite states farther east, from the Batavian Republic to the Helvetian, Cisalpine, and Ligurian Republics. While the French were thus occupied, the antirevolutionary powers in the east—Russia, Prussia, and the Hapsburg dynasty—carried out a truly revolutionary action by carving up Poland among themselves, provisionally in 1793 and again for good in 1795, thereby wiping an old and important member of the European family of nations off the map.

More than just reordering the continent of Europe was at stake, for the war leaped halfway around the globe and gripped the colonial empires; from India to the Americas a naval war raged for possession of the colonies and control of important sea routes. A virtual world war was under way, and if the flames died down in one place, they broke out in another, in altered constellations and with new force. For the first time in modern history the belligerents were contending for world domination and annihilation of their enemies, and until one of the major combatants—England, France, or Russia—was crushed, there was no prospect that the fighting would end.

Prussia, however, always caught between Russia and France both

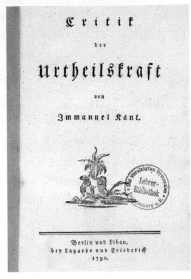

Early Editions of Works by Immanuel Kant: *Critique of Pure Reason* (Riga, 1787), *Critique of Judgment* (Berlin, 1790), and Second Edition of *Critique of Practical Reason* (Riga, 1792)

There was a paradox at the heart of Enlightenment thinking: Philosophers were concerned on the one hand with discovering the immutable laws that govern the workings of nature, but on the other with finding a philosophical foundation for individual human freedom. This gap was bridged by Immanuel Kant (1724–1804) of Königsberg, who wrote that reality does not manifest itself to us as it actually is, because the ability of the human mind to perceive the world around it is limited. The *Ding an sich*, the "thing as such" or actual physical reality, is hidden behind its apparent form. According to Kant, this distinction does not apply to the moral realm, however. Moral law—or the "categorical imperative" to "act at all times so that the principles on which you base your actions could be made into general laws"—manifests itself directly and fully to human perception, giving human beings the freedom to decide one way or another. We thus inhabit two worlds simultaneously, the realm of appearances, in which each of us is an insignificant atom in the grip of unalterable forces, and the realm of practical morality, in which we are free.

geographically and strategically, pulled out of the coalition against France and signed the Peace of Basel in 1795, ceding the Rhineland and abandoning its oath of loyalty to the German emperor and his empire. Prussia withdrew to the east, and for ten years peace reigned in northern and eastern Germany, guaranteed by Prussian military might—the peace that allowed the cultural world of Goethe and Schiller, of Novalis and Humboldt to develop and blossom. With this step Prussia gave the green light for a ruthless reconfiguration of the map of Germany, for a revolutionary concentration of territory and power that spelled the end of the Holy Roman Empire.

An unprecedented transfer of central European real estate began. While Spain and Portugal withdrew from the war exhausted, while Austria was handed one defeat after another, while Britain grew increasingly isolated and Russia showed a lack of interest, to the extent of allying itself with France against Britain in 1802, France swept from triumph to triumph. The French annexed Belgium and the Rhineland and proclaimed them part of their own national territory, transformed the Netherlands and the Swiss Confederation into protectorates, and divided Italy into satellite republics; reality, in the wake of the revolution, far exceeded Louis XIV's boldest dreams. France now possessed hegemony in Europe, together with Russia.

The losers in these developments—the German principalities of Bavaria, Hesse-Kassel, Württemberg, and Baden—found a way to emerge from the disaster not only at little cost to themselves but even with a profit, following the Prussian model. In return for ceding the Rhineland to France, they agreed among themselves to make up for their losses by seizing territory from those who possessed neither might nor powerful advocates: the small secular and ecclesiastical rulers, the free cities, and the imperial knights. The emperor himself, Francis II, followed suit in a secret codicil to the Peace of Campo Formio in 1797, thereby sacrificing the integrity of the empire to Hapsburg interests. The last word was spoken not even by the participating princes themselves but by France and Russia as guarantors of the empire: The two powers' plan for compensation was passed first by the Imperial Deputation, a committee of the Diet, and confirmed a month later by the full Diet of Regensburg.

The step made the splintered world of small German states a thing of the past. The number of territories and states attached directly to the empire dropped from 314 to 30, not counting the remaining 300 imperial knights. The changes were enormous; Württemberg doubled the number of its subjects, and Baden more than tripled its population in one stroke. Much disappeared, such as the colorful collection of independent cities and towns in Franconia and Swabia, most of them tiny places like Wimpfen, Biberach, and Buchholz, but also proud centers of culture and trade such as Ulm, Augsburg, and Heilbronn. The seats of many noble families—the Fürstenbergs, Leiningens, Fuggers, and Hohenlohes—lost their status as local capitals as well. While such places had always been modest in scale, they had nonetheless afforded a degree of affluence and pride to their inhabitants; now, ruled by the officials and commissars of a distant and invisible government, they sank into insignificance. The Maltese and Teutonic Orders were illegally stripped of their holdings in Breisgau and on the Lake of Constance; formerly independent bishoprics and abbeys were ruthlessly annexed, and the region of autonomous monasteries in southern Germany was carved up and swallowed, from Vierzehnheiligen in Franconia to Weingarten in Upper Swabia. It was the collapse of a political and legal tradition almost a thousand years old, and the revolutionary triumph of the modern centralized state, which now swept away everything in its path.

The most loyal adherents of the emperor and empire, the autonomous cities and the small secular and ecclesiastical territories, had been virtually wiped out. The middle-sized states that had enlarged their areas with French help saw the maintenance of close ties with France as their only possible course for the future. In the autumn of 1804 Napoleon Bonaparte, First Consul of France and its dictator for the previous four years, undertook an official tour through the Rhine-

land; the population received him with overwhelming jubilation. A few weeks later Napoleon crowned himself "emperor of the French" in Paris, and the scepter of Charlemagne—not known at the time to be a counterfeit—featured prominently in the ceremony.

Were there now two emperors in Europe? The Holy Roman

Emperor Francis II assumed the title of emperor of Austria and was ridiculed for it by Napoleon, who called his competitor a "skeleton brought to the throne solely through the merit of his ancestors." The death blow was then easily delivered. On July 12, 1806, the representatives of sixteen states in south and southwestern Germany signed an act that abolished their connection with the empire and established a protectorate under Napoleon known as the *Rheinbund* (Confederation of the Rhine).

On August 6, 1806, Francis II laid down the crown of the Holy Roman Emperor. Goethe noted that he found the news less interesting than an argument in which his coachman became embroiled, and like him, most people greeted the demise of the Holy Roman Empire of the German Nation with a shrug of the shoulders and returned to their daily concerns. An empire of this kind, that had lasted almost two thousand years since its founding by Julius Caesar, that had tottered many times but was always able to transform itself despite all the weaknesses and inconsistencies of its last few centuries—this was unique in European history. Among all the princes of the empire, the only one who seemed to have any notion of how the future looked was King Gustav IV Adolph of Sweden, a member of the imperial estates as ruler of West Pomerania. He announced the emperor's decision with sadness and respect, adding, "Although the most sacred bonds . . . have now been dissolved, the German nation can never be destroyed, and through the grace of Almighty God, Germany will one day be united once more, and restored to power and repute."

4

The Birth of the German Nation

(1806–1848)

The military success of the French citizen-soldiers who fought and won in the name of their "one and indivisible nation" was not a matter of luck; in the words of a graduate of the University of Halle named Laukhard, who had been taken prisoner by the French, served in the revolutionary army, and thus knew what he was talking about: The French shared "a characteristic with the noble defenders of ancient Greece, namely a warm love of their country that Germans do not know, because as Germans they have no country." For this reason it could appear as if the French armies were invincible.

In 1805 Napoleon defeated Austria's main forces near Austerlitz, and the ensuing Peace of Pressburg reduced Austria to the status of a medium-sized power. On October 14, 1806, the Prussian army met a similar fate at Jena and Auerstedt. The rout of the Prussians was so complete that no further serious resistance was offered: Napoleon

Queen Luise of Prussia
(Nikolaus Lauer, 1799)

The legends surrounding Queen Luise (1776–1810) sprang up during her lifetime and intensified following her early death. The humiliation she experienced at the hands of Napoleon, who in 1807 brusquely rejected her pleas for mild terms for Prussia's surrender, was felt to be symbolic of French treatment of the country as a whole. Her charm and unpretentious style of living won her the affection of the population, and the writer Novalis recommended in 1787 that "every educated woman and concerned mother should have the queen's portrait in her parlor or her daughter's room . . . Genuine patriotism could be created through such a continuous inclusion of the royal couple in our private and public life."

marched into Berlin, welcomed by a cheering population. In the following year the king of Prussia, Frederick William III, accepted the victor's harsh conditions, and Prussia would have vanished from the map of Europe had it not been for the fact that Napoleon and Czar Alexander I of Russia had a mutual interest in keeping a strategic buffer zone between their two blocs.

Up to this point "Germany" had been inconceivable without the surrounding mantle of the empire. This protective shell disappeared in 1806, and once it was gone, it became more difficult than ever to say what Germany actually was. The subjects of Prussia, Bavaria, Saxony-Gotha, or, say, Schwarzburg-Sondershausen might feel somehow "German," yet many identified themselves more broadly with a cosmopolitan bourgeoisie or more narrowly in terms of loyalty to their particular ruling house. When terms such as "nation," "fatherland," or "patriotism" cropped up, they could refer equally well to some vaguely defined Germany, to the specific political unit in which one lived, or to both at once.

A number of factors came together to alter this situation: the shock of defeat; a sense of humiliation; the onerous financial burdens imposed on the defeated states; the devastation caused by French armies as they marched through, living off the land and squeezing all they could out of the population; the rise in the cost of living connected with the system of French customs duties now imposed. All of these contributed to bringing about two major changes of a quite contrary nature: the administrative reform of the German states along French lines, and the discovery of Germany as a nation.

Where French satellite governments were installed, as in the kingdom of Westphalia and the Grand Duchy of Berg, administrative and legal systems were imposed directly by France. The states allied with France—the Confederation of the Rhine, meaning all the German states except for Prussia and Austria—took over French institutions and legal norms in different ways, often adapted to fit their own traditions. Constitutions were enacted, government administrations were modernized on the French model, and the *Code Napoléon* was adopted, which abolished the feudal basis of law and created a legal foundation for the postrevolutionary civil state. The states belonging to the Confederation of the Rhine had lost their outward independence, but through measures such as the introduction of a modern civil law code and elimination of both aristocratic privileges and serfdom, internally they became freer and more progressive than the rest of Germany.

However, even the two states that did not join the confederation but remained threatened by Napoleon—Austria and Prussia—essentially followed the French model in reforming some of their institutional structures. For the reigning monarchs and their chief officials, the primary goals were to overcome the defeats of Austerlitz and Jena, and to restore and then increase the scope of their power. Here France served as a model to the extent that it demonstrated how to win rather than lose; the reformers were determined never again to suffer the kind of defeat handed to them in 1805 and 1806.

In Prussia, which proved more purposeful and flexible in pursuing reform than the sluggish, unwieldy monarchy on the Danube, the new state was conceived as a previously unheard-of concentration of powers and control. The reforms were carried out by civil servants, that is, by officials, soldiers, and jurists who saw themselves as legitimate representatives of the country as a whole. Led by the chief ministers Baron Karl vom und zum Stein (1757–1831) and Karl August von Hardenberg, the Prussian reformers set about with almost revolutionary élan to create the new state through a series of decrees. The old mercenary army was to be replaced by an army of free citizens whose advancement through the ranks would depend on achievements and merit rather than noble birth; the government and its administrative bureaucracy were to be modernized and made more efficient; serfdom east of the Elbe River was to be abolished. Further goals were reorganization of local government both for cities and rural areas, emancipation of the Jews, modernization of the justice sys-

The Steps in Bonaparte's Rise and Fall
(drawing by Johann Michael Voltz, 1814)

This satirical drawing depicts the stages in Napoleon's career: The "Corsican lad" climbs the ladder to success, becoming First Consul with Josephine at his side, and then French emperor; things go rapidly downhill from there, as he is forced to withdraw first from Spain, then Moscow, and finally Germany. At the far right the rulers of Austria, Prussia, and Russia push him off the ladder, and at the bottom Father Time holds up a map of the island of Elba, while Napoleon sighs, "How small my realm has grown."

tem, and a loosening of restrictions on capital investment and commercial enterprise. The culmination was to be a Prussian national assembly, in which elected representatives of the people would determine policy in an equal partnership with the crown.

Yet at the same time the inhabitants resented the presence of French troops of occupation. The reforms proceeded slowly, and a growing number of citizens in different places felt that their government's submissiveness toward the vastly superior power of France was not diplomatic but weak and dishonorable. Their experience of occupation by Napoleon's soldiers gave words such as "fatherland" and "nation" new force, turning them into rallying cries. During the winter of 1806–1807 the philosopher Johann Gottlieb Fichte (1762–1814) delivered his "Addresses to the German Nation" in occupied Berlin, in which he declared that the nature of the German people was genuine and unspoiled, and that by fighting for their own identity and freedom from French military and cultural domination, Germans were serving the cause of progress. The popular writer Ernst Moritz Arndt (1769–1860) was even more outspoken: "Let unanimity be your church! Make hatred of the French your religion, and let freedom and fatherland be the saints to whom you pray!"

A national movement also began to take shape, organized mainly in secret societies such as the *Tugendbund* (League of Virtue) or the German League of Friedrich Ludwig Jahn, an ardent patriot and champion of healthy living and exercise who became known in Germany as the "father of gymnastics." There were also any number of more or less formal discussion groups. All of these circles shared a desire to urge a national struggle for liberation on leaders who seemed to them so hesitant as to be virtual traitors. Where the governments appeared immovable, bands of patriotic activists mounted small local insurrections in 1809, under leaders such as Colonel Wilhelm von Dörnberg in Hesse, Major Ferdinand von Schill in Prussia, and the "Black Duke" in Braunschweig.

However, armed resistance to Napoleon was offered only in the Catholic regions of Europe, in the name of religion and traditional rule; there were rebellions by peasants in the Vendée of western France, by the Army of the Holy Faith in Italy, and guerrilla warfare in Spain. In the German-speaking part of Europe the most serious insurrection was mounted by Tyrolean peasants led by Andreas Hofer (1767–1810), an innkeeper. Several times they managed to defeat Bavarian forces who were occupying Tyrol as allies of the French, but their own Austrian government failed to provide enough support, and they were forced to surrender in 1809. Hofer was executed in Mantua the following year. The real significance of such resistance lay in its symbolic and propagandistic value: the direct action proved a great stimulus to patriotic feeling.

This helps to account for the astounding shift of mood in Germany when the news arrived of the burning of Moscow and Napoleon's heavy losses during his retreat from Russia. The same people who, fascinated by Napoleon, had showed little interest when the Holy Roman Empire collapsed in 1806 now responded to the defeat of the *Grande Armée* in Russia with joy. When King Frederick William III of Prussia issued a call to arms on March 17, 1813, it triggered a mass enthusiasm similar in some respects to the popular uprisings of the French Revolution, fed by a flood of nationalistic, anti-French propaganda and verse. Hardly any German poet found it beneath his dignity to contribute; a rare exception was Goethe, the great cosmopolite, who was repelled by his compatriots' passionate nationalism and continued to wear the decoration he had been awarded by Napoleon long after it had become unpopular. The Wars of Liberation against Napoleon were regarded as truly a people's war. The poet Theodor Körner (1791–1813), who volunteered for service, wrote: "It is no cause to which crowned heads are privy, / 'Tis a crusade, it is a holy war." Well-educated burghers and laboring men alike rushed to join the volunteer corps, while women donated "gold for iron" and rolled bandages. For almost a year and a half people were seized by a fever of excitement that made the "German nation" a direct, personal experience.

Despite all this, victory hung by a thread at the start. Russia, England, Prussia, and Sweden were not enough to stop Napoleon's last concerted effort; it took Austria's entry into the coalition, after long hesitation, and finally a bolt by the troops of the Confederation of the Rhine to the allied camp, quickly followed by the member states' ruling princes. By the spring of 1814 the allies' armies had reached the outskirts of Paris. Napoleon abdicated, and a world war of more than twenty years' duration came to an end.

As the volunteers returned to civilian life, dreaming that their hopes would be fulfilled and the promises for a constitution and German unity would be kept, the statesmen and diplomats of the allied powers were meeting in Vienna, men whose greatest fear was that a new order among nations might arise in Europe. The key words of European diplomacy were restoration and return—restoration of the prerevolutionary system of nation states and a return to its political order. Once again all Europe came to the negotiating table with equal rights, the vanquished no less than the victors, and the outcome resembled the Peace of Westphalia at the end of the Thirty Years' War, in 1648. For the most part the frontiers of the great powers were redrawn where they had lain in 1792; only Prussia gained, receiving extensive areas along the Rhine as well as parts of Saxony, while Austria withdrew from Belgium and the Upper Rhine. This ended the centuries-old direct confrontation of France and Austria that had begun with the struggle between Francis I and Charles V over Italy and the Burgundian inheritance. Prussia thus replaced the Hapsburgs as France's German neighbor and potential chief opponent along the Rhine; the Prussian state now stretched from Aachen on the French border to Tilsit on the Baltic, like a clamp linking east and west Germany. Austria, on the other hand, turned its back on the west; it was a presence only on the eastern periphery of Germany and in the future would look toward southern and southeastern Europe, focusing attention on Italy and the Balkans as its sphere of influence.

A Break in Negotiations at the Congress of Vienna
(Jean Baptiste Isabey, 1819)

In the fall of 1814 representatives of the European nations met in Vienna to decide on a new order for Europe—including Germany—after Napoleon's downfall. The Duke of Wellington is shown standing at the left gesturing toward Foreign Minister Castlereagh of Britain, who has one arm draped casually over the back of his chair. The seated figure in the lower left-hand corner is the Prussian Chancellor Hardenberg, and standing between Wellington and Hardenberg is Chancellor Metternich of Austria. The diplomats on the right side of the picture are grouped around Talleyrand, the French foreign minister who survived all the political upheaval in his country. Wearing a long wig as a demonstration of loyalty to the Bourbon King Louis XVIII, Talleyrand looks like the *ancien régime* personified. Above all the negotiators hangs a portrait of Francis I of Austria, shown pointing toward the insignia of the Holy Roman Empire of which he has divested himself. Was he intended as a symbol of the past, or of the future as well?

Central Europe remained as fragmented as ever, held together now by the loose ties of the *Deutscher Bund* (German Confederation), a secularized descendent of the Holy Roman Empire. The most that could be achieved was a loose alliance of 39 states and cities, with the Federal Diet, a permanent congress of envoys, as its only shared constitutional body. It was presided over by the Austrian emperor, but

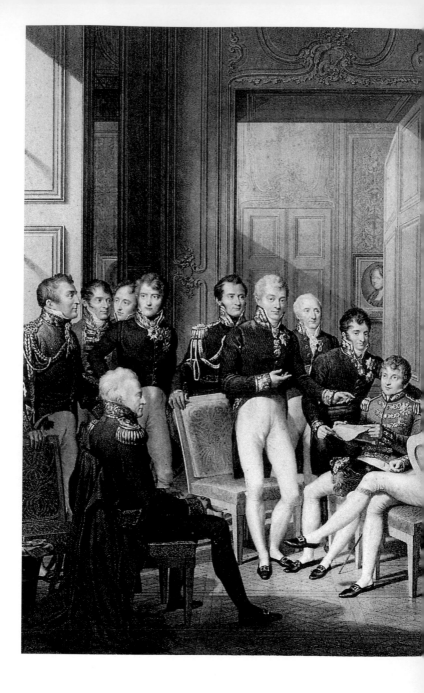

The Birth of the German Nation

votes were distributed so as to make it impossible for Prussia and Austria to dominate the other states. These two great powers belonged to the confederation solely by virtue of their possessions within the former empire, while the kings of Denmark, England, and the Netherlands were also members in their capacities as heads of the houses of Schleswig, Hanover, and Luxemburg. In this manner the political order in Germany was linked with that of Europe in a determined rejection of the principle of nationhood; it represented a last attempt to prevent Germany from becoming a compact power at the center and to maintain it as the playing field on which the other major powers could balance their interests. For the last time in European history, statesmen were able to pursue a policy, dictated by reason, of preserving a balance of power and securing peace, without being hindered by ideologies and national hatreds.

The political order in Germany and Europe, as agreed upon by the European powers at the Congress of Vienna in 1815, left it up to the various states to handle matters at home as they saw fit; both conservative and liberal constitutions were possible. However, public opinion in western and central Europe had been stirred up by the Wars of Liberation. Citizens began loudly demanding fulfillment of the promises for greater liberty, anchored in new constitutions, that their governments had made in desperate times. Students from most German universities gathered at Wartburg Castle and adopted their own tricolor of black, red, and gold, to match the uniforms worn by the volunteer corps of General von Lützow, which had operated behind French lines with many of these same students serving in it: red for the uniform coats, black for the trim, and gold for the buttons. The delegates to the conference called for a free, united Germany and threw books by authors they considered reactionary—because they were antinationalistic—onto a bonfire.

Two years later a student named Carl Sand fatally stabbed the writer August von Kotzebue, because he had mocked the idea of a national movement. Kotzebue's death created an enormous sensa-

Dreyse & Collenbusch Co. in Sömmerda:
The Factory, Offices, and Owner's Quarters
(after 1845)

The industrialization of Germany has begun but not yet taken on its later architectural form in this scene. The factory, offices, and living quarters of the owner are still located under one roof, and the well-tended formal garden is in the style of the previous century. The owner has not moved his residence away from the manufacturing tract, even though the company made a very modern product, the first practical breech-loading rifle, which was mass-produced and adopted by the Prussian army in 1841. The technical superiority of the model M41 rifle was demonstrated in the wars of 1864 and 1866.

tion—it was the first political assassination in Germany since John the Parricide had murdered his uncle, the Hapsburg King Albert I, in 1308. The dark side of the new nationalist spirit had revealed itself early on, confirming the worst fears of the architect of the new order, the Austrian chancellor Klemens, Prince Metternich (1773–1859). In August 1819 the chief ministers of the German states met in Carlsbad and agreed on a policy of ruthless suppression of all revolutionary and liberationist movements. It brought to a halt the development of new constitutions. Austria and Prussia returned to absolutism, and the movements for change were forced underground. While the dam against revolution appeared to be holding, Metternich knew there was no going back: "My most secret thought," he wrote in his diary, "is that the old Europe has reached the beginning of the end."

Germany entered on a phase usually referred to in retrospect as

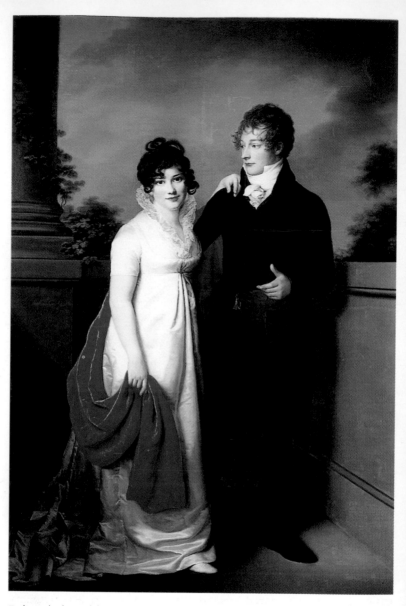

Emilie and Johann Philipp Petersen
(Friedrich Carl Gröger, 1806)

The Petersens were a prominent family of Hamburg merchants who provided the Hansa city with many senators and mayors over the centuries. This couple is depicted as unmistakably middle-class, both in their intimate and informal pose and the sober black and white of their attire. But they represent a middle class with new self-assurance, as indicated by the bright red of Mrs. Petersen's stole, a rather aristocratic article of clothing, and the column, an indispensable element in portraits of the nobility.

The Flooded River
(Antonie Waldorp, 1843)

The Biedermeier era was depicted in retrospect as an idyllic, preindustrial era of post coaches, and poets from Eichendorff to Lenau wrote verses in which this means of transportation appeared in the most romantic of lights. In reality coaches were uncomfortable, the roads were bad, and contemporaries complained bitterly of coachmen's rudeness and greed. When rivers rose and became impassable, as in this scene, coach passengers might be stranded for days.

Biedermeier. It was an era of reaction, yet it was also the longest period of peace that anyone could remember; for two decades there was no war in Europe. Political debate receded into the background, stifled to a considerable degree by censorship and government persecution of those who dared to speak up. In its place arose a mentality that valued the small scale, tidiness, economy of means, and homey comfort, *Gemütlichkeit.* The domestic idyll appeared to have triumphed. Germany became embodied by the figure of *der deutsche Michel,* the upright, small-town *paterfamilias* in his nightcap. Again and again we encounter him in various guises in the paintings of Moritz von Schwind or Ludwig Richter: sometimes romantic, sometimes a figure from fairy tale, sometimes a lovable old eccentric, but always loyal, good-natured, a little dreamy.

The era was intensely musical; Carl Maria von Weber's *Der Freischütz* had its premiere in Berlin to lively public acclaim and was celebrated as the Germans' national opera. Other opera composers such as Conradin Kreutzer or Albert Lortzing were just as popular as Weber, but Ludwig van Beethoven, Franz Schubert, and Felix Mendelssohn-Bartholdy enjoyed success, too, especially for their chamber music; it was typical of the times that people turned to *Hausmusik,* pieces for piano or string quartet and songs that could be performed at home, in private gatherings. In the field of literature, derivative writers carried the day, and small forms dominated—the essays of Ludwig Börne and the lyric poetry of August von Platen, Eduard Mörike, or Friedrich Rückert, but above all Heinrich Heine, whose deceptively simple and melodic verses captured the hearts of a whole generation.

In architecture, the classical style was exemplified in the clear forms and proportions of Karl Friedrich Schinkel's buildings in Berlin or Leo von Klenze's in Munich, although already threatened by an antiquarian approach that saw beauty in anything that looked old and had a whiff of history about it. Two venerable, never-completed structures were restored and finished about this time: Marienburg Castle in west Prussia, as a symbol of Prussian reforms connected with past traditions, and the Cologne Cathedral, to whose completion not only the different ethnic groups but also the different denominations of Germany were asked to contribute, in order to make it a monument of national reconciliation and unity. Gothic architecture was believed at the time to be a uniquely German style; only later was it discovered that the Cathedral of Amiens had served as a model for that of Cologne.

But the idyll was deceptive. This was already evident by 1830, when the July Revolution swept through Paris, sending shock waves

Type of food	1800	1835	1850
Grain	52%	44%	44%
Potatoes	8	26	28
Cabbage and other vegetables	25	19	17
Animal products	15	11	11
Total	100	100	100

Average Diet from 1800 to 1850

The potato did not become a major source of nourishment for the general population until the nineteenth century. Until about 1770 grains were the staple of most people's diets; then increasing prices made grain unaffordable for the poor. They began to eat cabbage instead—*kraut* in German—giving rise to the popular nickname for Germans in English-speaking countries. After 1835 consumption of potatoes rose so dramatically that potato blights led to famines and waves of emigration in the mid-1840s, just as in Ireland.

all across Europe. In several German states barricades were erected and fighting erupted; in its aftermath some rulers made concessions to the liberal *Zeitgeist*, permitting constitutions to be drawn up and allowing representative assemblies. Two years later, at the All-German Festival held at Hambach Castle in the Palatinate, the national movement proved itself to be very much alive. Consisting mostly of university students, the more liberal members of the bourgeoisie, and democratically minded working men and artisans, it now received further support from farmers who had formed protest groups in southwest Germany. The reason for their involvement lay in an extraordinary rate of population growth while food production remained stagnant. In rural areas the nonlandowning population of agricultural laborers had increased greatly, especially east of the Elbe River, leading to a genuine crisis of overpopulation. Those who could not earn a living or feed their families off the land migrated to the cities, where they swelled the masses of the urban poor. The skilled trades were particularly hard hit, for reforms in Prussia and the member states of the Confederation of the Rhine had earlier eliminated the old guild regulations; in consequence the skilled trades quickly became overcrowded, and many apprentices and journeymen could not find work. This phe-

Das Lied der Deutschen, The Germans' Song

(text by August Heinrich Hoffmann von Fallersleben, Hamburg, 1841)

Hoffmann von Fallersleben (1798–1874) wrote his *Lied der Deutschen* in August 1841 in exile on the island of Helgoland, which then belonged to Great Britain. It was sung for the first time, set to a melody from Haydn's "Emperor Quartet," by members of a Hamburg gymnastics club in honor of Professor Welcker, a prominent pro-democrat. The first verse, beginning with the words *Deutschland, Deutschland über alles*, was not aggressive or chauvinistic in the least; it merely placed German unity above the hodge-podge of principalities in the then-existing German Confederation. The rivers mentioned—the Meuse,

Memel (Klaipeda in Lithuanian), and Adige—along with the Belt, the sound between Schleswig and the Danish island of Fyn (Funen), represented the rough boundaries of the German Confederation or German-speaking territories belonging to the Confederation. In the nineteenth century the song was not nearly as popular as *The Watch on the Rhine*, and after the founding of the empire in 1871 was eclipsed by the official hymn *Heil Dir im Siegerkranz*, "Hail to Thee in Victor's Laurels." It was not declared the national anthem until 1922, when President Friedrich Ebert chose it as a conscious link to the revolutionary democratic traditions of 1848. Since 1952 the third verse has been sung as the national anthem of the Federal Republic of Germany.

nomenon of mass impoverishment was called "pauperism"; no one knew how to combat it.

Up to this point the shape of a future German national state had been visible only in the barest outlines. There were increasing references to the "German people" and the "German fatherland," but as a

City	1831	1844	1855
Berlin	80	127	195
Vienna	43	48	34
Leipzig	79	130	156
Stuttgart	15	36	55

Number of Bookstores in Cities of the German Confederation

In the period between the Wars of Liberation and the Revolution of 1848, the reading public grew as many more people attained literacy, although regional differences remained. In 1884 Berlin alone had more bookstores than the whole of Austria. Bookstores tended to be stocked primarily with fiction and nonpolitical nonfiction, partly in response to the tastes of the era but also as a result of censorship.

rule these terms were used to heighten the contrast with the enemy, the French, and occurred in vague and poetic contexts. They referred to a cultural and linguistic unity more than anything else, and did not begin to imply that the many separate German states would actually be consolidated into a single nation any time soon. When asked where his fatherland was, the writer Wilhelm Raabe replied that it could be found "where ancient custom places the mythical name Germany on the map, where the most upright people on earth have lived honestly and faithfully since time immemorial, and have given their governments not one cause for justified complaint since their original creation from the primal clay." With respect to the last claim, things were about to change, but it is true that during the Wars of Liberation in 1813 and 1815 the "German fatherland" had as yet no fixed shape. It was a poetic, historical, and utopian notion, an ideal that in its more earthly incarnation usually bore the name "Prussia."

It is conceivable that the various German states could have succeeded in retaining the loyalty of their subjects into the 1840s and even longer, and as a concept "Germany" would have meant little to anyone but geographers. But the reform efforts in the different states had stalled, and those reforms that had gone through, modernizing agriculture, commerce, and taxation, had been achieved at considerable social cost. Dangerous fault lines and tensions were appearing between social classes, and now the Prussian reformers, who had earlier borrowed ammunition from the "arsenal of revolution," would have to pay the price. They could hardly introduce general conscription, promise to improve standards of education throughout the country, stoke the fires of public opinion to white heat during the Wars of Liberation, and then expect the population to go back to its old docile submission to a small bureaucratic elite, however wise and enlightened.

During this period, known as the *Vormärz* ("pre-March," since the Revolution of 1848 broke out in that month in Germany), the growing social tensions added to the bitterness felt over broken promises to introduce real constitutional reforms. The behavior of the authorities gave even more cause for bitterness, since government leaders, alarmed at the radical tone adopted by opposition journalists and fearing a repeat of the French Revolution on German soil, clamped down harder on the press. And when citizens raised demands to combine economic liberalization with broader participation in politics, the leadership tried to stay in control of the situation by increasing police pressure. Through all these conflicts a broad wedge was driven between the society and the apparatus of the state.

Not only social tensions but also political unrest mounted again in Germany, and in general it is striking how the great surges of nationalistic feeling and political discontent in 1813, 1817, 1830, and later years coincided with crises in the economy and foreign affairs. After the events of 1830 the authorities managed to gain the upper hand again, but the mere fact that most German states now had representative assemblies whose liberal delegates could speak and publish freely without fear of punishment made it impossible to control public opinion. The liberal opposition gained vast numbers of new supporters. The idea of national unity gained strength as well during the Rhine crisis of 1840, when for the first time since 1815 France demonstrated an inclination to expand its borders in that direction. A spon-

Reading Room
(L. Arnoto, ca. 1840)

Around 1770, about 15 percent of adults in Germany could read and write; by 1840 the number had grown to roughly half—a true revolution. The book and newspaper market grew accordingly, supplying readers with political opinions and points of view which they could use to choose a political party. This created a well-informed public prepared to debate issues and increasingly able to force governments to deal with particular topics and aims. On the other hand, the press also made the public easier to influence than ever before.

taneous mass protest movement sprang up in Germany, directed in part at the German Confederation for reacting so lamely.

The years following 1840 saw a rebirth of German nationalism and strong growth in the organizations promoting it. The gymnastics movement *(Turnbewegung)* spread throughout Germany, with an accompanying ideology that linked the goal of physical fitness with the ideas of patriotism and national defense. Another important component of the national movement was the *Gesangverein,* or choral society. Local groups formed umbrella or-

The Silesian Weavers
(Carl Wilhelm Hübner, 1845)

Between 1815 and 1848 the total population of the German Confederation increased from 22 to 35 million people. Within one generation the population thus grew by more than 50 percent, and food production was unable to keep pace. Countless people suffered hunger, and their misery was exacerbated by the transition of German society from the old craft-based economy to the new industrial economy. This problem first arose in England—where a movement of "Luddites" sprang up who smashed machinery in textile factories in the Midlands—and then spread throughout the continent of Europe. One particularly hard-hit group in Germany was the weavers of Silesia, whose hand-woven cloth could not compete with the cheaper, factory-produced textiles. Inhumanly long working hours, child labor, and pitifully inadequate wages were the result. In 1844 the weavers mounted desperate revolts in villages in the regions of Langenbielau and Peterswalde, smashing mechanical looms and looting factory owners' homes. Prussian soldiers were sent in to suppress the uprising, but attention had been focused on the social problems; they remained on the political agenda and led to increasing tensions that exploded in the Revolution of 1848.

ganizations that sponsored the first national choral festivals and fanned nationalistic sentiment; members not only promoted patriotic songs at these gatherings—they also made inflammatory speeches. The first pan-German academic congresses took place in this era, where participants stressed the links between scholarship and the idea of nationhood. The decade was also the heyday of national monuments; in addition to the Cologne Cathedral, the monuments begun or finished in this period included the memorial near Detmold to Hermann of the Cherusci, the national hero who had defeated three Roman legions in A.D. 9, the Walhalla memorial to the war dead in Regensburg, and the Hall of Liberation near Kelheim on the Rhine. The idea of nationhood and the liberal opposition, it became evident, were two sides of the same coin.

The situation was ripe for both social and political unrest. All that was lacking for an explosive revolutionary situation like that of 1789 was an economic crisis, combined with some destabilizing political event. The former arrived not singly but doubly: In 1846–47 the last European crisis of the old type occurred, when poor harvests resulted in famine, migration to the cities, and overcrowding in the skilled trades, only to be followed in 1847–48 by the first "modern" crisis, precipitated by a collapse of prices for consumer goods. As spontaneous hunger revolts broke out all over Germany and governments sent in troops to suppress them, the liberal constitutional opposition began speaking out more insistently than ever.

On October 10, 1847, the leaders of this faction met in Heppenheim, near Mannheim, and issued a demand for a federal German state with a strong central government that would be answerable to a parliament. A month before the radical democrats, successors of the 1830 movement whose platform was to make Germany a single unified republic, had met in Offenburg. Further calls for action were issued by the social revolutionaries and socialists gathered around men such as Friedrich Hecker, Wilhelm Weitling, and Moses Hess, and also by the radical journeymen's associations in the German emigré communities of Switzerland, Paris, and London. The governments of the states in the German Confederation had no convincing arguments to counter this swelling chorus of discontent and protest; the writings and speeches of the opposition prepared public opinion for the open revolution that was soon to follow.

5

Blood and Iron

(1848–1871)

Just as in 1830, the events of 1848 began with the arrival of news from Paris that on February 24 a king had once again been deposed, barricades had been erected in the streets, and the first martyrs of the new revolution had fallen. The unrest spread across most of Europe; in many different places nationalist, social-reform, and liberal currents swirled and mingled, all directed against the antinational and antiliberal political order established by the Congress of Vienna in 1815. There was fighting in the streets in virtually every German territorial capital.

In state parliaments both the moderate liberals and radical democrats demanded freedom of the press and of assembly, and the rights to form political parties and bear arms, in the last case so that citizen

Allegory on the Suppression of the Revolution of 1848–49
(Düsseldorf school, ca. 1849)

One reason the revolution failed was middle-class liberals' hesitancy: They were in favor of revolution, but just a little one that would bring unity and liberty without overdoing the equality part. Their agenda definitely did not include a radical overthrow of the social order and bloodshed. But radical uprisings on the Rhine, in the Palatinate, Hesse, Baden, and central Germany made it look as if the Revolution of 1848 was headed for Jacobin terror and the guillotine. Thus most liberals were willing to ac- cept a few concessions in all haste, consolidate their gains, and turn to Prussia and Austria, the old conservative powers, to restore law and order. The allegory illustrates bourgeois fears: The angel with the flaming sword has cast the devil, clutching his red flag, back into the pit, and the personification of Order, identifiable by the for- tress shape of her crown, embraces the victims of anarchy. The restoration of tranquility is re- warded by the angel of peace, who pours riches from a horn of plenty.

militias could offer armed resistance to the old order and its standing armies. The protests culminated in demands that a German national parliament be called. The "March demands" were followed by the "March governments," whose cabinets of liberal leaders set about trying to transform the demands into reality. The mood of spring overflowed into national politics; the new Bavarian government even proclaimed itself the "ministry of the new dawn," and the black, red, and gold flag of the national movement was hoisted almost everywhere in Germany.

Everything now hung on what would happen in the two dominant powers of the German Confederation. In Vienna, within just a few days the moderate liberal faction was swept aside by an upsurge of radical democratic sentiment. Metternich fled to England, and the court took refuge in Innsbruck, while ethnic minorities throughout the multinational empire mounted their own patriotic rebellions. Within a few weeks Austria, on whose might Metternich's system of restoration had rested, became incapable of concerted action. In Prussia, it appeared at first as if Frederick William IV had succeeded in steering developments in the direction he wished and placing himself at the head of a drive for unification. But in fact the king hesitated too long, and his concessions came too late, so that on March 18 open revolt broke out in Berlin as well. He was able to placate the populace only by withdrawing his troops and promising to call a Prussian national assembly to draw up a constitution for Prussia.

On May 18, 1848, the German National Assembly—585 elected representatives—convened in St. Paul's Church in Frankfurt to draft and adopt a constitution that would guarantee basic freedoms and to elect a national government. The list of delegates reads like a roll of honor of liberal and intellectual Germany. Poets like Ludwig Uhland and Friedrich Theodor Vischer had been elected, along with leaders from the era of the Wars of Liberation like Ernst Moritz Arndt and Friedrich Ludwig Jahn, and historians like Friedrich Christoph Dahlmann, Johann Gustav Droysen, and Georg Gottfried Gervinus. But

A Session of the National Assembly in
St. Paul's Church, Frankfurt
(lithograph by Paul Bürde, after 1848)

From May 18, 1848, to May 30, 1849,
the 585 delegates of the National Assembly
met in St. Paul's Church in Frankfurt; they
had been chosen in a general election held
throughout the regions of the German Confederation, west and east Prussia, and
Schleswig, in which all adult males could
cast equal votes. The drawing shows Baron
Heinrich von Gagern standing on the president's platform, surrounded by the most important and popular delegates.

there were also Catholic priests
among them, such as Wilhelm
Emmanuel Baron von Ketteler, the
Bishop of Mainz, who wrote on
social questions, as well as leaders
from liberal political groups of
every stripe. At midcentury the
educated and professional bourgeoisie was still the main pillar of
support for the idea of national unity.

But what regions would be part of the new Germany? There had
never been agreement on this question, and the delegates meeting at
St. Paul's were hopelessly divided over the issue. Two possible solutions emerged. The first was *Großdeutschland,* "Great Germany," which
would consist of all German regions including Austria and be headed
by a Hapsburg emperor. This was opposed by adherents of the second

Eine Whistgesellschaft! Vorerst nur ein Tisch mit einem Strohmann.

A Whist Party: Usually I Play with a Scepter, Crown, and Orb
(Wilhelm Storck, 1848)

The reactionary rulers forced to flee by the Revolution met in England: King Louis Philippe, from whose capital the revolution had once again spread; Prince Klemens von Metternich, the architect of the reactionary post-Napoleonic peace order of 1815, who was forced to resign on March 13, 1848, and could barely escape the hostile population's fury; and Prince William, the king of Prussia's brother and later successor, who had made himself highly unpopular in the days of the March revolution in Berlin by calling for ruthless suppression of the uprising and earned himself the nickname the "Bullet Prince."

solution, *Kleindeutschland*, "Small Germany," which would exclude the Austrian areas and be ruled by a Hohenzollern emperor. A conflict erupted over the questions of frontiers and future supremacy and dragged on for months. Meanwhile, in southwest Germany radicals took to the barricades to fight for a third option: a democracy. Their revolt was suppressed by the troops of the confederation. Finally the assembly managed to adopt a constitution in the venerable tradition of the American, French, and Belgian models and to create a provisional central government. But the constitution was not recognized, and the government had no power. Revolutions are won by those who can decide the question of power in their favor, and the Frankfurt parliament was utterly powerless.

This became evident at once when a crisis arose in Schleswig-Holstein. The estates there had proclaimed their independence from Denmark on March 24, 1848, had formed a provisional government and appealed to the German National Assembly for help. The fate of the two duchies aroused intense public interest, and in the eyes of the German nationalists the only way for the Frankfurt parliament to establish its legitimate authority would be by succeeding in making them part of the new Germany. But the National Assembly had no military forces of its own; it had to borrow Prussian troops, who advanced well into Jutland. Then the other European powers protested, and the Prussians were forced to withdraw. In a pointed demonstration of superior might, British warships took up positions in the North Sea, Russian troops massed on the east Prussian border, and French diplomats intervened with the different German governments. The spread of German nationalism to the possessions of the Danish crown confirmed the fears at other European courts that a unified German state in the heart of the continent would disrupt the overall balance of power. It now became all too clear that changes in central Europe—and particularly German unity—could not be achieved against the will of the major powers in the current system.

The National Assembly was thwarted not only by the reigning political constellation in Europe, however, but also by the danger that the revolution would become radicalized. The forces of the liberal bourgeoisie who had been dreaming of a constitutional nation state favorable to economic development saw a second revolution approaching, one that would bring Jacobin terror and the guillotine. They forged a deal with the growing antirevolutionary faction in Berlin and hastily tried to consolidate what gains they had already made. Thus when a constitution was granted for Prussia in November 1848, it was enough to bring the revolution to a virtual halt there—when a little military pressure was thrown in for good measure. Late in the

Die deutsche verfassunggebende Nationalverfammlung hat beschlossen, und verkündigt als Reichsverfassung:

Verfassung
des deutschen Reiches.

Abschnitt I. Das Reich.
Artikel I.

§. 1.

Das deutsche Reich besteht aus dem Gebiete des bisherigen deutschen Bundes. Die Festsetzung der Verhältnisse des Herzogthums Schleswig bleibt vorbehalten.

§. 2.

Hat ein deutsches Land mit einem nichtdeutschen Lande dasselbe Staatsoberhaupt, so soll das deutsche Land eine von dem nichtdeutschen Lande getrennte eigene Verfassung, Regierung und Verwaltung haben. In die Regierung und Verwaltung des deutschen Landes dürfen nur deutsche Staatsbürger berufen werden.

Die Reichsverfassung und Reichsgesetzgebung hat in einem solchen deutschen Lande dieselbe verbindliche Kraft, wie in den übrigen deutschen Ländern.

§. 3.

Hat ein deutsches Land mit einem nichtdeutschen Lande dasselbe Staatsoberhaupt, so muß dieses entweder in seinem deutschen Lande residiren, oder es muß auf verfassungsmäßigem Wege in demselben eine Regentschaft niedergesetzt werden, zu welcher nur Deutsche berufen werden dürfen.

§. 4.

Abgesehen von den bereits bestehenden Verbindungen deutscher und nichtdeutscher Länder soll kein Staatsoberhaupt eines nichtdeutschen Landes zugleich zur Regierung eines deutschen Landes gelangen, noch darf ein in Deutschland regierender Fürst, ohne seine deutsche Regierung abzutreten, eine fremde Krone annehmen.

§. 5.

Die einzelnen deutschen Staaten behalten ihre Selbstständigkeit, soweit dieselbe nicht durch die Reichsverfassung beschränkt ist; sie haben alle staatlichen Hoheiten und Rechte, soweit diese nicht der Reichsgewalt ausdrücklich übertragen sind.

The Constitution of the German Reich, 1849

The German constitution of 1849 was an estimable document informed by the spirit of popular sovereignty and human rights. Although it never went into effect, it remains one of the most important and impressive documents in German constitutional history and still seems modern today, both clear in its overall conception and precise in its details. Although not placed at the beginning, the catalogue of fundamental rights was formulated with special care; it codified the view of natural human rights developed in the Enlightenment and created a sphere of individual freedoms for citizens that was protected from the power of the state. The present Basic Law of the Federal Republic of Germany was derived in considerable measure from this constitution.

day the assembly also tried to acquire some real power by abandoning the solution favored by the majority of delegates—Great Germany—and offering the Prussian king the crown of a "small German" empire instead, but this attempt failed, too. While Frederick William IV would have been delighted to become supreme ruler of Germany, he was willing to receive such a title only from the hands of the other princes, not from a parliament. The crown offered to him by the delegation from the assembly was "filthy," he wrote to the Grand Duke of Hesse, "a diadem of foul dirt" with the "stench of revolution" clinging to it. In addition he rightly feared that accepting it would arouse protest from the other European powers and lead Austria to intervene. A peace-loving man who avoided conflict when possible, the king had no interest in starting another Seven Years' War.

On the surface it may have appeared as if the Revolution of 1848–49 had failed. However, the conflict between the forces of the status quo and those of movement had at least ended in a compromise. All over Germany, rulers had bound themselves to written constitutions and now shared their law-making powers with parliaments. On the other hand the dream of the March rebellion of 1848—to have a Great German national state based on popular sovereignty and human rights—had failed for two reasons, namely resistance from the major powers and lack of unity within the revolutionary ranks. But one thing had changed for certain: The revolution had made the alternatives for a future solution to the German question quite clear. The proponents of a German national state had split into two camps, the Great German faction on one side and the Small German faction on the other.

The Small German camp was stronger from the start, the reason being that in the area of economic policy their goal was already a reality. The German Customs Union had been formed in 1834 under Prussian leadership, primarily as a result of the efforts of Prussian finance minister Friedrich von Motz (1775–1830); by 1848, 28 of the 39 German states had joined. Metternich observed these developments with mistrust, for he viewed them as increasing "the preponderance of Prussia" and promoting "the extremely dangerous doctrine of German unity." And in fact the Austrian-dominated German Confederation was an instrument of the status quo, designed to prevent all innovation, whereas the Prussian-led Customs Union represented a forward-looking economic community, one that was experiencing continual growth and exercising a magnetic attraction on neighboring states.

This new and relatively large economic bloc could not become truly unified, however, as long as the system for transporting goods remained slow and unwieldy. It was largely owing to the efforts of the economist Friedrich List (1789–1846) and several industrialists from the Rhineland that the first German railway line was able to open on December 7, 1835, after a long battle against prejudice and conservative opposition to technology. The track ran from Nuremberg to Fürth, a grand total of 3.7 miles—at a time when Belgium had 12.5 miles of railroad, France 88 miles, and Great Britain 340 miles. But the rail network in Germany grew very rapidly after that; on the eve of the 1848 revolution it covered over 3,000 miles, more than twice the length of the French network, and more than four times the length of the Austrian. Without the railroads the Customs Union could never have become a single market, but now a unified economy in the region became possible, in which supply, demand, and prices were subject to the same competitive pressures everywhere. The growth of the railroads led in turn to an unforeseen boom in the iron-processing industry. As the need for locomotives, machines, railroad cars, and tracks increased, factory output rose, and production was stimulated across a whole spectrum of supply industries.

This much groundwork had been laid for industrial development by around 1848. And since in the aftermath of the revolution entrepreneurs no longer needed to fear political upheavals, they could begin to make long-term plans for expansion. At the same time, due to the discovery of sensationally rich deposits of gold in California and Australia, the capital supply increased enormously, making credit cheap, while prices rose and demand grew. A golden era for entrepreneurship dawned. New banks were established everywhere, stimulated first and foremost by the need for capital for railroad construction. Stock companies were founded, and between 1850 and 1857 the

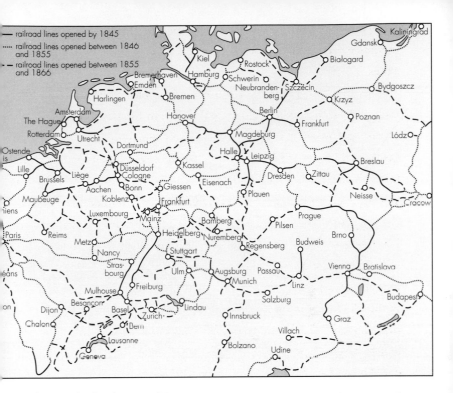

Development of Railroads in Central Europe up to 1866

The network of railroads throughout the lands of the German Confederation grew denser from year to year. Bold new constructions of riveted steel supports permitted engineers to build bridge spans that would have been unimaginable only a short time before.

amounts of money in circulation, bank deposits, and capital investment within the German Customs Union increased more than threefold.

One further circumstance contributed to the economic boom: Labor was cheap. The new factories drew people like magnets. The destitute masses were happy simply to find regular employment and steady wages. Despite all the criticism that has been justly leveled at the deplorable conditions in which this first generation of factory proletarians lived and worked, one should keep in mind that in comparison with the poverty of the preindustrial masses the average worker was now better off. Unemployment and underemployment were reduced, as was the undercutting of wages through cottage industries and competition from Britain and Belgium. Thus, even though bad

The Ludwig Rail Line
(painted and lacquered papier-mâché box, ca. 1836)

The first German rail line opened on December 7, 1835, and ran a grand total of 3.7 miles from Nuremberg to Fürth. The *Stuttgarter Morgenblatt* described the first run: "Horses shied on the nearby road as the monster neared; children started to cry, and many people could not suppress a slight shudder." Nonetheless, the reporter observed a "feeling of elation" among the thousands of spectators: "No skeptic will be able to shake their new faith in the human spirit and its power, all the less so as this spirit is joyful and uplifting."

harvests caused food prices to soar again in 1852 and 1855, Germany experienced no more hunger revolts. Pauperism, the great social threat to Europe's future in the first half of the century, faded away, and young people of the next generation knew of it only from their elders' accounts.

Industrialization transformed German society. The old world disappeared not as the result of a political revolution but through a revolution in the economy and the world of labor, accompanied by a fur-

Numbers of German Emigrants from
1820 to 1913

1820–1829	50,000
1830–1839	210,000
1840–1849	480,000
1850–1859	1,161,000
1861–1870	782,000
1871–1880	626,000
1881–1890	1,343,000
1891–1900	539,000
1901–1910	280,000
1911–1913	69,000

ther revolution in transport and communications, from railroads to the telegraph; all of them were interconnected and interdependent. A population explosion in rural areas and worsening conditions there led people to try their luck elsewhere. As reports reached them of secure jobs in the new industrial areas of Silesia, Saxony, the region around Berlin, the Rhineland, and the Ruhr valley, the greatest mass migration Germany had yet seen set in. First a stream of people seeking work poured out of the agricultural region east of the Elbe River toward Berlin; later the wave rolled into central Germany, growing constantly and finally reaching the Rhine–Ruhr industrial zone about 1860. Within the new factory proletariat, unskilled agricultural migrants mingled with local urban artisans pushed out of their guild organizations as the demand for their handmade wares was outstripped by the rising demand for cheap, mass-produced factory goods. Not until the 1880s and the invention of the electric motor—the little man's energy source—did the small workshop become competitive again, thereby preventing fulfillment of Karl Marx's prophecy that artisans would die out in the industrial age.

Broad segments of the middle classes were affected by the new trend toward mobility as well. The Prussian economic reforms had released large amounts of capital and labor, attracting formerly rural trades to the cities and entrepreneurs from medium-sized towns to the developing industrial metropolises, where markets were larger. Governments made a point of sending their growing numbers of bureaucrats as far away from their home towns as possible. In short, the old hierarchically organized and agrarian society of Europe disinte-

The Emigrants' Farewell to the Homeland (Antonie Volkmar, 1860)

Between 1830 and 1913 more than six million people left Germany, more than half of them after 1861. Poverty was the main but not the only cause of emigration abroad, especially to the "Promised Land" in North America. The great increase in emigration to the United States following the Revolution of 1848–49 was also connected with people's hopes for a freer and more democratic life on the other side of the ocean.

grated, to be replaced by a modern, urban, and industrial society, divided into a proletariat and bourgeoisie.

The predominant feeling of the era was one of uprootedness: Family ties were broken, traditional loyalties abandoned, religious attachments weakened. Industrial settings, factories, and bureaucracies offered no replacements for the old ties; people felt like interchangeable atoms whirled about in the grip of anonymous forces. In brief, a previously unknown sense prevailed that familiar norms had been lost, leaving a whole society uncertain of its orientation, and in the throes of an identity crisis.

Where religion and fixed social norms no longer provided support, a variety of myths and modern philosophies filled the gap, competing and battling with one another, most of them categorically excluding the others. Liberals, for example, believed in freedom, the pursuit of happiness, and individual self-determination in both the economic and political spheres—the secular antithesis of the prevailing authoritarian structures, which dated from the prerevolutionary era and were dominated by absolutist and aristocratic thinking. Connected with all this was the idea of national unity, which would represent an incarnation of the common will. Alongside this view, the century's other great ideology opposed to the status quo took shape, in the form of socialism as the solution to class conflict. Socialism appealed for solidarity among the masses to counter the self-serving ruling class, whose affluence would not be possible without the labor performed in factories.

The old world mobilized its defenses in turn, developing ideologies with a mass appeal of their own: Traditional leadership circles developed a conservative philosophy as a defensive shield against the rebellious "rabble," but also against the rise of liberal capitalism. The Catholic political movement flourished in Silesia, the Rhineland, and southern Germany, where the more traditionally oriented population had not experienced as great a loss of the old social norms; it represented a reaction to the largely Protestant, Prussian liberal movement and its aggressively presented demands for power.

Thus there arose a considerable number of competing ideas for the ordering of society and the legitimation of political power, which found expression in various parliamentary factions and political journals and eventually crystallized into political parties. This became clear when the effects of an economic slump and new developments in the European political constellation stirred up German politics again at the end of the 1850s. An independent German workers' movement emerged and formed organizations that would become a fixture on the political scene. Ferdinand Lassalle (1825–1864) drew up the platform of the *Allgemeiner Deutscher Arbeiterverein* (General German Workingmen's Association) in 1863, while at the same time

August Bebel (1840–1913) and Wilhelm Liebknecht (1826–1900) established the *Vereinstag deutscher Arbeitervereine* (Federation of German Workingmen's Associations). The latter served as a core around which the *Sozialdemokratische Arbeiterpartei* (Social Democratic Workers' Party) would develop, which was founded in 1869. These early organizations were the forerunners of the present-day Social Democrats in Germany.

Parliamentary liberalism revived as well. In Prussia, King Frederick William IV had gone mad; his brother William I, who became regent in 1858 and later succeeded him, surprised everyone by loosening censorship restrictions and nominating a liberal cabinet. He quickly ran afoul of the liberal majority in the parliament, however, when over its objections he attempted to increase the size of the standing army, lengthen the period of service for draftees, and also reduce the strength of the *Landwehr,* the citizen's militia that was controlled by the middle classes and served as a counterweight to the professional, aristocrat-dominated army. The liberals raised a storm of protest, and in Prussia the conflict hardened between the liberal parliamentarians on the one hand and the ruling alliance of the monarch, the landowning aristocracy, and the military on the other.

One additional factor brought the political situation into flux: Napoleon III, nephew of the great Corsican general, who had imitated his uncle by declaring himself Emperor of France, also tried to carry on old French policy by striving for influence in Italy. In 1859 he entered into an alliance with the kingdom of Piedmont-Sardinia, thereby challenging Austrian supremacy in northern Italy.

For the first time since the failure of the Revolution of 1848 the German public was seized by a wave of nationalism. The old hostility toward the archenemy France that had inflamed national sentiment in 1813 now flared up again, and in thousands of leaflets, pamphlets, and newspaper articles, activists and journalists demanded the swift creation of a sovereign German nation state that would possess real military power and be able to intervene effectively in foreign affairs.

Napoleon III and Bismarck on the Morning after the Battle of Sedan
(Wilhelm Camphausen, 1877)

"Yesterday morning [September 2, 1870] General Reille woke me with the news that Napoleon wanted to talk to me. I rode toward Sedan, without having washed or eaten breakfast, and encountered the emperor in an open carriage with three adjutants, waiting on the road. I dismounted, greeted him just as politely as if we had been in the Tuileries, and inquired about his orders. He wished to see the king [of Prussia] . . . In Fresnois we discovered a little chateau in a park, and there we concluded the capitulation, by power of which between 40,000 and 60,000 Frenchmen became our prisoners, I don't have more exact figures. Yesterday and the day before cost France 100,000 men and one emperor. Today the latter departed for Wilhelmshöh near Kassel, with all his courtiers, horses, and carriages" (Bismarck to his wife, September 3, 1870).

The surge of national feeling reached a climax on November 10, 1859, in the observances for Friedrich Schiller's 100th birthday, which was celebrated throughout the German-speaking regions. At the same time it became evident that the opposing fronts which had emerged within the national movement during the Revolution of 1848 still existed; now they hardened their positions in formal organizations. "Small German" and "Great German" were their watchwords, and Prussia's political lead over Austria was reflected in the victory of its forces. The Small German *Deutscher Nationalverein* (German National Association), founded in Coburg in 1859, was better organized and financed; above all, however, its propaganda proved so much more effective that it routed the Great German opposition, composed chiefly of the smaller states and those that were predominantly Catholic. Their organization, the *Deutscher Reformverein* (German Reform Association), not founded until 1862, entered the fray too late; it was further plagued by internal disunity and lacked rousing slogans.

The Small German national movement had one major handicap, however. Its politically most powerful supporters, the liberal members of the Prussian parliament, were at loggerheads with the very institution that was supposed to bring about the kind of national unification they wanted: the Prussian government. On September 24, 1862, William I named a new prime minister, the arch-conservative Otto von Bismarck (1815–1898), who had become notorious as the personification of the counter-revolution during his brief tour of duty as Prussian ambassador to France. Bismarck had persuaded the king to place him at the head of his government in the course of a long talk in the gardens of Babelsberg Palace, when he assured William that he could stabilize the power of the monarchy and put an end to the liberals' domination of parliament. The German public perceived Bismarck as the embodiment not only of all antiliberal strivings but also—since liberalism and nationalism represented two sides of the same coin—of all the antinational forces.

In fact, however, Bismarck was misunderstood by both his opponents and his highly conservative friends. He viewed the job of Prussian prime minister not as a goal but only as the means by which he could achieve a higher aim. His real intent was to consolidate and expand Prussia's might in a Europe beset by revolutions, and he was convinced that the path to success lay in establishing Prussian hegemony in Germany at Austrian expense. However, he hoped to reach this goal with the consent of the other great powers as far as possible, for the failure of the dreams to create a nation state in 1848–49 had shown that no alterations to the central European frontiers could be achieved over their resistance.

When Denmark formally annexed the Duchy of Schleswig in November 1863—the Danish king also bore the title of Duke of Schleswig—Germany was once again seized by patriotic fervor. Both public opinion and parliamentary factions demanded a pan-German declaration of war. As in 1848, Schleswig-Holstein represented the German *irredenta,* the region with historical and cultural ties to the mother country that was as yet "unredeemed"; it also symbolized the expansion of German nationalism beyond the borders drawn at the Congress of Vienna in 1815, then so feared by the European powers. It was characteristic of the blindness of all German nationalistic factions that they ignored the general European political situation in their debates. National movements in all European countries, not just in Germany, regarded the political order established in 1815 as a reactionary obstacle that deserved to be opposed with all possible means.

It is one of the ironies of German history that the liberal nationalists' bitter opposition to Bismarck contributed to the success of the very policies they so hated. Nothing would have hindered his plans more than an alliance with the national movement, whose ultimate aims to bring down the existing system were as clear as day. Bismarck needed their opposition as a screen to operate behind, concealing his strength and real intentions until the moment when he could take action and catch everyone off guard. Disregarding the upsurge of national sentiment, he therefore recognized the rights of the Danish royal house to rule Schleswig-Holstein, a move that placated England, France, and Russia. At the same time, however, he planned an invasion, on the grounds that old rights of the province had been violated by its incorporation into the Danish state. The two largest German powers, Prussia and Austria, surprised everyone by acting in concert. While the only difference between their stand on the issue and that of the nationalists was thus of a purely formal, legalistic kind, their recognition of Danish rights and the old order of 1815 enraged the German patriots. After Prussian and Austrian troops marched into Jutland in January 1864 and made significant military gains, liberals' fury knew no bounds—with good reason, as it turned out, for the peace treaty signed on October 30, 1864, by no means integrated the liberated duchies into the German Confederation as a new state. Instead, it turned them into an Austro-Prussian condominium, under the joint sovereignty of the two states.

Many liberals were forced to conclude that while Bismarck's policies might appear utterly unprincipled, on the other hand they were clearly successful—in contrast to the nationalist movement. The ruthless realism of his prophecy to the parliament in 1862 now proved to have been accurate when he horrified liberals by stating, "The great questions of the age are not settled by speeches and majority votes—that was the error of 1848 and 1849—but by iron and blood."

Bismarck's first step had been accomplished: Although the national movement and liberal public opinion were vocal, he had exposed them as powerless to act. Denmark had been maneuvered out of the German Confederation, and Prussia had acquired considerable territory. Now it was time to realize his great goal, the one he had been working toward since the revolution: the establishment of lasting Prussian hegemony in Germany and a final reckoning with Austria. This would be the culmination of more than a century of Prussian policy that had begun with Frederick the Great's grab for Silesia in 1740. Since 1848–49 the two predominant German powers had existed in an uneasy balance, in which their rivalry had always been palpable. Between them had stood the smaller states of the "Third Germany," which had tried to maintain their independence from both great powers and the existing federal structure of the confederation by tactical seesawing between north and south.

With the Danish war a fundamental change had occurred. For the first time the lines on the map of central Europe had been redrawn without any of the powers on the periphery intervening; this was owing not only to Bismarck's brilliant strategy but also to the Crimean War (1853–1856). That conflict disturbed the previous harmony of the "Concert of Europe" (general accord, especially the Quadruple Alliance between Britain, Austria, Russia, and Prussia after the defeat of Napoleon); Russia and Britain became involved in open hostilities and thus temporarily incapable of concerted action on the Continent. It opened a historical window of opportunity for a few brief years. A central European power under resolute leaders with firm goals in view now had greater latitude for action than had existed for a long time before or would exist for a long time afterward.

By the beginning of 1866 the cabinets in both Vienna and Berlin realized that the decisive battle for supremacy in Germany was imminent. Each was searching for a pretext that would allow it to present its opponent as the aggressor. A pretext was found when a newly united Italy allied itself with Prussia, precisely according to Bismarck's calculations. The Italian declaration forced the council of ministers in Vienna to mobilize Austrian troops on March 21, 1866, putting a chain of events in motion that came to an abrupt halt at the battle of Königgrätz on July 3, 1866. It was an unforeseen and stunning victory for the Prussians over the allied armies of Austria and Saxony, won not only through the Prussians' superior weapons technology and training, but also through the skill of the Prussian chief of staff, General Helmuth von Moltke (1800–1891). For the first time in history a military commander had used the resources of railroads and telegraph to coordinate large-scale troop movements from all directions toward a single point. It was the largest single European battle of the nineteenth century.

The war that ended at Königgrätz has been seen in retrospect, in the light of the Prussian victory, as a step toward German unity. Had the Austrians won, the actual circumstances would have emerged more clearly. In fact it was Prussia that had declared the constitution of the German Confederation null and void and broken with the old order before embarking on the war, while Austria acted as the presiding power of the confederation. It was thus not a war between Prussia and Austria but one between Prussia and Germany. The South German confederate troops that fought on the Austrian side accordingly wore the black-red-gold colors on their uniform sleeves when they faced the Prussians, whose colors were black and white.

With the Treaty of Prague that followed, Austria was ejected from Germany, and the German Confederation became a thing of the past. What remained of it became a federal state with twenty-two small and middle-sized members north of the Main River, totally dominated by Prussia in both the military and economic sectors. Renamed the North German Confederation, it was connected with the other German states south of the Main through a military agreement and the strong links of the Customs Union, which continued in existence. Altogether it was a peculiar construction of international law that—in view of the discrepancy in real power between north and south in Germany—could not survive for any length of time.

Now it was the aggressive foreign policy tactics of the French that helped to bring about the very German unity that the French government wished to prevent at all costs. The task of unification could be completed only under pressure from the outside, as Bismarck was well aware, and the desired pressure was provided by Napoleon III. The French had emerged from the year 1866 with empty hands; Bismarck had brusquely rejected their requests for compensation after the founding of the North German Confederation, and the result was a sense of wounded pride that needed an outlet.

In 1870 the Spanish throne was vacant, and in the spring of that year the Spanish parliament offered the crown to a member of the house of Hohenzollern-Sigmaringen, the Catholic collateral branch of the ruling Prussian dynasty. In France the step aroused ancient fears of encirclement, and Napoleon made his strong objections known. Bismarck would have let the matter drop, only he recognized that France was isolated, as England and Russia showed no interest in becoming involved. While Bismarck was not actively seeking war, he was not trying to avoid it either. For his part, King William I was even prepared to accede to French demands and leave the Spanish throne to a candidate from outside Germany. For the alarmed French public this was not enough. The French ambassador Benedetti traveled to Bad Ems near Coblenz, where the Prussian king was staying, and delivered a demand for guarantees that no Hohenzollern prince would ever be a candidate in the future. William I judged this accurately for what it was, a diplomatic slap in the face, and refused.

Back in Berlin, Bismarck received a communiqué describing these events in a dispassionate tone, edited it to make the snub to the French sound sharper, and released the altered text of the "Ems Dispatch" to the press the same day, on July 13, 1870. He knew the French government was weak and that domestic political pressures would not permit it to let a diplomatic defeat go unanswered. His assessment of Napoleon III was correct; the French emperor rose to the bait and reacted aggressively, rushing to declare war on July 19 without waiting to make sure he had backing from other powers.

Unlike the "cabinet war" of 1866, the Franco-Prussian War of 1870–71, which grew into a Franco-German war as the southern German states were called on to honor their pacts with Prussia, was fought with modern technology and large armies for which whole nations were mobilized, foreshadowing the horrors unleashed in the total warfare of the twentieth century. In its first phase the technical and tactical superiority of the Prussian general staff under Helmuth von Moltke's leadership played a key role. The German side was better at mobilizing and deploying troops and at moving large armies long distances. The course of this part of the war was decided not by the epic border battles of Mars-la-Tour and Gravelotte but at Metz and Sedan, where the Germans encircled the French with minutely planned precision. These two great battles were masterpieces of strategy designed at general staff headquarters, leaving little room for initiative on the part of field commanders, who were in fact too close to events to be able to see the whole picture. Although Metz and Sedan cost far fewer casualties than the previous encounters, they nonetheless drove the French armies to capitulate.

The second phase of the war was conducted by the newly created French Republic, which fielded huge armies in a *levée en masse,* hoping to crush the enemy as it had in 1793. These tactics led to setbacks for the German forces, without, however, seriously damaging their chances for victory. A truce was negotiated on January 28, 1871, followed by a preliminary peace accord on February 26, as German troops were besieging Paris and could thus witness the rise and fall of the Paris Commune from close by. Such a thing, agreed the watching conservative German politicians and military leaders, with a glance over their shoulders at the German Social Democrats, must never be allowed to happen in Germany.

The peace treaty of Frankfurt signed on May 10, 1871, which in essence cost France the provinces of Alsace and Lorraine as well as payment of a war indemnity of 5 billion francs, made it even more evident that the old days, in which ministerial cabinets directed wars to be fought for the achievement of limited and rational goals, were gone forever. Bismarck realized clearly that he had not achieved his own goal, which had been to eliminate the danger of war on Germany's western border; in fact the peace treaty itself contained the seeds of future conflict. But he was unable to override both public opinion, which was virtually unanimous in demanding the "recapture of ancient German lands," namely Alsace and Lorraine (the negligible number of those opposed included the co-leaders of the Social Democrats Wilhelm Liebknecht and August Bebel), and the Prussian general staff, who for purely strategic reasons had declared the goal of the war to be capture of the Vosges heights and the fortress of Metz.

Political unification of the allied German states proceeded in tandem with the events of the war. The fever pitch of patriotism in both public and press placed such pressure on southern German governments that their cabinets could see no viable path other than joining the North German Confederation, on whatever terms might be offered. German unification by no means came about solely on orders from above, from the ruling princes and their governments, but also as a result of clamor from below, from the forces of the liberal, middle-class national movement, and the result was accordingly not a Great Prussia but a German Empire. It was not the princes who first proclaimed King William I of Prussia as German emperor in the Hall of Mirrors at Versailles on January 18, 1871, but the deputation from the North German Federal Diet *(Reichstag)*, who had already asked the king to accept the imperial crown a month earlier, on December 18, 1870. Their leader, Eduard von Simson, president of the Diet, was the same man who had offered the imperial throne to Frederick William IV as head of the deputation from the Frankfurt parliament in 1849 and been so brusquely snubbed.

From the very beginning, therefore, the legitimation of the new German Empire was twofold: It had received the approval of the second estate, the nobility, and had also been confirmed by parliamentary votes and plebescites. The new German state indeed bore two faces, but there was also a symptomatic contrast between the civilian delegation of legislators in their gray suits, which lent the ceremony a sober, workaday air, and the princes and generals, whose glittering uniforms dominated people's memories when they recalled the founding of the nation.

6 German Possibilities:
A Digression

After the empire's foundation in 1871, there seemed to be no point in pursuing the question of whether it had been necessary to create a German nation state and, if so, whether it had to take the present form. In the minds of contemporaries and the next two generations, Bismarck's state appeared a historical necessity, for which no alternative existed. And after all, weren't there good arguments for this view? Hadn't the Germans merely caught up with the rest of Europe and taken a step most countries had put behind them a long time ago, making Germany—in Helmuth Plessner's phrase—a "belated nation"? Wasn't the growing strength of national feeling, which was becoming the ideology of the masses, a strong argument for Bismarck's solution, along with economic modernization

The Strike
(detail, Robert Koehler, 1886)

Mann der Arbeit, aufgewacht!
Und erkenne deine Macht!
Alle Räder stehen still,
Wenn dein starker Arm es will.

Brecht das Doppeljoch entzwei!
Brecht das Joch der Sklaverei!
Brecht die Sklaverei der Not!
Brot ist Freiheit, Freiheit Brot!

(Georg Herwegh, "Anthem of the General German Workingmen's Association," 1863)

Awake, ye workers! Understand
That the might is in your hand!
It is in your power to say
That no wheels will turn today!

Break the double yoke each bears—
Of slavery and hunger's cares!
Break in two this double dread!
Bread is freedom, freedom bread!

and the increased heft of economic structures? Does it make any sense to raise the question of historical alternatives?

The question must be asked, for only by reconstructing past possibilities and opportunities can we liberate ourselves from fatalistic attitudes and come to an accurate assessment of actual historical developments. And from the perspective of political observers at the time, the circumstances leading to the unification of the German Empire represented only one of several possible chains of events, and perhaps not even the most likely one.

Many possible solutions existed to the German question. One was the *Deutscher Bund* (German Confederation) of 1815, and important facts argued in its favor: the remnants of tradition left from the Holy Roman Empire; consideration for existing ruling interests; the division of power created by its constitution (which realistically gave the two largest members considerable scope but without allowing them to dominate the other states); and finally the interest of the major powers in maintaining a balance of power in Europe, an equilibrium that appeared threatened by any progress toward unification in the divided center. All the same, the German Confederation could not last, mainly because the stalemate between Austria and Prussia, while preventing any centralization of power, also blocked every modernization, and secondly because its legitimation of power and its mechanisms for maintaining power were based on an outmoded ideology incongruent with the major currents of nineteenth-century political thought and belief systems that spoke to the masses.

The second possible solution had been tried out in 1848–49, namely the creation of a modern, centralized German nation state based on popular sovereignty and human rights. This model had also proved incapable of surviving; it failed in part as a result of the social and ideological heterogeneity of its liberal and nationalist supporters, but also due to the resistance of the major powers, who saw the spread of German nationalism beyond the frontiers of the German Confederation as a revolution threatening the balance of power in

Raising the German Flag at Fort Vanves outside Paris, January 19, 1871
(Eugen Adam, 1878)

On January 18, 1871, William I was proclaimed German emperor at the Palace of Versailles. The following day the besieging German troops—Bavarian soldiers in this scene—hoisted the new German flag at Fort Vanves southwest of Paris. The flag's colors are those of the North German Confederation: black, white, and red. Since 1848 the king had regarded the colors black, red, and gold with suspicion; they had a whiff of revolution and democracy. Bismarck attached little importance to the flag's design: "To tell the truth, I couldn't care less about the colors. As far as I'm concerned, they can use green and yellow and roses in springtime, or the flag of Mecklenburg-Strelitz. It's just that the old Prussian trooper [i.e., the king] won't hear of black-red-gold." How black-white-red came to be chosen is not clear. All that mattered to Bismarck is that this combination was not associated with any party inside the country. They were not declared the national German colors until 1888.

Europe. Yet no national parliament could have hoped for legitimacy in the eyes of German patriots if it rejected the need for "liberation" of the German *irredenta*, Alsace and Schleswig-Holstein.

After the collapse of the Revolution of 1848 there was no lack of further possibilities; once the national movement revived around 1859, they were heatedly debated, and every idea had its own camp of supporters. One such possibility was Great Germany, which included Austria but also Bohemia and northern Italy. It was the headiest and most exciting concept, since it opened the broadest perspectives and possessed the greatest emotional appeal in its recall of a glorified imperial past. Nonetheless, even by the early 1860s this program had the most hopeless prospects of all. The main obstacle did not necessarily lie in Prussian claims to hegemony—these were put forward mostly by the top echelon of the Prussian civil service, whereas the king and arch-conservative aristocracy had considerable respect for the privileges of the Hapsburgs. But rational economic considerations argued against Great Germany in view of the degree of integration achieved by the Customs Union, the relative backwardness of the Austrian monarchy, and its hopelessly antiquated mercantilist economic policies. Furthermore, Austria had long since begun to drift away from Germany; it was involved in extraterritorial conflicts in the Balkans and Italy, and its multinational constitution would have created insoluble problems if any attempt were made to absorb the Hapsburg state into a Great Germany.

Another possibility was dual hegemony of the dominant powers within the German Confederation, a solution Prussia had favored for a time and tried to establish in its reform proposals for the confederation. This amounted to a division of Germany into two parts along the Main River, with a Prussian–north German federation on one side and a south German–Austrian federation governed from Vienna on the other. Bismarck had proposed this solution, which would have simultaneously resolved the century-old conflict between Prussia and Austria, as late as 1864. It was a realistic alternative to the actual course of German history; it failed because the Austrians mistrusted the Prussians' self-restraint—with some justification—and feared that a stream of new demands would come later.

And finally there was the triad idea supported by the German states in the middle, who feared Prussian supremacy and Prussian-Austrian joint hegemony in equal measure. Was it not in fact a rather obvious solution—to amalgamate the many purely German territories into one nation state, and let Prussia and Austria, both of which included regions outside the borders of the old Holy Roman Empire and had large percentages of non-Germans in their population, go their own ways as European powers? The concept of a Third Germany had been a formative element in German history for centuries already; again and again the small and medium-sized territories had banded together to protect their traditional freedoms and to ward off larger powers' attempts to dominate them. The Third Germany had always been loyal to the empire in the sense that whatever constitution happened to be in force always seemed the best guarantor of individual principalities' rights. However, there was always a temptation to seek support from one great power to resist pressures from others—the model of the League of Princes of 1785 under Prussian patronage was just as conceivable as alliances with foreign powers, ranging from the Swedish-dominated Heilbronn League of 1633 to the Confederation of the Rhine (Rheinbund) created in the Napoleonic era.

The states of the Third Germany grew active again after 1859, seeking to alter the federal constitution so as to strengthen their rights and prevent Prussia and Austria from encroaching on the federation's jurisdiction. It soon transpired that the reform plans of Bavaria, Saxony, and Baden diverged too widely to devise a single common strategy, but the third bloc was nonetheless strong enough to maneuver between Austria and Prussia and play them off against one another in the Federal Diet. Each state still possessed the right, based on the federal constitution of 1815, to enter into alliances with powers outside Germany, and a replay of the Rheinbund policy was not unthinkable.

The solution ultimately found for the German question—a Small Germany dominated by Prussia—was thus only one option among many, and although the existence of the Customs Union, Austrian weakness, and, for a time, liberal sympathies favored it, its realization was by no means a foregone conclusion. Bismarck once confessed that he carried the dream of national unity in his heart, but added, "If Germany achieves its goal of nationhood in the nineteenth century, that will seem to me a great thing, and if it were to happen within the next ten years, or even five, it would be something extraordinary, an

The Proclamation of the Emperor in the Hall of Mirrors at Versailles
(Anton von Werner, 1878)

At the time of its founding the German nation state saw itself as reviving a historic legacy, so the proclamation of William I as emperor at Versailles was staged as an allegory of Roman-Germanic militarism: In this picture there is not a single civilian in sight. But Versailles was also associated with notions of hereditary enmity between Germany and France. The proclamation of the emperor on French soil was thus intended as "a symbol of revenge taken by Germany for centuries of injustice, as a symbol of the victories by which we regained the city of Strasbourg that Louis XIV stole from us," in the words of William's adjutant general. The French saw their humiliation in similar terms, so that fifty years later they took their own revenge in the same setting.

unhoped-for gift through the grace of God." That was in May 1868, not quite three years before the founding of the empire. For unification to succeed, two things were necessary: an international crisis that made it impossible for the great powers to intervene, and Prussian leadership capable of recognizing the opportunity and seizing it.

As far as the first was concerned, the Concert of Europe had been disrupted since the Crimean War, when England and France hastened to defend Turkey from Russian attack—not from any virtuous motives but simply to prevent the czar from expanding his sphere of influence into the Mediterranean. The Crimean War had stirred up public opinion on both sides profoundly, so that England and Russia, the two powers on the European periphery, regarded one another with grave suspicion by the time the war ended, making a joint intervention such as had occurred in 1848 when Germany marched into Denmark more unlikely. In France, Napoleon III courted Vienna and Berlin equally, hoping that, if it came to a showdown between them, he would benefit no matter which side emerged the victor. For these reasons Prussia's maneuvering room was temporarily increased, although no clear limits had been set. The risks involved in exceeding them were enormous, and failure would have meant relegation to the status of a minor power. A different leader in charge of Prussian policy, French intervention in the Austro-Prussian War of 1866, Russian or Austrian intervention in the Franco-Prussian War in 1870, or even a different outcome in one battle—any one of these things could have altered the course of German history.

7

A Nation State in the Center
of Europe (1871–1890)

Das deutsche Reich, the German Empire born on the battlefields of France in 1871, was an alliance between the ruling princes of Germany, supported by Prussian military might and legitimated by the enthusiastic approval of middle-class nationalists. They had vainly attempted to found a nation state based on popular sovereignty and human rights in 1848, and they now saw their dream of an all-inclusive German state realized through Bismarck's power politics.

The foundations on which the empire rested—the princes' alliance, Prussian arms, and the popular plebescite—were reflected in the constitution that was now drawn up. It provided for an upper chamber in which the princes were represented; the German Empire was in fact not a monarchy but an oligarchy of federated princes. Complementing this *Bundesrat* (Federal Council) was a second chamber, the *Reichstag* (Imperial Diet), a representative assembly chosen in free elections in which all German men over the age of twenty-five were allowed to cast equal votes by secret ballot, based on the law passed by the revolutionary parliament of 1849. Laws had to be passed by both houses; the constitution, as it turned out, provided for an almost perfect balance between a popular democracy and an authoritarian state.

Otto von Bismarck
(Fritz von Lenbach, 1879)

There was a third element in the mix, however, that stood outside parliamentary jurisdiction and remained the prerogative of the princes: It consisted of the two real pillars of state authority, the army and the civil service. Furthermore, since three-fifths of all civil servants were Prussian, and particularly since the imperial army was made up mostly of Prussian troops and took its orders from the Prussian king in his capacity as commander-in-chief, there was a fourth significant power: the Prussian king himself, who occupied the position of president of the federation and through this was entitled to bear the title of German Emperor (*Deutscher Kaiser,* Article 11). In fact there was absolutely no relation, in terms of international law, between William I and the Hapsburg emperor Franz II, who had relinquished the Roman crown in 1806, just as the new nation of Great Prussia or Small Germany had nothing whatever to do with the transnational character of the former Holy Roman Empire of the German Nation. But the consciousness of those who supported the idea of nationhood, mainly the liberal bourgeoisie, had been shaped for generations by romantic, utopian images and myths, in which a supposedly glorious medieval German past would be resurrected in a new empire. The force of these associations was so great that no German nation state could disregard them and still appear legitimate in the eyes of its citizens—much to the irritation of William I, who regarded his title of emperor as no more than a necessary concession to the spirit of the age and felt that by accepting it at Versailles he was presiding over the funeral of the old Prussia.

The success of the new government was thus guaranteed from an ideological standpoint, and from an economic standpoint as well. After the end of the Franco-Prussian war the German Empire was gripped by a veritable fever of entrepreneurial activity and speculation, driven in no small measure by the inflow of French war reparation payments. Industrial capacity was increased without any guarantee of profitability, and huge fortunes were made within a very short span of time. Along with the boom of the *Gründerzeit* (Founders' Era) came a change in Germans' appearance. The traditional plain ways of the old upper class—dictated by the Prussian motto *Mehr sein als scheinen*, "Be more than you seem," and a chronic lack of money—gave way to excessive pomp and *nouveau riche* ostentation in all areas of life, including architecture, interior decoration, clothing, and personal habits. William I resisted the trend, stubbornly clinging to his plain customs—the rubber tub carried over to the palace from a nearby hotel once a week for the royal bath was the talk of Berlin— and issuing directives on sober, modest behavior to civil servants and army officers. But he seemed like a fossil. The boom was followed by the crash of 1873, when the Vienna stock exchange collapsed and the rich lost vast fortunes overnight. Only a few years later, however, the scars had healed; the economic barometer began to climb steadily again, and with it the affluence of the middle classes, a trend that held until the First World War.

It was not only society that altered its appearance: Before the backdrop of its economic triumphs, Germany took the final steps in its transformation from an agrarian to an industrialized nation. Across the landscape that fifty years earlier had been dotted with farming villages and sleepy provincial towns there now sprawled giant industrial tracts and acres of new housing. Essen, for example, which in 1850 was still a quiet country town with 9,000 inhabitants, had a population of 295,000 fifty years later—a 33-fold increase. The rail connections were complete from Aachen in the west to Königsberg in the east, and from Hamburg in the north to Munich in the south, making the economic unification of Germany as much a reality as the political one. There was one major exception, however: The gap between the industrialized western part of the country and the old colonized regions east of the Elbe River was growing wider and wider. Upon crossing the Elbe at Magdeburg, passengers on an eastbound train would leave the industrial landscape behind and suddenly find them-

selves in an agrarian world again, surrounded by the vast grain fields of manorial estates, dotted here and there with manor houses and the brick church towers of little market towns.

These differences were reflected in the class divisions of German society. At the top was the landowning aristocracy, which still possessed enormous political power under the provisions of the imperial

Kaiser William I as a Field Marshal in the Uniform of the First Infantry Regiment
(Paul Bülow, 1879)

Unlike his father, Frederick William III, and his brother, Frederick William IV, William I was a military man with a blunt and direct manner; his mother, Queen Luise, called him "straightforward, honest, and sensible." His horizons and his standards for making decisions were those of the army; it was no accident that he acquired the nickname the "Bullet Prince" during the Revolution of 1848. From 1858 on William ruled as regent for his brother, who had become mentally incapacitated; in 1861 he crowned himself king in Königsberg, following the example of his forebear Frederick I. After William named Bismarck prime minister in 1862, the two men developed a close relationship that was tested in many crises. He did not want to become emperor; on the morning of his proclamation he brushed off congratulations, exclaiming irritably, "I don't consider it worth a straw; Prussia is all that matters to me."

constitution; as the economic importance of their land dwindled, however, the source of their wealth was in rapid decline. The old middle class of educated professional men and civil servants was now augmented by the newly affluent property-owning bourgeoisie, the economic pillar of the empire and, as liberal or moderate liberal voters, its main political pillar as well. Next came the lower middle class with its core of craftsmen and artisans, who lived in constant fear of losing their livelihoods to machines and being sucked down into the anonymous masses of the proletariat; their anxieties tended to make them susceptible to antisocialist and jingoistic movements and slogans. And finally there were the ever-growing numbers of factory workers, the proletariat that now found its own identity as the fourth estate and began to join Social Democratic organizations or, in Catholic regions, the Center Party, and the corresponding labor unions.

The impression of a developing class society was heightened by the contrast between neighborhoods in industrial cities. At the west end of town were villas and tree-lined streets for the entrepreneurs and property-owning bourgeoisie; across town to the east, where the prevailing westerly winds blew the smoke and noxious fumes from the factories, were drab rows of apartment blocks for the poor.

This great variety of intersecting, often antagonistic social and economic interests solidified into political parties, mass organizations, and special-interest groups and was further increased by political and ethnic minorities. Problems related to minority groups had

Councillor Valentin Manheimer on His Seventieth Birthday
(Anton von Werner, 1887)

Rarely have the wealth and success of the propertied industrialist been presented in such compact visual form as in this painting by the dean of academic artists of the day, Anton von Werner. The ladies' sumptuous gowns and the suggestion of a grand columned arcade in the background appear to illustrate Germans' sense, after the founding of the empire, that they, too, had finally "arrived." The successful clothing manufacturer Valentin Manheimer typified the emancipated, successful Jewish entrepreneur in Berlin during the empire. Born as the son of a cantor in Gommern (near Magdeburg) in 1815, he became a textile merchant. In 1836 he went to Berlin, where he succeeded in consolidating the Berlin tailoring trade, placing it on a modern industrial footing, and opening access to international markets. He was named a councillor of commerce in 1873, and privy councillor of commerce in 1884. He created a charitable foundation for invalid workers and was worth 12 million marks when he died in 1889.

arisen with the founding of a German national state that contained considerable French, Polish, and Danish populations, and the role Jews should play within German society was hotly debated. "Internal consolidation" of the empire, the achievement of some kind of balance between the various groups making up the nation, was the most pressing problem of domestic politics. Bismarck's technique for solv-

At the Labor Exchange
(Fritz Paulsen, 1881)

The scene shows one of the 460 employment bureaus that existed in Berlin around 1880, where the thousands of young people streaming into the city from the agrarian regions of eastern Germany came to look for work. In the center a well-dressed couple is talking to a wetnurse from the Spreewald district; in aristocratic and affluent bourgeois circles young mothers often did not nurse their children themselves. At this period in Germany 23 percent of the women who held paying jobs worked as household servants. They lived in their employers' households, usually in cramped and poorly heated quarters, and had neither fixed working hours nor the right to regular time off. They enjoyed very little protection under the law: They were not permitted to go on strike, could be dismissed on trivial grounds, and could not sue for back wages. Thus few young women chose to remain "in service" for any length of time; those who did not marry usually found factory work preferable.

ing this problem was to declare powerful groups that could not be integrated into a monarchical authoritarian state as outsiders, "enemies of the empire."

The first such group was the Center Party, the parliamentary arm of political Catholicism, which since midcentury had been firmly opposing attempts to centralize political and cultural life in the Protestant state of Prussia. On the surface, the *Kulturkampf* (cultural struggle) that now set in involved the issues of state supervision of schools and the appointment of parish priests; in reality, however, it was an at-

ALLGEMEINE
ELEKTRICITÄTS-GESELLSCHAFT
BERLIN.

tempt on the part of the authoritarian Prussian-German government to interpose a measure of control over German Catholicism, with its transnational aspects and tendency to take independent political positions—half a millennium after the French and English states had waged their own battles against the church.

By the end of the 1870s a struggle had also begun against the SPD (*Sozialdemokratische Partei Deutschlands,* the Social Democratic Party of Germany). August Bebel, leader of the SPD group in the *Reichstag,* had terrified both rulers and property owners when he prophesied on May 25, 1871, that the Paris Commune was only a "small skirmish" in comparison with the revolution that would come to Germany. The antisocialist law of 1878 was the government's answer to this declaration from the "party of subversion," intended as a stern measure, even

Poster of the General Electric Light Company of Berlin
(Louis Schmidt, 1888)

Artificial light was one of the symbols of the industrial revolution. The ability to "turn night into day" meant that one of the basic limitations of nature had been overcome. Some towns and cities had introduced street lights in the eighteenth century, using either pitch or oil lamps; and from the 1830s on, gas-lights—which flickered and gave off a terrible smell—came into general use. But the real triumph of artificial light arrived with Thomas A. Edison's invention of the electric light bulb in 1879. Between 1880 and 1920 electricity transformed urban life, providing the power for local mass transit, elevators, the telephone, radio, movies, and more and more household appliances. For people at the close of the nineteenth century, electricity had become synonymous with energy and life.

though in the light of twentieth-century methods of political suppression it appears almost harmless: The SPD delegates remained in the *Reichstag* and grew in numbers with each succeeding election. But using another tactic, the government began in the 1880s to introduce a series of laws creating a system of government health, disability, and old age insurance that—although conceived in the spirit of Prussian paternalism—became a model for the rest of Europe. This legislation was designed to turn penniless socialists into contented backers of the conservative government. The whole strategy backfired, however, for after the antisocialist law was allowed to expire in 1890, the SPD registered more growth than ever.

The new empire needed more than safeguards against internal opposition. Its neighbors by no means regarded its existence as a normal fact of life, as a glance at maps of Europe from that era will make clear. The unification of the previously splintered center of the continent represented a new and unfamiliar element in the system and was viewed by other nations as a potential threat to their security. Benjamin Disraeli, leader of the British opposition, summed up the apprehensions of cabinet ministers in St. Petersburg, Paris, and London when he described the founding of the German Empire as the greatest revolution of the nineteenth century, greater even than the French Revolution of the previous century. In his view the dangers for the future were incalculable.

Bismarck's own greatest concern was to signal to the outside world that the empire's ambitions were "satisfied," that the ferment of

	1800	1850	1880	1900	1910
Berlin	172	419	1,122	1,889	3,730
Hamburg	130	132	290	706	932
Munich	30	110	230	500	595
Leipzig	40	63	149	456	588
Dresden	60	97	221	396	547
Cologne	50	97	145	373	516
Breslau	60	114	273	423	512
Frankfurt/Main	48	65	137	289	415
Düsseldorf	10	27	95	214	358
Elberfeld-Barmen	25	84	190	299	339
Nuremberg	30	54	100	261	333
Charlottenburg			30	189	305
Hanover	18	29	123	236	302
Essen	4	9	57	119	295
Chemnitz	14	32	95	207	287
Duisburg			41	93	229
Dortmund			67	143	214
Kiel	7	15	44	108	211
Mannheim			53	141	193

German nationalism had been channeled and rendered harmless, making the balance of power in Europe more secure rather than less. And in fact the dream of Great Germany that had inspired generations of German liberals faded surprisingly quickly after 1871. Austrian and Russian fears that Germans would consider further regions of eastern Europe "unredeemed" parts of the fatherland were not confirmed; Bismarck actively discouraged such dreams, and the Austro-German alliance signed in 1879 showed that, despite Königgrätz, the two German-speaking nations in the middle of Europe could join together and still not throw the entire European system out of kilter.

Urban Population Growth in the Nineteenth Century
(in thousands)

Growing overpopulation and unemployment in rural areas drove thousands of people to seek work in the cities in the nineteenth century, especially in the eastern part of the country. In 1800 90 percent of the population lived in the country and only 5 percent in large cities, but by 1871 more than 50 percent lived in towns with more than 5,000 inhabitants. While there were only two cities in Germany with populations above 100,000 in 1800, a century later there were 33.

The Workers' Gospel
(Jens Birkholm, 1900)

This painting depicts a meeting of Social Democratic activists in the late 1890s, dominated by a bust of the socialist prophet Karl Marx on a pedestal. Police officers are seated on the podium, ready to close down the meeting at once if the bounds of legality are overstepped. Facing the rapt audience is the speaker, proclaimer of the word, who has been given the features of traditional portraits of Christ and raises his right hand as if in blessing. Protestant industrial workers were particularly receptive to the uplifting message of socialism. In the parliamentary elections of 1871, 3.2 percent of Germans gave their votes to the Social Democrats; by 1912 the figure had risen to 34.8 percent.

From then on German foreign policy followed the guidelines laid down by Bismarck in his "Bad Kissingen Declaration" of June 1877. Its chief aims were first to create the impression among all the European powers that they could work together with the German Empire, and second to prevent coalitions from forming against Germany. In order to avoid this "nightmare of coalitions," as Bismarck put it, Germany would play the role of "honest broker" between the other powers. This policy achieved its greatest success with the Congress of Berlin in 1878, where the German chancellor played a major role in stabilizing the political situation in Europe and banished the threat of a major war over control of the Balkans.

Carrying out such a policy remained quite a feat, for it demanded a kind of political self-restraint that ran directly counter to the expansionist spirit of the age, among both nationalistic groups and industrialists, whose interests now ranged far beyond the borders of the old Customs Union in pursuit of spheres of influence and colonies, and also among liberals with imperialistic ambitions, who wanted to see Germany become a major maritime nation and world power. Above all it required a statesman of extraordinary skill at the helm of the new power in the center of the continent to balance the antagonistic interests of the other major powers and keep France from building anti-German coalitions. Bismarck succeeded through the Austro-German League, which was later joined by Italy, Romania, and, for a short time, Serbia, and by courting Russia. This policy led to the Three Emperors' Alliance of 1881 and finally to the mutual Reinsurance Treaty between St. Petersburg and Berlin in 1887 that formally cleared the way for Russia to take control of the Dardanelles.

Despite these successes, Bismarck's diplomacy remained a complicated "juggling act with five balls." His aim of ensuring that the threat of "one sword keeps the other in its sheath," as he put it, grew increasingly difficult as contrary forces and tendencies gained ground within all the nations of Europe. This was true of France as well as Germany, for example, where sentiment in favor of a war to avenge the defeat of 1871 and win back Alsace-Lorraine was so popular that no French government could afford to ignore it. It was also true of Russia, where the burgeoning Pan-Slav movement posed a threat to both Turkish and Austrian interests. Germany caught between Russia and France: The old Prussian fears of a war on two fronts remained very much alive; the danger that these two peripheral powers might join forces against the middle was obvious.

Bismarck's dismissal from office on March 20, 1890, had nothing to do with his conduct of foreign policy. He had fallen out with William II, who had succeeded to the throne in 1888 after the brief rule of his father, the "Hundred Days' Kaiser" Frederick III. The new emperor found the might of the "Iron Chancellor" oppressive, and they disagreed sharply on issues of social policy. William II, who wanted to reduce some of the gap between rich and poor, found Bismarck's opposition to the Social Democrats a stumbling block. And since the *Reichstag* proved unwilling to renew the antisocialist law, which was due to expire in 1890, Bismarck had no leverage. During his last days in office the renewal of the Russo-German Reinsurance Treaty, the cornerstone of Bismarck's system of alliances, was also placed in question. The emperor's lack of interest in extending the treaty contributed to the growing alienation between the two men.

With Bismarck's dismissal an era came to an end, as did the attempt to pursue foreign policy in the prerevolutionary manner. As mass emotions came to have an increasing influence on political decisions, the possibilities for maneuvering and negotiating between competing interests in the old style, with rational means and limited goals, faded. However, such policies were a necessity if a German nation state in the center of Europe was to survive.

8

Internal Unification and the Dream of World Power (1890–1914)

Kaiser William II embodied the spirit of the new age in many respects. In stark contrast to his grandfather William I, he cut an impressive figure in public. As a university student in Bonn he had learned that knowledge is power, and as a cadet in Potsdam he had acquired a fondness for military pomp and Prussian glory. Although he was innately gifted, with superb powers of memory and a sharp intellect, his education had filled him with bigoted and absurdly romantic notions, and a crippled arm and domineering mother had left psychological and emotional scars from his formative years. As commander-in-chief of the army during his reign, he remained an immature, arrogant cadet. As a dreamer infatuated with technology, he founded great research institutes yet loved to dress up as Frederick the Great or the "Great Elector" Frederick William. A man for many

The Emperor with His Family in the Park of Sanssouci
(William Friedrich Georg Pape, 1891)

An equestrian statue of Frederick the Great looks down on this Hohenzollern family idyll in the grounds of Sanssouci near Potsdam. Kaiser William II (1888–1941) is wearing the transitional uniform of the Second Regiment of Guards, a very restrained choice, given his preference for flashy military outfits. Empress Auguste Victoria is at his side, along with five of their six sons: Prince Oscar (dressed as a girl, as was then the custom for very small boys), and the princes Eitel Friedrich, August William, Adalbert, and Crown Prince Frederick William, with a dog. Like hundreds of thousands of other boys of the era, they are dressed in sailor suits; in Germany these outfits signaled national pride in the German naval fleet, which was a far more potent symbol than the army of Germany's might and its claim to equal status with Britain.

roles who possessed a secure identity in none of them, William II was a walking symbol of the people he ruled.

His coronation in the year 1888 marked a turning point in the history of the German Empire. The symbolic shift from plain-living William I, who saw himself as king of Prussia and hated the ermine trim of his emperor's robes, to his pomp-loving, theatrical, romantic grandson, who viewed himself—entirely without historical foundation—as successor to the medieval rulers of the Holy Roman Empire, corresponded to a

fundamental shift of mood within the country. Those so inclined may explain the latter on the basis of economic changes: After decades of free trade, a key tenet of the liberal bourgeoisie's creed, leaders of heavy industry in western Germany began demanding tariff protections against foreign competition, and the great landowners east of the Elbe, faced with growing worldwide grain surpluses, joined the cause. After long battles in newspaper columns and parliamentary debates, the protectionist interests—and the social and political forces behind them—carried the day.

Middle-class liberalism, the main pillar of support for Bismarck's policies in the first decade of the empire's existence, was pushed further and further into the role of the opposition, while the conservative parties moved to the fore. In consequence, although the largely liberal middle classes were making increasing economic gains, they lost political influence, whereas the opposite was the case with the great aristocratic landowners of the east. The importance of their es-

tates for the general economy was declining every day, but their stature rose socially as well as politically.

This trend was accompanied by an increase in the prominence and standing of the army, which was directly subordinate to the emperor and beyond the reach of parliamentary control in any case. The military leadership regarded itself as the sole guarantor of the country's and the monarchy's existence, not only against foreign enemies but also against internal opponents such as the Social Democrats, Catholics, and liberals. And it soon emerged that the general public preferred Prussian military officers as models over middle-class liberals. Respect dwindled for the civilian virtues of the professional and property-owning bourgeoisie, who had played such an important role in nineteenth-century German history, and was replaced by admiration for the tone and posture of a dashing lieutenant in the Prussian Guards.

Of course pockets existed where the more down-to-earth, middle-class self-image of the first half of the century prevailed, especially in the provincial capitals and prosperous towns of the Third Germany to the south. But the increasing political might of the Prussian trinity—emperor, aristocrats, and officers' corps—had a corresponding effect on Germans' view of themselves. The army in particular had stood in particularly high regard with citizens since the wars of unification of the 1860s and '70s; it was the pride of the nation. A bit of the glory rubbed off on each individual soldier, whose reputation in his own circles was thereby enhanced.

For this reason, compulsory military service was regarded as not so much a burden as a distinction and opportunity for social advancement. A romantic, glamorous aura surrounded sabers and uniforms; it was spread by newspapers and popular literature, with only a few liberal and socialist journals resisting the trend to glorify the military. The fact that a man had "served" also became an important factor in civilian life. Civil servants and teachers took pride in their status as officers in the reserves, and applied the standards they had learned in the army in offices and schools. Inevitably, the spread of military attitudes to other spheres of life began to have an effect on political opinion, first among the subjects of the empire, and then among its rulers as well.

Yet all this was not enough to form the style of a whole society;

under the showy, boastful gestures there was a lack of substance. Germans sought to cover up this lack—which they registered intuitively rather than through rational analysis—with a flood of superficialities. In architecture the neo-baroque style emerged; typically, the small and simple Berlin Cathedral that Schinkel had designed not sixty years earlier was torn down to make way for the present structure, Raschdorff's massive, overladen, and totally misproportioned church, built around the turn of the century. In the arts there was a flood of symbols and allegories, so randomly chosen that they revealed the absence of inner ties—philosophical, cultural, and spiritual—that could hold the nation together. Swaggering behavior masking uncertainty and the feeling that somehow this world could not last: That was "Wilhelmine" Germany in a nutshell.

The most important reason for the sense of doubt was a lack of progress in unifying the empire internally. Germany remained splintered; it was impossible to bridge the old territorial and religious divisions in a short time, and the same held true for the gaping fissures in society between industry and agriculture, aristocracy and bourgeoisie, capital and labor that had arisen in the wake of industrialization. The political parties, whose function should have been to represent these differences and negotiate between them, proved unequal to the task, in part because the German constitution, by not delegating political responsibility to the parties, did not force them to seek workable compromises. As a result, parties strove to develop philosophical and ideological programs instead of pragmatic policies, and served more as ersatz churches to their supporters than as representatives of their political interests. The German party system consisted of irreconcilably antagonistic groups, a jumble of fortresses surrounded by moats and palisades.

This political maze was made even more complicated by the fact that organized interest groups laid their own routes through, over, and around it. Beginning in the long deflationary phase after 1873, when the boom times ended and liberalism went into its long, slow

Baron Ferdinand Eduard von Stumm and Baroness Pauline von Stumm, née von Hoffmann
(Salvador Martinez Cubells, 1890)

Ferdinand von Stumm (1843–1925) came from one of the wealthiest families in Germany; his brother Karl was director of the family coal and steel company in the Saarland and generally known as King Stumm. The family was of middle-class origins and only raised to the nobility in 1888 by Frederick III. Ferdinand von Stumm entered the diplomatic service and was sent as German ambassador to Madrid; he resigned from this post in 1890, the year Bismarck was dismissed. Stumm commissioned these portraits of himself and his wife by a Spanish painter as a memento of his time in Spain. One might think he would have chosen to be painted in the splendid uniform of a diplomat, but instead he is shown as an officer of the reserves in the uniform of the Eighth Regiment of Hussars, even though the rank of ambassador was far higher than that of a major in the Prussian army: a telling example of the prestige enjoyed by the military in the public life of the empire.

decline, industrial and agricultural pressure groups sprang up. There were, for example, the German Agricultural Council, representing owners of small and middle-sized farms in Prussia, and the Catholic Central Federation of Agricultural Associations, but both were overshadowed politically by the *Bund der Landwirte* (Agrarian League), founded in 1893. This organization, whose membership came mostly from east of the Elbe, was dominated by the great landowners, and while its representatives achieved some success in cabinet ministries and legislatures, it operated most effectively in the highest circles of the imperial court and the Prussian Ministry of State.

Its counterpart in the industrial sector was the Central Association of German Industrialists, reinforced by the League of Industrialists after 1895. The first organization represented the interests of heavy industry, the second those of exporters. Similar groupings arose across the social and economic spectrum, all the way to workers' organizations at the opposite end, such as the Social Democratic Free Trade Unions and the Catholic Christian Trade Unions. All these configurations were complex and highly organized, with federations and umbrella organizations for every industry or branch of commerce, and a highly developed network of production, marketing, and price cartels. None of them talked to any of the others, or with the political parties—a lack of communication reflecting an ingrained inability and unwillingness to strive together for social and political stability. In a situation that demanded practical common sense, or a shared sense of higher values, each faction within the social system struggled against every other faction instead, weighed down by competing ideologies. They were linked by only one common sentiment, a sense of nationalistic enthusiasm for the empire that extended to much of the socialist and Social Democratic labor movement, despite the lip-service paid to international brotherhood.

With the passage of time this nationalism faded and grew stale, however. The founding of the empire meant the disappearance of the utopian vision that had provided a sense of direction and political strategies for two generations of German patriots. Its place was taken by economic aims; what was lacking was a broad-based civic culture based on common sense and time-honored ways of settling controversy, of the kind that regulated political affairs among Germany's neighbors to the west, and also a forward-looking vision or aim that could draw the nation together.

Only one institution was capable of defusing this comparatively dramatic situation, by placing all the efforts to resolve conflicts under its own aegis, including the problems of identity and purpose besetting German society, and this was the state—the Prussian-German authoritarian state that administered, educated, and trained the population, redistributed wealth, and declared itself responsible for everything from basic social welfare laws to cemetery regulations. Its institutions, its bureaucracy, and above all its military cherished the belief that they existed on a plane above the fray and represented the good of the whole, an idea that at its core is antidemocratic.

This tendency was only strengthened by a view of the *Reichstag*, the actual representatives of the people, as a crowd of jabbering, brawling incompetents. The legislature consequently received scant respect; as one conservative delegate put it, the emperor ought to be able to shut it down any time he liked, with one lieutenant and a squad of ten men. The model of an irresponsible populace and a wise "Father State" standing above its squabbles was pervasive; a sense of just how pervasive can be gained from a look at the German Social Democratic Party. It claimed to represent the polar opposite of this kind of state order, yet copied its spirit and structures down to the last detail. The lines, "We fight with greatest militance / Against the masses' ignorance," were not the motto of government bureaucrats but part of a verse from the Social Democratic "Workers' Marseillaise."

The deep fissures running through Wilhelmine Germany extended to areas on which the fame of the empire rested, apart from its military glory, namely science and the arts. The cultural domain was characterized by glaring contrasts, with academic taste and pomp on one

side, and the avant-garde on the other. The contradictions had never been so sharp. The ornate neo-baroque city hall in Hanover, for example, was built at about the same time as Peter Behrens's constructivist turbine assembly hall in Berlin and Walter Gropius's Fagus Works in Alfeld, a functional glass and steel structure flooded with light. In between the two extremes there was *Jugendstil,* the German variant of art nouveau, which was more a reflection of the crisis than a means of overcoming it, and in creative terms a blind alley.

In painting, one end of the spectrum was represented by academic

A Whole Size Too Big!
(cartoon by Bruno Paul, 1900)

Count Bernhard von Bülow (1849–1929), a sophisticated man of the world and favorite of Emperor William II, had just been named prime minister, the third to succeed Bismarck, when this cartoon was published. The caricaturist portrays him in Bismarck's cavalry uniform, and the verdict is merciless. In fact Bülow never did succeed in developing a coherent foreign policy that would extend Bismarck's program of alliances. He was well aware of many problems in both the domestic and foreign policy spheres, but unable to oppose the kaiser's wishes with sufficient force. Bülow resigned in 1909 and went to live in Rome.

artists who enjoyed the patronage of court circles, such as Anton von Werner and Hans Makart; they attached the highest value to magnificent colors and photographic exactitude. At the opposite end stood the avant-garde painters of the Munich, Vienna, and Berlin "Secessions," the *Blauer Reiter* (Blue Rider) movement, and the *Brücke* (Bridge) in Dresden; the works of such artists as Franz Marc, Gustav Klimt, and Max Liebermann pointed ahead to the modernism of the twentieth century.

In music, two very different trends developed, one begun by Richard Wagner and the other by Johannes Brahms. Brahms, who drew on the tradition of Protestant inwardness deriving from Schütz and Bach, combined the expressiveness of romantic music with the strict forms of older polyphony in a manner his contemporaries viewed as "academic." Wagner, on the other hand, whose aim was to create the *Gesamtkunstwerk,* the total work of art that would transcend all genres, began to dissolve traditional musical forms. One of the great revolutionaries in the history of music (who had actually stood on the barricades in Dresden in 1848), he came to be misunderstood by a growing segment of his mass audience, chiefly because they considered the subjects of his historicizing, heroic operas to be reactionary. These two giants of music history were followed by the late romantics such as Busoni and Bruckner on the one side, and on the other by innovators like Gustav Mahler and Richard Strauss. Both lines of development would be combined again in the bold music of Arnold Schoenberg. Wagner had powerful patrons—first King Ludwig II of Bavaria and later Emperor William II, who liked to think of himself as a new Lohengrin—whereas Richard Strauss overtaxed the emperor. "This is not my sort of music!" His Majesty exclaimed, and walked out of the Berlin premiere of *Der Rosenkavalier* in a huff.

Traditional and modern views collided everywhere. Plays by Gerhard Hauptmann and Georg Kaiser burst on the theatrical scene, which was otherwise dominated by the classical repertoire; in the field of literature, a deeply conservative writer like the novelist Theodor Fontane and the expressionist poet Georg Heym, killed in an accident while still a university student, seemed worlds apart although contemporaneous. New departures and decline existed in precarious balance, but a deep-seated feeling persisted that things could not last; the conviction that before too long something would happen to turn the world and society upside down gnawed painfully at the Wilhelmine era's sense of prosperity and security. Karl Marx, Friedrich Engels, and in their wake the major and minor socialist philosophers of the time were prophesying the coming of the revolution—what

Wilhelm Liebknecht called "the great hullabaloo"—within the lifetime of the present generation. Friedrich Nietzsche demanded the "revaluation of all values" and prophesied the advent of the "superman," who would liberate himself from morality through the "will to power," while Arthur Schopenhauer preached the meaninglessness of history to a bourgeoisie enamored with the idea of progress. The era's positivist belief in reason was undermined from other directions as well, no less by Richard Wagner's visions of a heroic antibourgeois future than by Sigmund Freud's discovery of the role of the unconscious and unconscious drives in human behavior.

The new prophets found great numbers of willing converts among

A Prayer to Light
("Fidus," Karl Johann Höppener, 1894)

The search for escape from the confines of bourgeois society in Wilhelmine Germany took many forms. The clothing of that era was like the society itself; stiff and formal, it restricted freedom of movement and choked its wearers. Looser and more comfortable clothing was one obvious way to break with convention, and those who wanted to shock the philistines even more could advocate nudism and sun worship. The painter and graphic artist who went by the name of Fidus (1868–1948) espoused the reform movement whole-heartedly; he often depicted his subjects naked and liberated from all the dross of social conventions, like the man shown here against a backdrop of open sky, greeting the return of life-giving light.

middle-class youth, who experienced the *belle époque* as a time of bloated philistinism and vacuous pretensions. Unlike their elders who had lived through the founding of the empire and looked with great pride on Germany's political and material achievements, much of the younger generation was repelled by what it saw as the hollowness and hypocrisy of the Wilhelmine state. The reactions of this generation can be described in abstract terms as a response to the violent social and technological upheavals of the industrial age. The shock set in late and expressed itself as panic and alienation—a "loss of the center," in Hans Sedlmayr's phrase.

For many young people, the search for a meaningful alternative vision led to radical departures and a total break with their parents' values: liberalism, moderation, social conventions, belief in reason, and human kindness. The norms of bourgeois culture met with vehement rejection. The parents were conservative, nationalist liberals, or free thinkers; their daughters and sons became racist nationalists, socialists, nihilists, or joined the *Wandervögel* ("migratory birds"), a youth movement that spread around the country from its beginnings at the *Steglitzer Gymnasium,* a high school in Berlin, in 1895. In this case the "movement" was literal; young people fled the cities to hike, cycle, and experience nature, simultaneously giving expression to their contempt for politics and the culture surrounding it. Experiments in antibourgeois forms of living abounded; alternative colonies and communes sprang up, inspired in equal measure by wishes to create art far from the demands of the marketplace, the longing to experi-

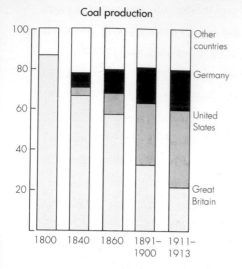

Coal production

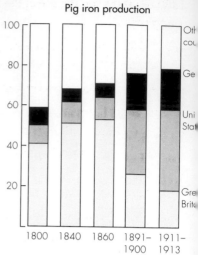

Pig iron production

ence real communal life, and romantic desires to "live off the land." From Monte Verità near Ascona in Italian Switzerland to the artists' colony in Worpswede, north of Bremen, communities flourished whose members hoped to renew the old unity between people and nature. Oases of anarchism, anthroposophy, and other

Production of Coal and Pig Iron, 1800–1913

(expressed in percentages of total world production)

Germany's growing economy after 1871 was based on the development of heavy industry. Germany never quite caught up with its economic rival Britain in the area of coal mining, but its rates of growth were comparable with those in the United States. The German iron industry owed its growth to both coal and the mining of ore in Lorraine. In 1910 German iron production was the largest in Europe; Germany produced 14.8 million tons, compared to Britain's 10.2 tons.

radically new lifestyles vied with one another to produce a new kind of human being; they all pulsed with vitality and creativity. From this soil grew the intellectual attitudes that would enable middle-class young men to march enthusiastically off to war in August 1914, into the longed-for apocalypse.

It was in large part the same young people who populated the lecture halls of German universities and institutes of technology, which were enjoying a worldwide repute unparalleled in their previous history. The number of students was continually on the rise; after stagnating until about 1860, enrollment skyrocketed from 11,000 in

1860 to 60,000 on the eve of the First World War, among them some 4,000 women, who were not permitted to enroll officially, however, until 1908. Education, and academic education in particular, remained the ticket of admission to the more lucrative and prestigious professions, and the government encouraged the trend, for the universities, especially the expanding law faculties, supplied it with capable civil servants, and the technical institutes provided the know-how on which the country's growing wealth and international prestige were based.

"Knowledge is power"—this motto applied to the country as a whole as well as to individuals, including members of the labor movement, who saw self-improvement as the best means to bring down social barriers. Workingmen's associations represented the first real centers of adult education in Germany. But the government not only organized and financed schools and universities; it also founded ultra-modern institutes for large-scale scientific research, with the intent of outpacing the British, French, and American competition. The Kaiser Wilhelm Society, founded in Berlin in 1911 and financed partly by the government and partly by industry, undertook both basic and applied research on a previously unknown scale. By 1918 its institutes had produced no fewer than five Nobel Prize winners: Albert Einstein, Max Planck, Emil Fischer, Fritz Haber, and Max von Laue. William II insisted on dedicating the first institute himself; the contrary tendencies of the age could not be better summed up than in the picture of the ardent romantic, who imagined himself the successor to medieval imperial glory, inaugurating the era of "big science" in a breastplate and Prussian helmet.

As their country's economic and political potential increased rapidly, many Germans began to see central Europe as too small a stage, as a cramped and confining theater. Without overseas territories, Germany was limited to modest economic development, within its own borders and an already saturated market. This was felt as humiliating by middle-class Germans, and—in comparison with their European neighbors—as discriminatory. Up to now national policy had meant achieving unification, and after that internal consolidation of the empire. But beginning in the 1890s national policy became international policy, in accordance with Max Weber's pronouncement in his inaugural lecture at the University of Freiburg in 1895: "We must grasp the fact that German unification was a youthful prank, although the nation was well advanced in years before undertaking it, and that we would have been better off without it, given the enormous costs it demanded, if it was to be the conclusion and not the starting point of a policy to become a world power." In other words, the completion and fulfillment of national unity required striving to acquire equal status with the other world powers.

That in turn meant a crucial break with Bismarck's policy, which had always been one of strict self-limitation to central Europe. The pressure to embark on imperialist adventures did not come from the old elite in Prussia; although foreign observers found the Prussian aristocracy uncivilized and fear-inspiring, it was in fact entirely occupied with defending its increasingly undermined position in society and domestic politics and possessed not the slightest ambitions with regard to foreign policy. The force behind these strivings was rather the liberal, property-owning middle class, the inheritors of the national movement, who now wanted to use their growing economic might to expand their influence and acquire a say in world affairs. It is difficult to determine in all this how much of a role was played by economic policy calculations and how much by a desire to compensate for the frustrations of having to watch French, British, and Russian imperialist expansion from the sidelines.

Bismarck had responded to the hue and cry for German colonies and overseas spheres of influence with reluctance and delaying tactics. That had been the era of colonial adventurers such as Carl Peters and Gustav Nachtigall, who had planted the German flag in east Africa and Cameroon and more or less forced the government to declare the regions German protectorates, with the aid of an insistent press and pressure from colonial organizations and representatives of industry. This changed under Bismarck's successors. New pressure groups with mass membership such as the German Colonial Society and the powerful Pan-German League, founded in 1887 and 1891 respectively, succeeded in making the establishment of German colonies in Africa and Oceania an official part of German foreign policy. Southwest Africa (present-day Namibia), east Africa (Tanzania), Togo, and Cameroon became German protectorates along with Tsingtao (Qingdao) in China and part of New Guinea. But the European nations could divide up the rest of the world without ceasing to behave like gentlemen; this was demonstrated by the Congo Act passed by an international conference in Berlin in 1885, the British-German Zanzibar Treaty of 1891, and finally the Treaty of Algeciras in 1906, which settled the question of Morocco.

Two other elements of German foreign policy proved more dangerous, the first being the attempts to extend the German axis of influence through Vienna and southeastern Europe all the way to Mesopotamia in the Ottoman Empire. These efforts reached their height with William's visit to the Near East in 1898 and commencement of German-financed construction on the Baghdad railroad in 1899. The Russians felt their ambitions in the Balkans and the Bosporus were threatened, while the British saw the events as hostile to their position in the Near East and India. It was inevitable that any conflict in these politically extremely sensitive spots would have a negative effect on peace in central Europe.

The second dangerous tack was the build-up of the German fleet. After Bernhard von Bülow was placed in charge of foreign policy and Admiral Alfred von Tirpitz appointed commander of the Imperial Navy Office almost simultaneously in 1897, the creation of a German navy that would be a match for the greatest maritime power in the world, at that time Great Britain, became a matter of priority. Clearly calculated power politics did not come into play here at all; the program was driven rather by a wave of patriotic enthusiasm and Ger-

Mt. Kilimanjaro in German East Africa
(Walter von Ruckteschell, 1914)

"The whole colonial business is humbug, but we need it for elections," said Bismarck in 1884. Only grudgingly did he give way to growing pressure and agree to turn the territories acquired in Africa by German traders and adventurers into protectorates of the German Empire. He believed he could turn the colonial propaganda to good use for the government, but his successors tended to do the reverse, placing the government increasingly in the service of colonial and nationalistic mass pressure groups. For the German public, these overseas possessions symbolized "world status" and were surrounded by an aura of romantic adventure. At 19,430 feet, Mount Kilimanjaro in what was then German east Africa—now Tanzania—was considered the "highest German mountain."

mans' desire to overcome the deep-seated feelings of inferiority that their "English cousins" inspired in so many areas. Momentum came from a true mass movement, spearheaded by the Naval League, with over a million members the largest German special-interest group. The fact that this policy would touch a most sensitive nerve in Britain and force it into a coalition with France and Russia, the two powers flanking Germany, played no role in the public debates. Just as in the earlier period leading up to unification, a mood of heated emotions and stirred-up public feeling prevailed once more, directed against the rational policy of maintaining a balance of power in Europe. This time, however, the movement had supporters within the government leadership, principally in the person of the emperor himself, who let no opportunity pass to disquiet and provoke the British with ill-considered, saber-rattling speeches.

Thus the conditions were created for a reshuffling of alliances along the lines Bismarck had foreseen in his worst nightmares. In 1904 Great Britain and France settled their colonial differences and concluded a far-reaching alliance, the *entente cordiale*. After William II's attempt to renew the old German–Russian alliance failed in 1905, there followed a treaty between the British and Russians two years later, in which the two powers resolved their rivalries in the Middle East. Germany saw itself encircled and politically isolated except for its ally Austria, which was so embroiled in the perennial Balkan crisis, however, that the alliance represented more of a burden than an advantage.

The feeling that they were surrounded by hostile powers aroused in Germans a stubborn determination to proceed, a "now more than ever" attitude that raised neurotic mass nationalism to an even greater pitch, as reflected in the stepped-up campaign of the Pan-German League. Military plans were also adapted to fit this situation. In 1905 Chief-of-staff Count Alfred von Schlieffen began developing a strategy for the war on two fronts that was now regarded as inevitable. Since Germany's military potential was insufficient to fight both Russia and France simultaneously, his plan counted on the Russians taking a long time to mobilize. He would therefore concentrate most of his troops in the west and, when war broke out, repeat Hannibal's tactics at the battle of Cannae on a giant scale and swing around in a huge arc with Metz at its center, sweeping through neutral Belgium and northern France to encircle and annihilate the French army within a few weeks. Then he would be able to devote his attention to the Russian campaign.

This strategy, which von Schlieffen worked out without consulting either the naval command or the architects of German foreign policy, had several disastrous features. The first was the automatic coupling that made war with France necessary from the outset if any military entanglement with the Russians should arise. A second was the intention of violating Belgian neutrality, which Great Britain had guaranteed; this would virtually force the British to enter the war against Germany as well.

Dark clouds were gathering on the horizon, not only over France and Russia but also in Germany itself. Peaceful coexistence between the different classes of society was threatened. The Social Democrats gained strength from election to election, and more frequent strikes demonstrated the growing self-confidence of the labor unions. Even the foundations of social order were attacked with impunity in both the press and legislatures. The feudal military regiments created resentments over the composition of the officers' corps, the preference given to the sons of the aristocracy, and the official tendency to look the other way in the matter of duels; it was a scandal that patricians could settle their affairs of honor without having to fear being brought to trial for murder or manslaughter afterward. And this was only a foretaste of the public outrage that erupted in November 1913 when word of the military's arrogance in the Zabern incident leaked out: Prussian soldiers had attacked civilians at Zabern (Saverne) in Alsace, yet their assault was first covered up and then defended by both military and civilian leaders.

The climate within Germany grew tenser and more oppressive from day to day, and thus the news of the assassination of the heir to the Austrian throne in Sarajevo on June 28, 1914, had the effect of the proverbial cleansing thunderstorm. The furiously escalating international crisis and threat of war united the German public again. The enthusiasm with which the outbreak of hostilities was greeted—the "spirit of 1914"—extended across the social spectrum, gripping even large segments of the progressive Social Democrats, and can be explained largely as an understandable psychological reaction to two phenomena: the pressure from abroad, which was felt to have taken on intolerable dimensions, and the loss of unity within the country in the preceding years.

It is one of the ruinous and tragic aspects of German history that the "internal unification" of Bismarck's empire came apart at the seams in times of peace; it could only be achieved through war, and then only for a short time. When in addition to everything else the war was lost as well, the inner unity of the empire was truly done for; the reality of the Weimar Republic would thus be a form of continuous civil war.

9

The Great War and Its Aftermath

(1914–1923)

"I do not recognize parties any longer, I recognize only Germans," proclaimed William II in the opening session of the *Reichstag* on August 4, 1914. In a way the emperor's statement helps to explain the general public's jubilation at the outbreak of the First World War in Germany, a reaction that is difficult to comprehend today. Celebrated in the propaganda output as the "spirit of 1914," it was not unlike the demonstrations of mass enthusiasm in London, Paris, and St. Petersburg. In the German political tradition, parties were symbols of narrow special interests, political infighting, and threats to national unity. Now, with the outbreak of hostilities, the parties lined up behind the government, and even the great majority of Social Democrats voted for the loans that were needed to fight the war, a war everyone believed would be over within a matter of weeks. And indeed it had to be over quickly: Schlieffen's plan, the basis of the

Winter in Wartime
(Hans Baluschek, 1917)

This painting shows the home front in the "rutabaga winter" of 1917. At the top of the picture is a coking plant, below it a railroad siding and shabby garden allotments, with huts flying the flags of the empire and the Prussian province of Saxony. At the bottom we see a family that has just buried a relative killed in the war; the son's hat identifies him as a crew member of the cruiser *Emden*, which made a hazardous voyage through the South Pacific at the start of the war. But by now the enthusiasm for the war is long gone, and the winter chill symbolizes the military situation. In the winter of 1917 alone 260,000 German civilians died of hunger, almost half the number of soldiers killed at the front in the same period (620,000).

general staff's strategy, could succeed only if the Germans won decisive victories soon. That the country's material resources were insufficient for a protracted war on two fronts was clear even to members of the cabinet without degrees in economics.

But the Schlieffen plan failed to work. The advance of the German armies through Belgium and France was stopped at the Marne, almost within sight of Paris, principally because the right wing on the western front was too weak. Ignoring Schlieffen's warnings, his successor, the younger Count von Moltke, had withdrawn men to shore up the left wing in Alsace, to prevent the French from breaking through into southern Germany. By October 1914 the troops in the west had already had to dig themselves in, and despite numerous offensives launched by both sides with horrendous casualties, the front lines were still in essentially the same place in 1918.

On the eastern front, on the other hand, German troops under the command of General Paul von Hindenburg, who had been summoned from retirement, were able to beat back the Russian army after its initial successes in east and west Prussia. Operations across large tracts of territory continued to characterize the course of the war in the east; battles from dug-in positions took place only occasionally, along limited stretches of the front. Aided by the Russian Revolution of 1917 and the complete demoralization of the Russian forces, German troops succeeded in occupying the Baltic countries, the Ukraine, and southern Russia up to the Caucasus by 1918.

As the war dragged on into the unforeseeable future, the original enthusiasm quickly faded, although the mood of the educated professional class remained fervent. In countless sermons and lectures, Protestant pastors and professors depicted the enemy as the embodiment of Satan, comparing the conflagration now consuming the world with the Last Judgment and urging the German people to see themselves as the agents of God's will. The nationalistic mass organizations experienced their greatest hour; the Pan-German League, the Fatherland Party, and similarly vocal groups competed with one another in proposing war aims that bordered on megalomania, supported by the National Federation of German Industry and military leaders who dreamed of a German empire stretching from Calais to St. Petersburg. Writers and intellectuals—including later supporters of democracy like Thomas Mann and Alfred Kerr—also came to worship at the shrine of battle, praising the war as the flames of purgatory that would cleanse the nation; their effusions rounded off the public's impression that enthusiasm for the war was universal.

But the reality of life in Germany was far removed from such flights of fancy. Food shortages occurred everywhere, despite ever stricter rationing and attempts to place production of at least basic commodities under government control. In the words of one contemporary critic, "As far as the management of food supplies was concerned, the war was already lost by the beginning of the third year." Armament workers in Berlin and Leipzig organized labor stoppages in April 1917 in protest against hunger, and in addition to demands for improved working conditions, calls began to be heard for negotiating a swift peace. Tensions mounted within the army and navy as well.

The temporary truce, agreed to by the parties and interest groups, to refrain from internal social and political agitation for the duration of the war began to crumble. In July 1917 the *Reichstag* was supposed to grant further war loans. Up to that time all of the parties, including a large majority of the SPD, had regarded this as their patriotic duty, in the conviction that Germany was waging a purely defensive war. The vehement debate over expansionist war goals had thoroughly destroyed this illusion, however, and the food supply appeared as precarious as the situation on both fronts.

Furthermore, the new Russian government brought to power by the February revolution had come up with a promising formula for ending the war: "A peace without annexations or reparations." And so the leaders of three delegations in the *Reichstag,* the SPD, the Center Party, and the left-liberal Progressive People's Party, joined together to form an Inter-Party Committee and planned a step no German parliament had dared to attempt since the Prussian constitutional crisis of 1862, namely to exert pressure on the government by threatening to withhold support for a major bill, in this case approval of the war loans.

The National Liberal Party then joined the effort as well, and on July 17, 1917, the new majority in the *Reichstag* declared itself in favor of a "negotiated peace . . . without forced annexation of new territories." With this step the *Reichstag* made itself into an independent political force, under the leadership of the same parties that would later form the backbone of the Weimar Republic. The first German democracy was born in the middle of the Great War, not after it.

Yet for the time being democracy was far from a reality. The attempt of the parliamentary representatives to rebel failed to impress government and military leaders, and fizzled. The military situation grew more acute; although the outbreak of revolution in St. Petersburg, now called Petrograd, caused large stretches of the Russian front to collapse, the United States had entered war against Germany on April 2, 1917. Large contingents of fresh, well-rested American troops began arriving at the western front in rapid succession, while the German forces continued to sustain huge losses of both men and materiel, without the prospect of significant replacements. Units at the front even had to halve their reserves of food to help stretch supplies at home. The chief of staff of a German group command in Flanders noted in despair, "Whole divisions are burned to cinders within a few hours, and a cry goes up for replacements that do not come. I pray to God this may be the last great butchery of the Great War; this morning thousands more went to their deaths."

In this situation people placed their hopes not in the delegates of the *Reichstag* but in the two military commanders Paul von Hindenburg and Erich Ludendorff. No other generals, and certainly no politicians, even approached these two men in popularity. After their victory over the Russian armies in East Prussia in 1914 they were venerated almost as twin St. Georges who had slain the dragon. Streets and squares were renamed after Hindenburg; every patriotic shopkeeper hung a picture of him in the window or behind the counter, and public opinion ranked him higher than the emperor. The appointment of Hindenburg to head the Army High Command on August 29, 1916, was like an unofficial plebescite and gave the military leadership a legitimacy in the people's eyes that the *Reichstag,* elected in 1912, no longer possessed.

It was not Hindenburg who gave the High Command its profile, however, but his deputy, First Quartermaster-General Erich Ludendorff. He was the first general from an untitled family in Prussian-German military history to achieve such a high position, and his perspective encompassed more than purely military tactics. Politics was always war, Ludendorff wrote later, turning the ideas of Clausewitz upside down, and peace an illusion of weak-minded civilians. In his opinion this meant that the military and political leadership of a country had to be one and the same. Only a military leader was capable of organizing a country to make it able to conduct total war, which required total mobilization.

The ideas that General Ludendorff, the man of middle-class origins, began to convert into reality at the end of 1916 emanated from the dark, long-repressed underside of bourgeois thinking: the unleashing of war from its traditional restraints, the attitude of "You are nothing, the people are everything" that provides a foundation for totalitarian dictatorship. It was no accident that later both Lenin and Hitler viewed Ludendorff's management of the wartime economy in 1917–1918 as a model of organization.

But it was to no avail. The situation continued to deteriorate, and both social and political conflict grew sharper. The Bolshevists' October revolution had supplied the protest movements arising out of the food shortages with political concepts, and now a revolutionary mood began to spread among workers in the armaments industry, among army draftees, and in the navy. The German troops at the front

August 1, 1914, in Berlin
(Arthur Kampf, 1914)

On July 31, 1914, Russia had mobilized itself against Germany and Austria. The German government responded by proclaiming a state of "imminent danger of war," and on the afternoon of August 1 the deadline in a German ultimatum ran out. Germany found itself at war with Russia. The painter shows a crowd of people gathered outside the royal palace in Berlin, waiting for the deadline to expire and in the meantime listening to a speaker. Here we see no exaggerated patriotism, nothing of the vaunted "spirit of 1914." The mood is quiet, even anxious.

were exhausted; the great German offensive in March 1918 proved a costly miscalculation, and the Allied counter-offensive in August ripped gaping holes in the German lines. Germany's allies Austria-Hungary and Turkey sent out peace feelers, and on September 28, 1918, Bulgaria capitulated. The following day Ludendorff suffered a nervous collapse. Fearing a renewed and decisive Allied breakthrough on the western front, he called for an immediate truce.

Ludendorff's request was only reasonable, and it was also reasonable that he insisted a new government be formed that would include the members of the Inter-Party Committee, since the Allies would consider only a government based on a parliamentary majority as capable of guaranteeing a reasonable peace agreement in the future. All the same, the timing and the consequences of these developments were to prove disastrous for several reasons. First of all, it was a catastrophe that the first German democracy emerged as the product not of an elected parliament and strong political parties but rather of a general staff at its wits' end. Second, the Weimar democracy came into being at the worst possible moment, in the hour of defeat, a circumstance that would always dog its existence. And finally, it was a calamity that truce negotiations would now be conducted by civilian politicians and not those in fact responsible for the outcome of the war, the generals of the High Command. By coupling his calls for a truce and parliamentary government, Ludendorff managed to shift the blame onto a convenient scapegoat. Here were the beginnings of the legend of the *Dolchstoß*, the supposed "stab in the back," a myth that would poison political debate throughout the Weimar Republic.

To transform the country from an authoritarian, almost absolutist state into a parliamentary democracy, only a few sentences in Bismarck's constitution needed to be changed. In the future, the chancellor would have to act with the support of the *Reichstag* and would be responsible for policy; his signature was required on officers' and civil servants' commissions, and the *Reichstag* would vote on all declarations of war and peace treaties. That was sufficient to bring about revolutionary changes in the German mode of government.

The German people did not grasp the sweeping nature of the changes. What they cared about now was not an alteration here and there in the text of the constitution but how progress toward peace was proceeding. Events swept forward with irresistible force. On October 29, 1918, sailors of the fleet in Kiel and Wilhelmshaven mutinied and formed revolutionary councils; the revolt spread in waves, first to army garrisons along the coast, then inland. The astounding aspect of all this was not the revolution itself, which represented little more than a cry of "Count me out!" from an utterly exhausted population, but the complete passivity with which the powers that had ruled hitherto accepted it. Houses that had reigned for centuries abdicated their rights without a murmur, nor did a single lieutenant of the royal guards leap into the breach to defend them. The public responded with virtual indifference to the abdication of William II, who went into exile in Holland on November 9, 1918; people had enough on their hands trying to deal with the catastrophe of defeat and their fears that they were in for a repeat of the Russian Revolution and its atrocities. Two days later Matthias Erzberger, still in office as a state secretary of the imperial government and a Center Party delegate to the *Reichstag,* signed the armistice in a railroad car sitting in a forest near Compiègne. The First World War was over; it had cost the lives of 10 million people, among them 2 million Germans. But the war continued in Germany, now in the form of civil war.

In the second week of November, after Germany's collapse, the situation was volatile, with three different factions vying for power. Along with the remnants of the old state, the army and the bureau-

German Posters from the First World War: Buy War Bonds! The Times Are Hard but
Victory Certain
(Fritz Erler, 1916; Bruno Paul, 1917)

In order not to jeopardize domestic stability, the German Empire financed the war effort not through taxes, which would have put it on a sound basis, but through war bonds promising 5 percent interest. The plan was to let Germany's defeated enemies cover them. From 1916 on the posters appealing to citizens to buy the bonds carried martial images. In the poster on the right, the war hero and Chief of the Army High Command Paul von Hindenburg personified the guarantee of victory and redeemability of the war bonds. Fritz Erler's drawing of the soldier at the front would be imitated thousands of times: His steel helmet, gas mask, and the barbed wire behind him symbolize the horrendous war in the trenches. The depiction of the soldier's eyes—fixed on a distant object and thrown into shadow by his helmet—made his gaze impersonal and elevated his portrait to an icon of war.

cracy, there were the moderate forces of the *Reichstag* majority of 1917—Social Democrats, Liberals, and the Center Party—who favored the transformation of the authoritarian monarchy into a modern democracy that would retain the basic prewar economic and social structures; in a sense their program was thus to carry to completion the Revolution of 1848. These forces of a black-red-gold revolution—the colors of the mid-nineteenth-century national-

The Council of People's Representatives
(postcard, Berlin, 1918)

The revolutionary government formed on November 10, 1918, called itself the Council of People's Representatives. Although two groups of Social Democrats—the "majority" and the "independents"—were given equal representation with three members each, the "majority" proved stronger from the start. The two chairmen of the Majority Social Democratic Party, Friedrich Ebert and Philipp Scheidemann, and Otto Landsberg, a lawyer located further to the right along the party spectrum, were tough and experienced political tacticians. The Independent Social Democrats—the upright and idealistic party chairman Hugo Haase, the colorless functionary Wilhelm Dittmann, and the representative of the revolutionary ombudsmen in the factories, Emil Barth—were seldom able to hold their own against their colleagues, especially since Barth frequently voted against Haase and Dittmann. In theory the executive council of the workers' and soldiers' revolutionary councils was supposed to control the Council of People's Representatives, but in fact this never happened.

ists—were opposed by the adherents of a Red revolution, a heterogeneous collection of leftist groups, chief among them the Spartacus League of Rosa Luxemburg and Karl Liebknecht, who were inspired by the Russian Revolution and favored a government based on workers' councils. They rejected parliamentary rule on principle and wished to see a socialist government established that would overthrow the existing economic and social order alike.

The outcome of this power struggle was essentially decided in the first few days of the revolution, in favor of the moderate camp. The official government was the revolutionary Council of People's Representatives, composed of Social Democrats and the more left-

Protect the Homeland!
(poster for the volunteer *Freikorps*, Lucian Bernhard, 1919)

Late in 1918 volunteer units known as *Freikorps* were formed, consisting of soldiers who had served at the front, with a high percentage of officers among them. These units played a central role in the civil war that ensued, as well as in the fighting along the eastern border against the Poles, and against the Russians in the Baltic region. They proved to be the only troops that could be depended upon, in contrast to the old regular army units and the hastily assembled republican units. The men of the *Freikorps* were desperadoes, determined fighters who feared only one thing: the idea of returning to civilian life. This attitude hardly qualified them as obedient servants of a democratic government, as became evident by the time of the Kapp putsch at the latest.

wing Independent Social Democrats (USPD), under the leadership of Friedrich Ebert and Hugo Haase. On November 9, 1918, Prince Max of Baden, the last imperial chancellor, had formally turned his office over to Ebert, leader of the SPD, although the constitutionality of his action was somewhat questionable. The civil service therefore placed itself at Ebert's disposal, and the military High Command came to a mutual agreement with the Council: The SPD would use its influence to moderate the radical soldiers' councils, while the new Quartermaster

General Wilhelm Groener would throw his support to Ebert's revolutionary government.

This alliance enabled the SPD to use troops of the old regular army and volunteer units to enforce its claims to political authority in clashes in Berlin and the rest of the country, where unrest was taking on the dimensions of a civil war. And it also enabled the party to force its more radical coalition partner, the Independent SPD, out of the government and to hold elections on January 19, 1919, for a National Assembly that would draft a new constitution. For the first time, both men and women went to the polls; while the men had fought at the fronts during the war, women had kept industrial production, transportation, and the civil administration going, and denying them equal political rights was now out of the question. Of the 423 assembly delegates elected, 41 were women, a total of 9.6 percent; none of the later *Reichstag* or post–World War II *Bundestag* assemblies has ever reached that high a percentage of women members.

The election results confirmed the claim to power of the black-red-gold forces, giving them *ex post facto* legitimacy: The SPD, Center Party, and left-liberal German Democratic Party (DDP) together received 76 percent of the vote. The first democratically elected national government thus had a broad basis of support. Philipp Scheidemann of the SPD became prime minister, and the National Assembly elected Friedrich Ebert president. This government faced two urgent tasks: It had to consolidate the power of the new republic against opposition from the left, and it had to conclude a peace treaty with the Allied victors. It succeeded in the first aim with the help of the old regular army and the new volunteer units known as *Freikorps.* As far as the second was concerned, the government expected terms that would not be too harsh, at most a few territorial concessions and the kind of manageable reparation payments that France had been made to pay in 1871.

However, this illusion was shattered when the Allies announced their conditions on May 7, 1919. The amount of territory Germany

What We Will Lose!
(poster, Louis Oppenheim, 1919)

This propaganda poster opposing the conditions of the Treaty of Versailles listed what Germany would lose: 20 percent of its territory, 10 percent of the population, one-third of its hard coal production, one-quarter of its grain and potato production, four-fifths of its iron ore reserves, and all its colonies and commercial fleet.

was to lose exceeded the most pessimistic predictions; the requirements for demilitarization would leave an army that looked more like a police force and render Germany incapable of defending itself. The extent of Allied economic and financial demands was not yet fully clear, but the tenor of the document gave cause for grave concern.

The German reaction was almost universal opposition to the terms. Scheidemann publicly declared he would refuse to sign such a treaty unless major concessions were granted. But the Allies continued to insist on most of their demands. Finally the National Assembly, under pressure from the continuing Allied blockade of food supplies and the threat to resume hostilities if Germany did not accept the treaty unconditionally, declared its willingness to sign. On June 28, 1919, two representatives of the German government, Foreign Minister Hermann Müller (SPD) and Postal Minister Johannes Bell (Center Party), presented themselves in Versailles to accept the final and most severe consequence of defeat. The signing ceremony took place in the Hall of Mirrors in the palace of King Louis XIV, the very same room in which the founding of the German Empire had been declared and William I proclaimed kaiser not fifty years earlier. Now as then, it was chosen to symbolize the victors' triumph and underscore the enemy's defeat: The losers would not only have to pay, they would also have to eat humble pie.

Despite their harshness, it was not so much the material consequences of the Versailles Treaty that influenced the future destiny of the Weimar Republic as the prevailing sentiment among Germans that unjust terms were being forced on a defenseless country. Lloyd George, the British prime minister, recognized the dangers early on, declaring, "When nations are exhausted by wars . . . which leave them tired, bleeding and broken, it is not difficult to patch up a peace . . . What is difficult, however, is to draw up a peace which will not provoke a fresh struggle when those who have had practical experience of what war means have passed away."

Instead of breaking up the former German Empire into a number of small states again, as the French generals were demanding, or accepting the new Weimar Republic as a legitimate member of the family of Western democracies, the Allies determined upon a destructive middle course. With the Treaty of Versailles, Germany was placed under legal sanctions, deprived of military power, economically ruined, and politically humiliated. From the German perspective the "dictat of Versailles," as it was later called, looked like an arbitrary instrument of Western might. And democracy appeared just as unacceptable as the European peace order of 1919; it was seen as the form of government of the victorious powers, which had been imposed on Germany as a result of its defeat.

Most Germans thus saw the new order of peace in Europe, as spelled out in the Treaty of Versailles, and democracy as one and the same thing. Any politician who now called for moderation and rational compromise with the former enemy was automatically vulnerable to accusations of weakness, or even betrayal. This was the soil in which Hitler's totalitarian and aggressive regime was ultimately able to grow.

In the meantime, however, the republic seemed to achieve a degree of consolidation during the second half of 1919. The serious revolts, which extended all the way to the creation of a socialist republic in Bavaria, had been suppressed, and the proclamation of the Weimar constitution on August 14, 1919, established the basic machinery of government. The revolutionary era was over. But the threat to the republic that had hitherto come from the left now manifested itself on the right. Disappointment over the terms of the peace treaty, continuing economic difficulties, and the dreary, oppressive conditions of everyday life all combined to alter the mood of the general public, making it more receptive to the propaganda campaigns of nationalist and monarchist groups.

This was reinforced by the necessity, under the terms of the Treaty of Versailles, of significantly reducing the strength of the armed forces. Most of the soldiers given discharges belonged to the *Freikorps;* these were the men who had defended the republic in the period of civil unrest and fought against Poles and Soviet Russians on the eastern border. Now they felt betrayed and abandoned by the republican government, which they despised in any case. On March 13, 1920, *Freikorps* units occupied Berlin, enabling a group of conservatives representing agrarian interests to mount a putsch under the leadership of Wolfgang Kapp, director general of the East Prussian agricultural credit banks. The leaders of Chancellor Gustav Bauer's legitimate government managed to flee to Stuttgart, where they began organizing resistance to the coup and issued a call for a general strike in conjunction with the labor unions. The putsch attempt was defeated after

AN DIE DEUTSCHEN MÜTTER!

72000 jüdische Soldaten sind für das Vaterland auf dem Felde der Ehre gefallen

Christliche und jüdische Helden haben gemeinsam gekämpft und ruhen gemeinsam in fremder Er

12000 Juden fielen im Kampf !

Blindwütiger Parteihass macht vor den Gräbern der Toten nicht Hal

Deutsche Frauen,

duldet nicht,dass die jüdische Mutter in ihrem Schmerz verhöhnt wird

Reichsbund jüdischer Frontsoldaten E.V.

only five days, due in the main not to the general strike but to the loyalty of civil servants in Berlin and the army leadership, who refused to carry out Kapp's orders.

The election that followed on June 6, 1920, was a catastrophe for the republic. The black-red-gold coalition, the only bloc committed to the democratic constitutional order, lost the two-thirds majority it had commanded in the National Assembly; in the new *Reichstag* it won only 43 percent of the seats. Henceforth the SPD, Center Party, and DDP, the only reliable supporters of the republic, would never again succeed in gaining a parliamentary majority that would enable them to form a govern-

To German Mothers!
(leaflet published by the Association of Jewish Veterans, 1920)

For the German public, the outcome of the Great War was an incomprehensible and undigested catastrophe. The military defeat, economic misery, and humiliation felt at the "dictat" of the Versailles Treaty could be borne only if the insults suffered could be blamed on a scapegoat. Given the fatal European tradition, the obvious candidate for such a scapegoat was the Jews. Anti-Semitic propaganda increased considerably in the postwar years, and desperate appeals for tolerance, such as this leaflet from the Association of Jewish Veterans, had little effect. In fact German Jews had done their part in the war; the number of German Jewish soldiers killed in battle matched the percentage of Jews in the total population.

ment. Parliamentary governments could now be formed in only two ways, both of them pernicious: Either the indisputably democratic camp entered into a coalition with openly or latently antidemocratic parties, or a minority coalition formed a government dependent on support from its opponents. Under these circumstances, a cabinet's chances for developing and pursuing long-term, decidedly prodemocratic policies were hopeless, and the likelihood of its remaining in office for a normal length of time was just as slim.

The republic experienced a succession of sixteen different governments, on the average a new one every eight-and-a-half months. A vicious circle was set in motion, for the weaker a government appeared, the more tempting it was for voters to switch to the alternative parties on the right or left that were promising authoritarian rule if they got into power. It is hardly surprising that the Weimar Republic ultimately came to grief. The wonder is that it managed to survive for fourteen years under such tremendously difficult conditions.

In the meantime the solution to the problem was the *Bürgerblock,* an alliance of moderate to conservative parties. In a coalition that would become the norm for the Weimar Republic, the Center Party and the DDP joined forces with the nationalist *Deutsche Volkspartei* (DVP, German People's Party) of Gustav Stresemann, which was essentially monarchist in outlook. The SPD, the true mother of the republic, ceased to be a member of the ruling coalition, without becoming altogether powerless, however: Not only did the president of the country, Friedrich Ebert, come from its ranks, but also Otto Braun, prime minister of Prussia, who together with the Prussian minister of the interior, Carl Severing, managed to run the largest state in Germany, covering three-fifths of its territory, with an effective combination of socialist and traditional Prussian approaches. For this reason, democrats of the Weimar era regarded Prussia as a bulwark of the republic.

Nonetheless the political crisis was not entirely over; it merely shifted from the domestic to the foreign policy arena. The next three years were characterized principally by sparring between the German

and Allied sides on implementation of the peace treaty. The fact that in cases of disagreement the German government always emerged the loser contributed decisively to the dwindling respect accorded it by the population and thus also to the undermining of the republic's legitimacy in general. And this is precisely what happened in early 1921 when news began to leak out about the amount of war reparations being demanded. The Reparations Commission of the postwar Entente powers had based its calculations on the estimated cost of total war damage and added to that all benefits the victors would have to pay to their veterans—a staggering sum. What followed was a replay of the peace negotiations; the German government rejected the terms as outrageous, to the cheers of the population, and was forced to ac-cept them in the end after all: 132 billion marks in gold, to be paid off with 6 percent annual interest.

That the government ultimately undertook to fulfill these demands was unavoidable, for it was the only way to disprove France's con-tention that the Germans were re-fusing to honor the terms of the treaty they had signed. The only way to force a revision of the reparation demands was to prove that the country was bankrupt. At the same time, however, this "policy of fulfillment" of the terms of the Versailles Treaty provided right wing opponents of the government with the slogans that provoked fanatic nationalists to murder; these were the years of the radical right-wing conspiracies that led to the assassinations of Matthias Erzberger, who had signed the Armistice, and Walter Rathenau, the German foreign minister.

In this series of defeats and humiliations for German foreign pol-icy, there was only one ray of light, the Treaty of Rapallo, concluded between Germany and the Soviet Union on April 16, 1922. It con-tained nothing more than the agreement to forgo reparation pay-ments on both sides and to resume trade relations. However, the "eastern policy" favored by Chancellor Joseph Wirth, Army Chief of Staff General Hans von Seeckt, and the foreign ministry, which was to culminate in an alliance of the two losers of the First World War against the Western Entente, never became a reality; it was obvious that this was not the way to force a revision of the Treaty of Versailles.

The German attempts to obtain Allied concessions regarding repa-ration payments convinced French Prime Minister Poincaré and his government that if the Germans were unwilling to pay what they owed, France would have to take it by force. Accordingly on January 11, 1923, French and Belgian troops occupied the Ruhr district, the site of Germany's largest coal mines, with the intent of taking the coal directly in lieu of money. The German government adopted a strategy of passive resistance and joined with political parties and labor unions in the area in calling for a strike against the occupying forces. In fact the occupation of the Ruhr cost France more than it brought in, since the production of coal dropped steeply. Yet for Germany the cost was even higher. Millions of people in the occupied region needed government assistance to survive; the coal no longer coming from the Ruhr had to be bought abroad; and since huge sums in taxes and customs tariffs were lost as well, the government ran up an enormous deficit that could only be made up by printing more money. In consequence the inflation rate, which had been rising since the end of the war, soared out of control. Germany entered the traumatic phase of galloping inflation, in which people had to convert their wages into goods immediately, because only a few hours later the money would buy practically nothing. In the end, burning a bundle of bank notes created more heat than the amount of coal one could buy with them. The money economy broke down altogether, and people reverted to the age-old practice of barter.

On August 13, 1923, Gustav Stresemann took over as chancellor with a cabinet of ministers extending across the political spectrum from the SPD to the DVP, the Great Coalition. He hoped to master the situation; and to the amazement of all, he succeeded. Stresemann needed only a short time to grasp the fact that once again the only way to survive was capitulation. On September 26 the government announced it was abandoning its policy of passive resistance in the Ruhr; on the same day a German wanting to buy one U.S. dollar would have had to pay 240 million marks. Not since 1871 had the country been so close to total dissolution. In the occupied territories Rhinelanders were contemplating secession, with the benevolent support of France, while in Saxony and Thuringia to the east workers' groups formed popular-front governments and began assembling their own armies in preparation for civil war. Stresemann resolutely sent in regular army units at once, and the rebel governments resigned.

The situation was even more dangerous in Bavaria. There it was troops from the regular army, the *Reichswehr,* that refused to follow orders from Berlin any longer and took an oath of loyalty to the government of Gustav von Kahr, an aristocrat and state commissar general of Bavaria. Von Kahr intended to clamp down in Bavaria and from this "cell" proceed to restore order in the rest of the country, especially in the "Marxist pigsty" of Berlin. His allies in this undertaking were General von Lossow, *Reichswehr* commander of the Bavarian region, and Adolf Hitler, who had managed to unite the numerous racist-nationalist right-wing groups in Bavaria under the aegis of his National Socialist German Workers' Party (NSDAP) and had plans to maneuver his allies von Kahr and von Lossow out of the picture and seize power for himself as soon as an opportunity presented itself. He showed his cards too early, however, and on November 9, 1923, a march led by Hitler and Ludendorff to a patriotic monument, the *Feldherrnhalle,* was broken up by the Bavarian state police, and Hitler and his associates were arrested.

The Bavarian division of the *Reichswehr* did an about-face and declared itself once again loyal to the chief of staff, General von Seeckt, who had assumed charge of the government when a state of emergency was declared. A return to calm was aided further by restabilization of the mark; this was achieved through a prohibition against printing more bank notes and the introduction on November 13, 1923, of the *Rentenmark,* a currency named after the newly created *Rentenbank* (Pension Bank) that issued it, which had no disastrous history conducive to immediate distrust like the old national bank.

The crises of the fall of 1923, which could be overcome only by extreme—and extremely unpopular—measures on the part of Stresemann's government, exhausted the willingness of the parties of the

A two-pound loaf of bread cost:	
December 1919	2.80 marks
December 1920	2.37 marks
December 1921	3.90 marks
December 1922	163.15 marks
January 1923	250 marks
April 1923	474 marks
July 1923	3,465 marks
August 1923	69,000 marks
September 1923	1,512,000 marks
October 1923	1,743,000,000 marks
November 1923	201,000,000,000 marks
December 1923	399,000,000,000 marks
January 1924	30 marks

The Price of Bread, 1919–1924

Great Coalition to work together. On November 23 Stresemann lost a vote of confidence in which the SPD, until then a member of the coalition, refused to support him any longer. However, in the succeeding government he was named foreign minister, and it was in this role that he achieved a series of successes in foreign policy which resulted in the "golden years" of the Weimar Republic, so called because of their relative lack of political strife both at home and abroad.

The positive tone of the era was due in large measure to a shift in the overall climate; new governments had come to power in both Britain and France that responded with greater openness to German wishes and hardships than their predecessors. The first indication of this change was approval of the Dawes Plan on April 9, 1923, which for the first time combined a retreat from Allied positions with a revision of reparations policy. France withdrew from the cities of Offenburg and Dortmund and held out the prospect that it might withdraw its troops from the Ruhr within the next year.

With these measures, the long, dark shadow of the postwar years, which had actually been a continuation of the Great War on the home front, finally receded. The catastrophe had lasted from 1914 to 1923, but now Germany and Europe as a whole were emerging from the darkness and entering into a long period of peace and returning prosperity, or so it appeared to contemporaries. Bernhard Harms, a distinguished economist at the University of Kiel, concluded one of his lectures with the words, "If we cannot achieve heaven on earth, at least we can reach for the stars."

METROPOLIS

MANUSKRIPT: THEA v. HARBOU ★ REGIE: FRITZ LANG

AN DER KAMERA: KARL FREUND / GÜNTHER RITTAU
BAUTEN: OTTO HUNTE ★ MUSIK: GOTTFRIED HUPPERTZ

IN DEN HAUPTROLLEN:

BRIGITTE HELM ★ GUSTAV FRÖHLICH
ALFRED ABEL · RUD. KLEIN-ROGGE · THEODOR LOOS · FRITZ RASP · HEINRICH GEORGE

10

Weimar: Brief Glory and Decline (1924–1933)

On the surface, the years that followed ushered in an era of calm and serenity on the domestic political front. Moderate cabinets governed under the middle-of-the-road chancellors Wilhelm Marx and Hans Luther, and if the cabinets collapsed from time to time, they soon regrouped and returned to office with virtually the same lineup. Political continuity was represented chiefly in the person of Foreign Minister Gustav Stresemann, who pursued limited foreign policy goals with some success and also, in his role as leader of the *Deutsche Volkspartei* (DVP, German People's Party), guaranteed the loyalty of important industrial and nationalistic groups to the present constitution and system of government. The Social Democratic Party (SPD), exhausted after its thankless task of holding the country together in the postwar years of crisis, gradually regrouped and played the role of leader of the opposition, most of the time lending its support to Stresemann's policies, which the right-wing parties detested.

Metropolis
(film poster, Werner Graul, 1926)

The expanding German film industry profited from an unprecedented level of interest in cinema after the war; in the 1920s Germany produced more films than all the other countries of Europe combined. In addition to many mediocre productions, German film output included outstanding works of art such as Fritz Lang's utopian silent film *Metropolis*, first shown in 1927. An exemplary commentary on modern working conditions, it nonetheless failed at the box office.

The Social Democrats also remained a considerable force in national politics through their dominance in the powerful and stable state government of Otto Braun in Prussia. Between 1924 and 1928 the *Reichstag* of the Weimar Republic experienced its only full legislative session without early elections having to be called.

Stresemann's policies were based on a fully developed plan having as its goals a revision of the Treaty of Versailles and a return to a concert of powers in Europe with Germany in a preeminent role. In practical terms this translated to avoiding ties or alliances with either East or West that might tip the balance of power in one direction. With the two blocs in balance, Germany could have room to maneuver. In Stresemann's own words, the aim was "to finesse and sidestep any major decisions."

The next few years saw great successes in his policy toward the West. After the Dawes Plan of 1924, the treaties of Locarno followed in 1925, which guaranteed the inviolability of the shared German, French, and Belgian borders and were to be supervised by Great Britain and Italy. The next step in Germany's return to full freedom in its conduct of foreign affairs was admission to the League of Nations; this goal was achieved in September 1926. The Young Plan followed in 1930, granting a further reduction in German reparation payments. With the Soviet Union, Stresemann reached an agreement in the Berlin Treaty of 1926, which guaranteed that each nation would remain neutral if the other were attacked by a third power; this pact released Moscow from the nightmare that Germany could ally itself with the Western powers and permit Britain and France to use its territory as a staging ground for an attack on the Soviet Union. In addition the *Reichswehr* and the Red Army concluded a secret assistance pact in case Poland attacked either East Prussia or the Ukraine, although it is not clear how many members of the German government were informed of its existence. At all events the situation bore a certain resemblance to Bismarck's juggling act with five balls. The Russian Revolution had driven a large wedge between East and West; for Ger-

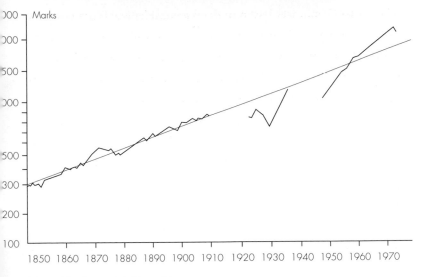

Marks

)00	
)00	
500	
)00	
500	
300	
200	
100	

1850 1860 1870 1880 1890 1900 1910 1920 1930 1940 1950 1960 1970

Net National Product per Inhabitant of the German Empire and the Federal Republic of Germany, 1850–1975
(calculated for the total territory of each, in the prices of 1913 in marks)

A line has been added to the curve to show the trend of German economic growth in the period between 1850 and 1975. (For the years 1914–1923 and 1939–1949 there is a lack of usable data.) Between 1850 and 1913 economic growth is continuous; after 1949 a relatively long lasting high rate of growth sets in. The curve for the period 1924–1939 departs strikingly from the overall trend. The plunge during the worldwide Depression of 1929–1932 is apparent, as is the fact that it took until the outbreak of the Second World War for levels to rise once again to match the long-term trend. The chart also makes clear that the crisis of 1929 was not preceded by any significant increase in growth: the curve for the "Golden Twenties" remains flat, and the net national product per inhabitant did not attain the levels of 1913 until 1928, only to plunge again immediately.

many, sitting between the two blocs, this represented an opportunity but also a temptation to exploit it.

Maintaining this balancing act required considerable skill, and it made some politicians very nervous to watch. One of them was Konrad Adenauer, the mayor of Cologne; he also chaired the executive council of the government in Prussia, but was a stranger to the classic Prussian policy of maneuvering between St. Petersburg or Moscow on the one hand and London and Paris on the other. Adenauer pointed out early on that in the long run peace in Europe depended on good relations between Germany and France. Stresemann was aware of this, but in his view the two nations had basically different interests; still, he attempted to cultivate the limited amount of common ground he saw. Adenauer, on the other hand, wanted to stake everything on the French card; he urged that solid political and economic links be forged between the countries, so that the national interests of Germany and France could never again diverge.

Adenauer's ideas would have their day later, but in the 1920s they were in fundamental conflict with German *Realpolitik* as it tried to balance East and West, the "unsteady rocking" that Adenauer criticized in Stresemann's approach. Meanwhile Stresemann had to operate under continual attack from "national" forces—including a wing of his own party—who regarded even limited concessions to France as bordering on treason. His French colleague Aristide Briand, who was awarded the Nobel Peace Prize jointly with Stresemann in 1926, fared no better at home. Worn down by the constant struggle, in which domestic rather than foreign opponents played the major role, Stresemann died of a heart attack on October 3, 1929, and was mourned by all of Europe.

Economic recovery was also necessary if true stability was to be achieved. German industry had survived the galloping inflation reasonably well, to the extent that it had used the plunge of the mark as an opportunity for investments. Recovery was further helped by the foreign capital that began to flow into Germany following adoption of the Dawes Plan, which stimulated the first large loan from Wall Street. A financial circulation system arose that kept the transatlantic economy flourishing for several years: Germany was able to make its reparations payments to the powers of the Entente; they repaid their war debts to the United States, and from there the money flowed back to Germany in the form of loans. This wonderful system revived the German economy with unusual speed; between 1924 and 1929 German production increased in volume by 50 percent, and many industries were able to regain their former dominant position in world markets.

But the upswing was largely limited to the export trade; domestic economic activity remained modest. Not until 1927 did the German gross national product reach the prewar level of 1913, and soon thereafter it began to decline again. Industrialists' willingness or ability to invest remained far below what it had been before the war, and labor productivity figures stagnated, without ever returning to prewar levels. The introduction of the eight-hour workday was one of the great achievements of Weimar social policy, but the opposite side of the coin was stagnating productivity. And people who could recall the prewar era could not help noticing that even in 1927, the Weimar economy's best year, unemployment figures stood far higher than in the worst prewar years.

The economy was basically unhealthy, due in large part to increasing concentration and the development of cartels, which punished entrepreneurs who tried to react flexibly to the markets. It was also due to the fact that agriculture and heavy industry received the lion's share of subsidies and loans, to the detriment of other branches of industry with greater potential for the future. A final factor was high wage costs. Since the presence of foreign competition meant production costs could not be passed on to consumers, disproportionately high wage costs reduced companies' willingness to invest, and this in turn kept employment figures down.

If the mid-Weimar period is nonetheless recalled as the Golden Twenties, the principal cause was neither political stability nor the deceptive appearance of an economic upturn but a cultural flowering that has become legendary. It was a time of enormous intellectual ferment and artistic creativity, from Walter Gropius's Bauhaus to Thomas Mann's *Magic Mountain,* from Paul Hindemith's *Cardillac* to Werner Heisenberg's uncertainty principle, from Oswald Spengler's *Decline of the West* to George Grosz's *Gesicht der herrschenden Klasse* (Face of the Ruling Class), from Erwin Schrödinger's quantum mechanics to Joseph von Sternberg's *Blue Angel,* from Ernst Jünger's *Der*

Arbeiter (The Working Man) to Erich Maria Remarque's *All Quiet on the Western Front.* All this and much more burst on the scene within one short decade, a shimmering kaleidoscope of previously unimagined shapes, colors, and themes.

Nonetheless "Weimar culture" was also a myth, cultivated by the many intellectuals who had given shape and color to the 1920s and were then forced to flee or stripped of their citizenship. What appeared from the perspective of the cafés of Prague and Paris, or the emigré colonies of New York and California, as an exotic flower brought forth by the republic that the *Sturmabteilung* (SA, storm troopers) of the NSDAP trampled under its boots in 1933, had in fact begun to blossom long before. The real roots of Weimar culture lay in the avant-garde of Wilhelmine Germany, and in the intellectual turmoil within the bourgeoisie around the turn of the century; the 1920s produced nothing essentially new. What *was* new was the retreat by proponents of the old official, academic culture, which left the field open for the former outsiders. The loss of the war and the period of catastrophic inflation that followed had shaken the confidence of bourgeois society and ended its role as a distinct class that dominated the cultural scene. But this does not imply that the new art was in any way more representative of mass culture or popular tastes.

Of the thirty-four German book titles that sold more than half a million copies between 1918 and 1933, only three were written by figures identified with Weimar culture: Erich Kästner's *Emil and the Detectives,* Remarque's *All Quiet on the Western Front,* and Thomas Mann's *Buddenbrooks,* which was in fact first published in 1901. The broader public favored very different authors, such as Hermann Löns, Hans Carossa, Walter Flex, Hans Grimm, and Clara Viebig; the adventure novels of Karl May and popular romances of Hedwig Courths-Mahler also enjoyed great success. Like all other instances of great cultural achievement, the artistic flowering of Weimar Germany took place within elite circles. The whole phenomenon was limited to a relatively narrow stratum of writers, painters, musicians, philosophers, patrons, critics, and their small audiences, located on the fringe between the professional classes and bohemians.

Weimar culture was both deeply bourgeois and at the same time infected by strong antibourgeois sentiment; it received its characteristic stamp from the experience of the Great War. The leftists had learned from it that everything to do with killing, the military, and uniforms was evil and senseless, while socialism was good. A man such as Carl von Ossietzky, editor of the *Weltbühne,* fought for the republican cause in the name of morality and human rights— not for the existing Weimar Republic, however, which struck him and so many other intellectuals of the era as lacking in principle, immature, boring, and bourgeois, but rather for an imaginary socialist and pacifist republic. To help such a republic into the world he was prepared to advocate the election of Ernst Thälmann, leader of the German Communist Party, as president.

At the other end of the cultural spectrum were the rightists, who had been equally affected by their war experiences but had drawn the opposite conclusions from them. They recalled the war not in terms of horror and inhumanity but in terms of the fiery furnace in which a new kind of man had been forged of blood and iron. Right-wing intellectuals like Ernst Jünger also fought the republic at every opportunity, in the name of an ideal that remained vague, somehow martial and nationalistic, but often with socialist aspects. The lack of clarity in their goals led many of them to take up with Hitler, who knew exactly what he meant by "national" and "socialist." Only a few, such as Jünger, kept their distance from larger movements.

The far left and far right made up the great majority of the Weimar cultural scene; they were ideological enemies, diametrically opposed to one another politically and yet in complete agreement when it came to mocking and attacking the existing democratic government in the name of their different ideals and ideologies. Only a few artists and writers were prepared to defend the republic, among them Thomas Mann, who had once been a vocal opponent of "bourgeois" democracy. In 1922 he appealed to students at the University of Berlin to support the present democratic government, but without success; he remained a voice in the wilderness.

The unwillingness of most intellectuals to lend their support to the republic became evident in other areas as well, including the press. There were several outstanding liberal newspapers, such as the *Vossische Zeitung,* the *Berliner Tageblatt,* and the *Frankfurter Zeitung,* which provided excellent coverage not only in their reporting and editorial commentary but also in extended articles in weekly supplements that remain models of political journalism. But these were not representative; the newspapers with mass circulations belonged to syndicates such as the nationalistic Scherl concern, later absorbed into the press and film empire of nationalistic media czar Alfred Hugenberg. One of the government's most outspoken critics was the *Generalanzeiger* press—a group of nationalist, pro-monarchy newspapers which attacked the republic daily. Conservative, nationalistic teachers were the norm in secondary schools, along with monarchist professors in the universities and antidemocratic clergymen in the pulpits.

Reactionary intellectuals coexisted with progressive science and technology. While the great majority of scholars longed for a return of the past era, the steamship *Bremen* of the North German Lloyd line set a record for the fastest Atlantic crossing; Fritz von Opel raced his rocket-propelled automobile on the Avus track in Berlin; German engineers built the Junkers G 38, the largest airplane of the day, and the largest seaplane, the Do X; the first television images were transmitted in Berlin; Mayor Konrad Adenauer of Cologne opened Europe's first superhighway, the *Autobahn*, between Cologne and Bonn, and the Kruckenberg rail zeppelin covered the distance from Berlin to Hamburg in under two hours.

However, it was not just intellectuals who had their difficulties with the current government. The Weimar government could not count on the loyalty of its own officials. The great majority of professional civil servants were monarchists with a deeply conservative

Obituary Notice for President Ebert
(*Illustrierte Reichsbanner-Zeitung*, March 7, 1925)

view of the state; it was almost a badge of their office and status. Yet their philosophy also attached more importance to formal legality in the exercise of power than to the political goals of those exercising it. Since the last chancellor of the empire, Prince Max of Baden, had formally turned power over to the revolutionary socialist Friedrich Ebert, the appearance of legality was preserved, and the bureaucracy thus owed loyalty to the present authorities. In their eyes the legally elected government continued to exist during the Kapp putsch, and as a result the administrative apparatus supported Ebert, even though many of its members privately sympathized with Kapp and his aims.

For precisely the same reasons, the civil service would later place itself at Hitler's disposal when he became chancellor. In principle the civil service was expected to remain above party politics, but this did not mean it was apolitical. Overall, civil servants tended to support the model of an authoritarian, centralized state, although they could not say so explicitly, and Brüning's government came close to fulfilling these ideals. And how could it have been otherwise? No one could expect bureaucrats to act differently from the majority of the population, which was increasingly withdrawing its support from the republican government. Furthermore, the constitution did not establish explicit standards for what kinds of actions were permissible. The civil service did not undermine the foundations of the democratic constitutional order, since there was precious little to undermine in any case. But neither did civil servants lift a finger to support the republic or save it from destruction.

As for the army—the little 100,000-man *Reichswehr,* under chief of command General Hans von Seeckt—it maintained a haughty distance from both the democratic institutions of the government and party politics, pursuing a secret build-up behind the back of civilian authorities in accord with Seeckt's maxim, "The army serves the state and only the state, for it is the state." After Seeckt's fall from power in 1927 things changed under the army's new strong man, General Kurt von Schleicher. From then on the leadership of the *Reichswehr* fol-

WÄHLT
HINDENBURG

*JCH REICHE JEDEM DEUTSCHEN
DIE HAND, DER NATIONAL DENKT
UND DEN KONFESSIONELLEN U.
SOZIALEN FRIEDEN WILL·*

(AUS HINDENBURGS OSTERBOTSCHAFT·)

Vote for Hindenburg
(poster for the presidential elections
of 1925)

lowed political events within the country closely, attempted to influence new government coalitions and appointments, and lobbied actively on behalf of the interests of the military and those social strata that provided much of the officers' corps, the aristocracy and conservative upper-middle class. Ultimately these efforts had catastrophic consequences, as General von Schleicher's failure as chancellor in January 1933 would make abundantly evident.

Various groups within society also kept their distance from the new form of government and its institutions. To be sure, the members of the working class with either a Social Democratic or Catholic orientation could be mobilized to support it, as emerged during the

Kapp putsch and later after Rathenau's assassination. But when the republic fell into a state of crisis in the 1930s, it became clear that workers' readiness to support a democratic government was directly tied to the social welfare benefits they received from it. In times when paychecks were losing their purchasing power and unemployment was high, loyalty to democracy faded, a decline reflected in the rising numbers of working-class Germans who voted for the Communists or joined the National Socialist Party.

The middle classes lived in a permanent awareness that their country was in crisis. They felt threatened by the rapid social and economic changes taking place around them; middle-class income grew more slowly than in virtually all other strata of society, and any savings they had been able to accumulate were wiped out overnight in the era of inflation, unless it had been invested in real estate. The resulting catastrophic drop in their standard of living, which hit an entire class of society, was generally blamed on democracy and the republic. These voters favored politicians who combined protests against what had happened to them with promises to create a new sense of community, which would provide for internal harmony but also bring back the old distinctions of rank and status. The rich, both entrepreneurs and property owners, regarded the Weimar government with suspicion, because its social and financial policies aimed clearly at a redistribution of wealth in favor of those who were worse off. Despite the fact that heavy industry and agriculture received massive state subsidies, these circles remained hostile toward the republic.

In good times, when there was plenty of money to go around, these deep social and political cracks could be papered over to some extent with economic policy and appropriations to various groups; for a time it appeared as if even the die-hard monarchists had come to accept the new reality. Ironically, this seemed to be the case after Friedrich Ebert's death from appendicitis, for which he had delayed seeking treatment because he was occupied with fighting a court judgment against him. Three ultra-nationalistic judges had found him guilty of treason for involving himself in the Berlin armaments workers' strike of 1918; the president rightly felt that this highly unjust verdict reflected on his personal honor. By a small majority Paul von Hindenburg, the chief of the Army High Command during the Great War, was elected to succeed Ebert as president.

To the amazement of people in his own circles, Hindenburg made no attempt to reintroduce the monarchy, dashing the hopes of his political backers. Instead he proved determined to be as good a president of the republic as he could, without either vacillation or deception. His backers had misjudged Hindenburg's attitude toward an oath, a matter in which he was a Prussian of the old school. If he had sworn an oath of loyalty to the constitution of the republic, then he would uphold it, every bit as staunchly as he had once enforced the field-service regulations of the Prussian army. The fact that Hindenburg had accepted the new order made it easier for many moderate conservatives to come to terms with democracy.

Nonetheless, the new president had one major drawback: Although well-intentioned, he had little grasp of politics and relied heavily on advisers. His declining mental powers, owing to his age and the onset of senility, made him even more dependent on assistance. Unfortunately, his circle of advisers was not appropriate for the president of a republic; it consisted of old Prussian army officers and the cream of the landowning aristocracy from east of the Elbe, virtually all people whose narrow view of politics was further clouded by their hatred of republicanism.

The era of the *Bürgerblock* cabinets came to an end with the national parliamentary elections of May 20, 1928. The SPD won considerable gains and formed a coalition government in which its new party leader, Hermann Müller, became chancellor; other SPD politicians were placed in charge of a number of important cabinet departments. The coalition once again ranged all the way across the spectrum to Stresemann's conservative DVP, making it as broad as the Great Coali-

You Must Slave for Three Generations!
(propaganda poster against the Young Plan
for the plebescite of 1929)

In Article 73 the Weimar Constitution provided for plebescites in which voters could
influence political decisions directly. Three attempts were made to conduct plebescites on
the national level, all of which failed because not enough people participated. In
one of these instances voters were asked to
take a stand on the Young Plan, which determined the amounts and duration of German
war reparations payments. The National Socialists, the German National People's Party,
and the veterans' organization *Stahlhelm*
(Steel Helmet) with close ties to the latter
party responded with a propaganda campaign opposing the plan. The proposal put
to the voters was a Freedom Bill that abolished all obligations arising from the Treaty
of Versailles and prescribed a penitentiary
sentence for any member of the government
who signed the Young Plan. As always in
such referenda, the demagogues had their
moment of glory, but in spite of their efforts,
not quite 14 percent of the electorate turned
out on December 22, 1929, to cast their
votes in favor of the bill. Fifty percent would
have been required for the bill to pass. The
referendum was the first time conservative
politicians allied themselves with the Nazi
Party, the first indication that a "national unity
front" of right-wing opponents of the republic
was forming.

tion of 1923. But what appeared at
first glance to promise domestic
political stability was in fact a shifting and volatile combination, "a
cabinet with a permanent crisis
built in," as the *Berliner Tageblatt*
observed on the day its members
were announced.

In fact the democratic parties
had already used up what common
ground they had, and every new
topic was a potential minefield.
The coalition almost broke up
over the plan for a new armored
cruiser to replace an outdated
warship. When the Social Democratic cabinet ministers at last
agreed to their conservative colleagues' proposal, they had to endure the humiliating spectacle of
their own party delegates in the
Reichstag voting against them. Un-
employment figures were rising dramatically; strikes were increasing;
there were demonstrations and fighting in the streets—in short a
whole variety of circumstances that eroded parties' willingness to
compromise. Party pressures wore down the cabinet; ministers
looked for ways to shift responsibility that was becoming more and
more onerous and uncomfortable.

Finally the point arrived when Hermann Müller could no longer
hold things together; a disagreement between the parties of this coalition over what appeared on the surface to be a minor matter—an increase in unemployment insurance premiums—led him to submit his
resignation on March 27, 1930. With the breakdown of the coalition

the last parliamentary government of the Weimar Republic came to an end. Julius Leber, an SPD delegate in the *Reichstag*, noted: "Without giving it all too much thought, the leadership of the Social Democratic Party sailed back into the comfortable and familiar harbor of the opposition. It occurred to very few people that the 'presidential government' we now faced was obviously the last possible form of government compatible with the constitution. People talked a great deal about the threat to democracy and the danger of fascism, but that was just fuel for the propaganda mills, they didn't really believe it. The SPD would still be there in the opposition, and that would be sufficient protection."

The failure of the republican parties to reach a workable consensus was symptomatic of the overall political collapse of the republic, which broke apart into factions at war with one another. On May 1, 1929, there was shooting in the streets of Berlin for the first time since 1920, with violent clashes between the police, under Social Democratic leadership, and Communist demonstrators. Growing unemployment swelled the ranks of German Communist Party (KPD) supporters, although the KPD contributed to its own isolation by following orders from Moscow and denouncing the Social Democrats as "social fascists." At the other end of the political spectrum, the DVP, now more nationalistic than ever under the leadership of press czar Alfred Hugenberg, and the veterans' organization known as the *Stahlhelm* (Steel Helmet) allied themselves with the ultra-nationalist right wing, Adolf Hitler's National Socialist German Workers' Party (NSDAP).

The NSDAP, born out of the collapse of the short-lived revolutionary Munich republic and the mood of the following years, which approached civil war, was the creation of one man, its Führer, Adolf Hitler, and totally dependent on his demagogic talent and charisma. Hitler was actually the founder of a sect, who relied on his supporters' conviction that he alone proclaimed the true faith. His message was a crude mixture of all the ideas and ideologies that had been in circulation during the postwar period and proved effective with the mass of the public. The catch-phrase "national socialism" itself had been created before the First World War as a means to unite a variety of nationalistic organizations in the battle against "international socialism." The term was designed to appeal to the working class, but it also proved attractive to young people from the middle and upper classes with romantic notions of *Volksgemeinschaft,* a "popular" or "national" community.

This model of community, originally developed as part of romantic Catholic doctrine on the corporative state, seemed to promise a solution to the class tensions of modern industrial societies. The racist anti-Semitic doctrine served as the vehicle for an aggressive sense of Germans' missionary role in world politics, a hyperbolic distortion of the old dream of a Great German Empire in the heart of Europe. Both concepts, nation and race, built on one another: The first goal was to free the nation from the chains of the Versailles Treaty, a demand popular in all social classes and political camps; and after this had been achieved, the second goal was expansion toward the east, the conquest of *Lebensraum* for the allegedly superior German "race," at the expensive of "inferior races."

It was not mainly a political program or the content of his speeches that drew people to Hitler's meetings, however; it was his effectiveness as a public speaker. He could collect the hopes and longings of his audience as a lens collects rays of light, then focus them with fascinating, vivid language and project them back onto the people. This accounts for the success of National Socialism: Hitler brought people's fears and prejudices out into the light of day from the preconscious, irrational depths of collective awareness and articulated them in terms of his worldview. In this respect the Nazi party proved more modern than all its rivals across the political spectrum, who believed that in order to win people over, all they needed to do was present them with rationally formulated platforms. Hitler played to the emotional needs of the masses, which the established parties ignored.

In consequence, the NSDAP was truly a party of the people, far more so than any other party of the Weimar era. Unlike the other parties, it did not depend on a particular set of voters defined by their social class, economic status, or religious affiliation; it had supporters in every stratum of society and profession, although not equally distributed. Blue-collar workers and farmers were under-represented—though the percentage of workers rose continu-ally—while white-collar, middle-class voters were overrepresented. The evidence also shows the party had less success in areas where older institutions and belief systems had not lost ground. Groups that proved relatively immune to National Socialism included the core of the Social Democratic labor movement (whereas Communist voters often switched over to the NSDAP and vice versa), upper middle-class and property-owning Protestants, and the traditional Catho-lic milieu of western and southern Germany and Silesia. Hitler's party made inroads even here, however. While the political parties traditionally favored by these groups struggled to attract supporters among the young, the sons and daughters of their members flocked to join the NSDAP. Hitler's party was not only a sect of believers and a party of the people; it was also a youth movement.

The party's opportunity arrived with the worldwide economic cri-sis that followed on the heels of Black Friday and the collapse of the New York stock market on October 25, 1929. Because overall the German economy had already been performing poorly for some time, Germany was particularly hard hit. What looked at first like a tempo-rary low grew into an unprecedented catastrophe, in which economic decline and political radicalism reinforced each other in a vicious circle.

This became clear in the results of the *Reichstag* elections of Sep-tember 14, 1930, at the latest. The National Socialists won 130 seats in a sensational success that shook foreign investors' confidence in German stability profoundly. The withdrawal of capital that had set in some time before swelled to a flood. And as always happens in economic crises, customs barriers went up all over the world, with the result that the German economy lost not only the foreign investment on which its own lack of capital made it dependent, but also its earlier profits from exports. Since the economy relied so heavily on the export trade, the consequences for both production and employment were catastrophic.

Within a year unemployment figures soared from 9 percent to 16 percent, but this was only the first stage of the Great Depression. By the middle of 1931 insufficient liquidity was causing the first bankruptcies, which in turn sucked the largest manufacturing concerns into the downward spiral. The economic crisis expanded into a financial and credit crisis. By 1932 Germany's industrial production had sunk to half the levels of 1928. The stock index dropped to only a third of its former level in the same period, whereas over those four years unemployment more than tripled, from 7 percent in 1928 to 31 percent in 1932.

The economic crisis affected all the countries in Europe, but its effect in Germany was particularly devastating. This was due in part to the inherent weakness of the democratic Weimar government. To prevent civil war, it had attempted to curry favor with voters by approving subsidies and policies to redistribute wealth. It had listened to all the organized pressure groups that approached it with requests for support and granted their wishes to a far greater degree than had prewar governments. While the tax rate had doubled between 1913 and 1929, rising from 9 percent on the eve of the First World War to 18 percent, tax revenues going to unemployment compensation and other social welfare programs had risen over the same period from

337 million marks to 4.751 billion marks annually, more than a thirteen-fold increase. With this strategy the unpopular Weimar government had courted the various special-interest groups with promises of support and entitlements, all of which would have to be fulfilled in a time of crisis.

When the bill came due—when the economies of the industrialized nations faced their greatest test in modern history after Black Friday, when banks were going under, when industrial production in Europe sank by 50 percent within three years, when one-third of the German workforce was unemployed and all the entitlements promised by the government had to be paid out—the pressure to solve all these problems at once proved to be more than the German government could withstand. In Britain, where the economic slump was almost as dramatic as in Germany, responsibility for shouldering the problems of society was divided among many different administrative and social organizations, and the constitutional foundations of government survived undamaged. But in Germany the Weimar state broke down under the weight of the expectations harbored by so many segments of the population. And since the majority of the German people's loyalty to their constitution depended on the success of its institutions in solving conflicts related to the distribution of wealth, when the social welfare state could not make good on its obligations, its constitutional underpinnings were seen as having failed also. Thus, through its efforts to establish itself securely, parliamentary democracy in Germany had pulled the rug out from under its own feet.

The parliamentary forces proved helpless in this situation. When the majority of the *Reichstag* rejected unpopular measures to reduce

There Will Be No Third Reich!
(leaflet published by the Iron Front, Hamburg, January 1932)

The Iron Front formed in response to Hitler's alliance with Hugenberg; it was an alliance of the Social Democratic Party and other similarly minded organizations. However, it was demonstratively rejected by almost all nonsocialist groups, remaining a "Red" rather than a "black-red-gold" national opposition movement. The disintegration of the Weimar coalition could not be halted even in a time of crisis. Nonetheless, the Iron Front did not capitulate; their mass demonstrations matched the rallies of the right-wing antirepublican forces in vehemence and carefully choreographed pomp.

P.D. A.D.G.B. Afa Bund A.D.B. Reichsbanner Arbeitersportkartell.

Die eiserne Front ruft auf zur

DRUCK u. VERLAG: S.P.D. HAMBURG.

ÖFFENTLICHEN KUNDGEBUNG
AM DONNERSTAG 14. JAN. 20 UHR BEI SAGEBIEL
KARL HÖLTERMANN FÜHRER DES REICHSBANNERS
FRITZ WILDUNG BERLIN — FÜHRER DES A.T.u.Sp.B.
UND VERTRETER DER ORGANISATIONEN
SPRECHEN ZU DEM THEMA

DAS DRITTE REICH KOMMT NICHT!

EINTRITT: MITGLIEDER 20 PF. ERWERBSLOSE 10 PF. NICHTMITGL. 30 PF.

the budget deficit in July 1930, the new chancellor and former Center Party delegate Heinrich Brüning (1885–1970) fell back on Article 48 of the Weimar constitution, which provided for such a crisis by allowing the president to proclaim emergency measures without consulting the legislature. This opened a new chapter in constitutional history, or rather turned back to an older one, for with the default of the legislature and a government supported only by the will of the head of state, Germany had in effect reverted to the constitutional monarchism of the nineteenth century, with President von Hindenburg in the role of ersatz emperor. And in fact Article 48, the "substitute" Weimar constitution, functioned quite well for a time, when there was a need for swift action in the area of budget and finance policy and for firm measures to uphold government authority in the face of increasingly violent, politically motivated street clashes organized by both the extreme right and the extreme left.

Drastic policies in times of crisis can never be popular, however. Brüning's policies were particularly unpopular because his "deflationary" measures, consisting mainly of extreme reductions in government expenditure, drove unemployment even higher. The chancellor was prepared to accept the cost of his program—vastly increased economic distress in the population—because such misery represented an irrefutable argument in his efforts to eliminate German reparations payments; he counted on it to expose the great gap between Germans' willingness to fulfill their obligations and their ability to do so. To a certain extent Brüning's economic policy was thus merely a function of his foreign policy, and he proved successful with the latter. At the end of 1931 an Allied commission determined that the country was insolvent, signaling the end of reparations, a step formally approved by the Lausanne Conference in July 1932. An international disarmament conference that had begun in Geneva in February also recognized Germany's fundamental right to arm itself on an equal status with the other nations of Europe. Brüning thus had some grounds for believing he was only "a hundred yards short of the finish line," as he put it, when he was dismissed by the president on May 30, 1932.

There were numerous reasons behind Brüning's fall from power. For one thing agrarian circles opposed him, believing they had received too little support in the profound debt crisis affecting large landowners east of the Elbe. Then the army, which believed it needed the support of the "excellent human material" of the NSDAP for its

Ar·J·Z

ERSCHEINT WÖCHENTLICH EINMAL • PREIS 20 Pfg., Ke. 1,60
30 GR., 30 SCHWEIZER RP. • V. b. b. • HEUER DEUTSCHER
VERLAG, BERLIN W 8 • JAHRGANG XI • NR. 42 • 16.10.1932

DER SINN DES
HITLERGRUSSES:

Motto:
**MILLIONEN
STEHEN
HINTER MIR!**

Kleiner Mann bittet um große Gaben

The Real Meaning of the Hitler Salute

(cover of *AIZ* magazine, John Heartfield,
October 16, 1932)

Marx and Lenin's script for world history had
no role in it for a "revolutionary" but anti-
Marxist mass movement. For the orthodox
left, the phenomenon of National Socialism
thus remained inexplicable. The conspiracy
suggested here between "monopoly capitalism" and Hitler was in fact an illusion; Hitler's capital was not the bank accounts of
captains of industry but his grip on people's
minds.

armament and militia plans, saw
its interests jeopardized by a ban
on the SA. President Hindenburg
surmised correctly that the chancellor was unpopular. To be sure,
his successor, Franz von Papen
(1879–1969), a conservative Center Party back-bencher largely un-
known to the general public, was vastly more unpopular. The ministers of Papen's government, recruited largely from the aristocracy
and great landowners and announced on June 1, 1932, became
known collectively as the "cabinet of the barons" on account of their
titles. In order to win support from the NSDAP in the *Reichstag*, Papen fulfilled Hitler's demands to rescind the ban on the SA, to dis-

WIR WÄHLEN HINDENBURG!

Albert Grzesinski,

Dr. Bernhard Weiss,

Georg Bernhard,

Dr. h. c. Hirtsiefer,

Dr. Magnus Hirschfeld,

Otto Hörsing,

Dr. Bell,

Dr. Rudolf Hilferding,

Minister Stegerwald,

Crispien,

Wir wählen Hitler!

Hermann Göring,

Alfred Rosenberg,

General v. Epp,

Hauptmann Röhm,

General Litzmann,

Gregor Strasser,

Hans Schemm,

Graf Helldorff,

Dr. Goebbels,

Dr. Frick,

Schau Dir diese Köpfe an, und Du weißt,
wohin Du gehörst!

Hindenburg's term as president expired in the spring of 1932. The candidates for the next election formed strange alliances. The veterans' organization *Stahlhelm* nominated Duesterberg, their own president, rather than their honorary president Hindenburg; the Nazis nominated Hitler and the Communists Thälmann. Hindenburg was thus forced to accept support from the parties of the Weimar coalition, from which he had been eager to distance himself since 1930. Hindenburg won only in the second round, in which his remaining opponents were Hitler and Thälmann, receiving 53 percent of the vote. Hitler received 37 percent, showing that the poisonous anti-Semitic mudslinging his campaign indulged in had been effective.

solve the legislature, and to call for new elections. Since the pro-democracy black-red-gold state government was still in office in Prussia, despite heavy losses at the polls, and responding with equal force to both National Socialist and Communist insurgents in the streets, Papen persuaded Hindenburg to issue an emergency decree placing him in charge of the Prussian government. Once he was named national commissioner for Prussia on July 20, Papen chased Prime Minister Otto Braun and his cabinet from office. The Prussian bureaucracy and police, both important institutions for the exercise of power within the country, now stood under the command of the executive branch of the national government.

The results of the *Reichstag* elections of July 31, 1932, matched the agitated mood of the times. The NSDAP almost doubled its already substantial percentage of the vote; the moderate *Bürgerblock* shriveled dramatically. Together the Communist Party and National Socialists won an absolute majority of the seats, and they gladly exploited the situation, working hand in hand to sabotage government measures, although naturally unable to form a genuine governing coalition. To prevent the new *Reichstag* from bringing down the Papen government with a vote of no confidence, the legislature was dissolved again immediately on the first day it assembled. A wave of unprecedented political violence swept the country; elections were held again on November 6, and although the Nazis lost some votes, a result that gave some cause for hope, the change was not significant. Hindenburg then finally named as chancellor the man who already held real power in the country, General Kurt von Schleicher (1882–1934), the minister of the army.

Schleicher now attempted to carry out the desperate plan of a "transverse front": first to mobilize the trade union wings of all the parties across the board in support of his policies and second to divide the NSDAP. To achieve the latter, he sent out feelers to see if he could win over Gregor Strasser, the head of organization for the Nazis and Hitler's strongest rival within the party. But Schleicher's plan failed. The leaders of the SPD refused to allow the heads of the affiliated Free Labor Unions to enter into any dealings with him, and the NSDAP, hearing of what was afoot, made short work of Strasser's attempted revolt.

Schleicher then tried to persuade Hindenburg to dissolve the *Reichstag* yet again, but the president was worn out and unwilling to continue governing by invoking Article 48. Instead Hindenburg instructed Papen to form a government with parliamentary backing. Papen negotiated first with Hugenberg, the head of the DNVP, and then with Hitler, who agreed to participate in a new government on the condition that he himself receive the office of chancellor. Hitler agreed to the appointment of conservative friends of Hindenburg and Papen as cabinet ministers, and since he had previously demanded a totally free hand or no cooperation, his new conditions seemed modest and reasonable. Papen and Hugenberg accepted them.

President Hindenburg had resisted naming Hitler as chancellor as long as he could, but in the end he proved unable to hold out against his advisers, who without exception favored a government of "national concentration" under Hitler's leadership. And Hitler, unlike the previous candidates for chancellor, was not demanding to govern on the basis of emergency decrees; instead he announced his intention to hold new elections for the *Reichstag,* "one last time," as he said, with a secret ambiguity he alone could appreciate. After that, he promised, a broad majority coalition of NSDAP and DNVP would provide parliamentary backing for a Hitler-Hugenberg cabinet.

Hindenburg found this reassuring: Hitler would be surrounded by conservative men the president trusted, and Hindenburg himself would be relieved of the burden of responsibility for the undemocratic, emergency-paragraph regime. He could stop performing his nerve-wracking balancing act at the razor's edge of unconstitutionality. And yet he still hesitated. Finally, rumors that Schleicher was planning a putsch against him—unfounded but fabricated on purpose to rattle him—tipped the scales. Hindenburg became convinced that there was no longer an alternative to Hitler. On January 30, 1933, he appointed Hitler chancellor, sounding the death knell for the republic of Weimar.

11

German Megalomania
(1933–1942)

On the evening of January 30, 1933, no one doubted that the Weimar Republic was dead, but people differed in their visions of what the future held. Only supporters of the National Socialist Party were jubilant; they celebrated the day as if it were the Second Coming. The general public displayed more reserve than suited the propaganda mills of the new government, which began grinding at once. The British ambassador reported from Berlin that the press had reacted to "the appointment of Herr Hitler to the Chancellorship with almost philosophic calm," and added, "the populace took the news phlegmatically."

The pro-democracy parliamentary forces had no thought of banding together to ward off the danger. Leaders of the Social Democrats compared the present with Bismarck's laws against the socialists; they

Storm Troopers' Parade at the Nazi Party Rally in Nuremberg, 1933
(gouache, Ernst Vollbehr, 1933)

At the National Socialist Party rallies, which took place annually in Nuremberg in early September, the "community of the people" the Nazis were endeavoring to create became a palpable experience. The conferences and discussion meetings themselves were more or less incidental; the real appeal lay in the carefully orchestrated mass marches, parades, roll calls, memorial services, and demonstrations of weapons. The artist Ernst Vollbehr has succeeded in capturing the essential quality of these rituals: Individuals have been reduced to specks in an enormous and precise geometrical construction of military uniforms. Only one recognizable person stands out from this almost mechanical pattern: the Führer, with the blood-red swastika flag above him like an exclamation point.

believed that things could hardly get worse. Hitler's conservative backers took an optimistic view of the future. They were convinced that Hitler was "hemmed in" with conservative cabinet ministers who would keep him in line. Papen told one of his friends, "What are you worried about? I have Hindenburg's full confidence. In two months we'll have Hitler backed into a corner and whimpering."

In order to understand the tenor of such remarks in retrospect, one must keep in mind that in assessing the National Socialist regime in 1933 Hitler's contemporaries had no experience to go on. The Second World War and Auschwitz were still covered by the mists of time, and the few people who had read *Mein Kampf*, Hitler's announcement of his future program, tended not to take it seriously. Experience had shown that in general there was a large gap between ideological declarations of principle and practical political strategy. Furthermore the reversion to an authoritarian regime did not come as a shock. From 1930 on Germans became inured to the idea that parliamentary control over political developments was tenuous at best, and if they looked around the rest of Europe, things did not appear all that different elsewhere. Governments were headed by dictators in most countries, and where that was not the case, as in the popular front government in France, domestic political unrest was at such a pitch that it hardly served as an advertisement for democracy. There was a widespread perception that the Great Depression had exhausted democratic governments, and that the immediate future belonged to the strong men of every country.

Mussolini in Italy was a prime example, a dictator whose rule had received openly admiring commentary even from liberals like Theodor Wolff, editor-in-chief of the *Berliner Tageblatt,* and socialists like Kurt Hiller. If Hitler was totally misjudged by the public, this was because he was in fact not an ordinary politician but an ideological fanatic and revolutionary. The traditional concepts of European politics were foreign to him; they meant nothing to him in any case, for in the

Unbeugsamer Glaube u. fanatischer Siegeswille führten zum 30. Januar 1933.

Indomitable Faith
(souvenir postcard, 1933)

Hitler built his success on, among other things, the emotional deficit other political parties failed to address: "The driving force behind the tremendous upheavals that have occurred on this earth has always lain not so much in a scientific knowledge of what governs people's behavior as in a fanaticism that inspires them, and sometimes in a form of hysteria that impels them forward. Anyone who wants to win over the broad mass of people must know the key that opens the door to their hearts. It is not objectivity, that is to say weakness, but will and power" (Hitler, *Mein Kampf*).

last analysis he had only one goal: to establish world dominance for a "superior race" over the dead bodies of its "inferiors." He never took his eyes off this aim, although he often kept it concealed behind a veil of tactical maneuvers.

To reach it, Hitler first had to establish National Socialist rule irreversibly and make the party a dominant presence everywhere in the country. What is usually referred to as the "seizure of power" was in reality a process that took a year and a half to complete. The first step consisted of eliminating the separate units within German politics, namely the parties and the separate states or *Länder.* The *Reichstag* fire of February 27, 1933, was probably not a provocation planned by the Nazis but the act of a single anarchist. However, the precise cause was immaterial for the developments that followed. The ensuing "Decree for the Protection of the People and the State" repealed basic civil rights guaranteed by the Weimar constitution—although the constitution itself remained in force on paper—and created a permanent state of emergency that enabled the regime to hunt down its opponents with an appearance of legality. The SA, which by late January had unleashed a campaign of terror more or less on its own initiative, dragging outspoken antagonists off to "unofficial" concentration camps where they were tortured and murdered, was declared an adjunct of the police force.

The last multiparty elections took place in this climate of intimidation on March 5, 1933, yet even under these circumstances the NSDAP won only 43.9 percent of the vote. The Nazis were thus never elected by a majority of the German people, for the later plebescites with outcomes of over 90 percent took place under the peculiar conditions of a totalitarian dictatorship, in which such election results are the norm.

The new *Reichstag* no longer had any Communist delegates, for the emergency decree that followed the burning of the parliament's building had outlawed the party. On March 23, 1933, Hitler presented the new legislature with a bill for an Enabling Act that would give the government the right to decree laws without the participation of the *Reichstag* and the upper house, the *Reichsrat,* thereby circumventing altogether the legislature and the oversight bodies provided by the constitution. The political parties were faced with the question of whether they should formally assent to their own demise. Finally, prompted by a mixture of force and enticements, they passed the law, with one holdout: The SPD delegates admirably refused to vote for the Enabling Act despite pressures that amounted to terrorism; and, refusing to be intimidated, SPD chairman Otto Wels delivered a courageous eulogy to the deceased democracy before a backdrop of shouting storm troopers.

The SPD-affiliated Free Labor Unions made efforts to arrive at a formula for coexistence with the new regime but were banned on May 2, 1933, despite this; the SPD itself was dissolved a month later. Many of its leaders were transported to concentration camps; some were killed. The moderate parties preferred voluntary *Gleichschaltung* (coordination), the term in Nazi jargon for the dissolution of political associations and/or their absorption into NSDAP organizations. By mid-1933 only one party existed in Germany, the party of Adolf Hitler. The independence of the *Länder,* the states of the federation and Germany's oldest historical legacy, was also eliminated within a few months, in a process as swift and brutal as a coup d'etat. The state prime ministers were replaced by *Reichsstatthalter,* governors who served as officials of the central government and reported to the minister of the interior. The unified revolutionary state had become a reality.

The seizure of power involved not only the elimination of irritating competitors but also the acquisition of control over the instruments of government authority. The two chief pillars of government power were the bureaucracy and the military. Following promulgation of the Law for Restoration of the Professional Civil Service on April 7, 1933, the National Socialists dismissed a whole range of undesirable officials—democrats and liberals, but above all Jews—and replaced them with NSDAP members. The regime had a harder time with the military, for apart from a few young officers, the army looked on Hitler and his party with attitudes ranging from skeptical to hostile. Many conservative officers found the Nazis' swaggering and boastful "low-class" behavior and aggressiveness offensive. They took a particularly dim view of the party's own armed force, the SA, which was raising ever more insistent demands for a second revolution, a "night of the long knives" to deal with bastions of bourgeois society and the conservative organs of the old state. The SA claimed to be the "real" army of the National Socialist state, and for the *Reichswehr*, which viewed itself as the sole guarantor of government authority, this amounted to outrageous presumption.

The interests of the army leadership overlapped with Hitler's on this point, however, for Hitler was enough of a realist to see that the *Reichswehr* was more useful as an instrument of power than the SA; he was also beginning to fear the ambition and revolutionary zeal of the storm troopers' chief of staff, Ernst Röhm. Thus it came about

"Through Light to the Night"
(cover of *AIZ* magazine, John Heartfield, Prague, May 10, 1933)

The *Arbeiter Illustrierte Zeitung* (Workers' Illustrated News) was an intellectual, pro-Communist publication that by May 1933 had been forced abroad; this issue was published in Czechoslovakia. This photo montage shows the *Reichstag* burning in the background; the National Socialist "minister for propaganda and national enlightenment," Joseph Goebbels (1897–1945), appears in a characteristic pose in the foreground, next to a pile of burning books. On the same day as the magazine appeared, book burnings took place on the *Opernplatz* in Berlin and in other university towns, organized by students' groups; the books tossed into the bonfires were mainly works that had made Weimar culture world famous (such as *The Magic Mountain* and *All Quiet on the Western Front*) and were now defamed as "destructive writings of authors who cannot be tolerated."

that the army participated in the elimination of the SA as a rival force during the "Röhm putsch" of June 30, 1934, implicating itself in Röhm's assassination and the murders of a large number of Hitler's other opponents. The fact that the *Reichswehr* remained silent even when its own generals Schleicher and Bredow were killed made its leaders accomplices of the unlawful regime whose basic principle was formulated after the wave of assassinations by Carl Schmitt, professor of constitutional law and a leading Nazi apologist: "The Führer protects the law." With this dictum the arbitrary will of the dictator was made the highest law of the land.

Yet Hitler's aims were not fully achieved by wresting control of the institutions of government. A totalitarian dictatorship is not firmly established until it also controls the minds of the people. Liberal, democratic, and socialist intellectuals and artists were persecuted and forced into emigration if they were not interned in concentration camps first. Their books were publicly burned, their paintings

Erscheint wöchentlich einmal. • Preis Kč 1·60, 30 Gr., 30 Schweizer Rappen, 20 Pfg.
In Nordamerika und Kanada 10 Cents • V. b. b. • Jahrgang XII • Nummer 18 • 10. Mai 1933

AM 10. MAI WERDEN IN DEUTSCHLAND ALLE MISSLIEBIGEN BÜCHER VERBRANNT

DURCH LICHT ZUR NACHT

Also sprach Dr. Goebbels: Lasst uns aufs neue Brände entfachen, auf dass die Verblendeten nicht erwachen!

Bilder deutscher Rassen 1

Formen: Großwüchsig, schlank; langköpfig, schmalgesichtig; Nase schmal; Haar wellig.

Nordische Rasse

Farben: Sehr hell, Haar goldblond, Augen blau bis grau, Haut rosig-weiß.

Formen: Sehr großwüchsig, wuchtig; langköpfig, breitgesichtig; Nase ziemlich schmal; Haar wellig oder lockig.

Fälische Rasse

Farben: Hell, Haar blond, Augen blau bis grau, Haut rosig-weiß.

Formen: Kleinwüchsig, schlank; langköpfig, mittelbreitgesichtig; Nase ziemlich schmal; Haar wellig oder lockig.

Westische Rasse

Farben: Sehr dunkel, Haar schwarz, Augen schwarz, Haut hellbraun.

or music declared "un-German" and attacked as "degenerate" *(entartet)*. From September 1933 on, cultural life in Germany was largely manipulated and made to serve the needs of the National Socialist state by Joseph Goebbels, minister of propaganda, through the newly created National Chamber of Culture, although some latitude re-

mained for nonconforming writers and artists until the outbreak
of war.

The battle for hearts and minds
continued. At the universities, un-
congenial professors and faculty
members were dismissed and often forced out of the country,
while no small number of their
colleagues hastened to place the
institutions of higher learning,
which had once existed far from
the tumult of day-to-day politics,
at the disposal of the new rulers in
brown shirts. Similar developments occurred within the churches. In
the Lutheran Church the German Christian movement flourished,
which took its orientation from the racist-nationalist ideology and
Führer-principle of the Nazis. At the Barmen Synod held in May 1934
their opponents formed the Confessing Church, whose members
tirelessly attacked the National Socialists despite government repri-
sals and arrests. Sympathy for the new regime was not lacking among
the Catholic clergy, especially after the concordat signed with the
Vatican on July 20, 1933. Yet resistance also increased within the Roman Catholic Church as news spread of the Nazis' euthanasia plans,
reaching its height with issuance of the papal encyclical *Mit brennender
Sorge* (With deep anxiety) in 1937.

Where attempts to silence intellectual leaders did not suffice, state
terror set in. It is associated above all with the names Heinrich
Himmler and Reinhard Heydrich, and with the SS (*Schutzstaffel,* defense formation); this elite National Socialist "security unit" became
the supreme police force of the Third Reich, an all-powerful instrument for punishing, terrorizing, and purging the population of undesirable elements. Its headquarters on Prince Albrecht Street in Berlin

housed administrative offices and torture chambers, the main office of the Gestapo (the shortened form of *GEheime STAatsPOlizei*, Secret State Police), and the head office of Reich Security. The campaign against enemies of the regime was managed from Prince Albrecht Street: political, ideological, and racial enemies, meaning first and foremost Jews. The SS spread its nets all over the country, from police departments to the sinister world of the concentration camps. The SS also contained a special unit at the personal disposal of the Führer that later formed the core of the wartime *Waffen-SS* (Armed SS) and maintained ties with the Race and Resettlement Headquarters, the bureaucratic division formed to carry out Hitler's racial policies.

Autobahns in the German Reich
(poster, ca. 1936)

Plans for superhighways based on the American model were developed in the closing years of the Weimar Republic, but construction of the first autobahn designed to run from Hamburg to Basel via Frankfurt was interrupted by the Great Depression. The National Socialists, who took up the plans again and promoted construction, turned them into a spectacular job-creation program. In 1936 about 120,000 men were employed on the project, and supervisors purposely dispensed with machines in order to give even more men work. The military and strategic value of the autobahns proved to be small, and in the late 1930s the amount of effort going into their construction was reduced, so that more labor and raw materials could be invested in the armaments industry.

The muddled Manichean racial doctrine of National Socialism required as a foil for "Aryans," the bringers of light and redemption, a group of people who merely by belonging to a particular "race" embodied everything evil, bad, and deviant. The National Socialists had no difficulty in identifying a group to occupy the position of outsider, given Europe's thousand-year tradition in this respect: It was the Jews. The persecution of the Jews was not planned and prepared long in advance; it depended on circumstances both abroad and within the country, but it always constituted one of the regime's ultimate ideological aims. The campaign made use of terror and propaganda actions designed by the party to appear as if they had erupted spontaneously from the population, "from below," beginning with the boycott of Jewish merchants organized by Goebbels on April 1, 1933, and

REICHSAUTOBAHNEN
IN DEUTSCHLAND

reaching fever pitch with the *Reichskristallnacht,* the night of shattered glass, on November 9, 1938.

In alternation with such tactics, the government imposed new laws "from above." Among the very first was the Law for Restoration of the Professional Civil Service, which empowered the government to dismiss Jewish officials, followed by the Defense Law of May 21, 1935, excluding Jews from military service. The remaining rights of Jews were greatly reduced with the proclamation of the Nuremberg Laws on September 15, 1935, which made proof of Aryan descent a pre-requisite for exercising the rights of citizens or holding elective office; they deprived Jews of full citizenship, and prohibited marriage be-tween Jews and non-Jews. These measures, a twisted perversion of the rule of law, created a juridical foundation for permanent discrimi-nation and persecution of German Jews.

Persecution and violence were one side of the regime, enticement and fascination the other. It began with the fact that hardly a social group, political interest, or collective hope existed that the National Socialists did not promote or furnish with some benefit. Blue-collar workers were impressed by spectacular job-creation programs like the construction of the autobahns, improvements in workers' bene-fits, and free-time activities provided by the party's own recreation department, whose slogan was *Kraft durch Freude,* strength through en-joyment. Retail merchants profited from the fact that their competi-tion, the despised big department stores, were required to pay higher taxes, and members of the skilled trades appreciated the stricter measures limiting the number of new master's licenses that could be issued. Farmers welcomed protective tariffs and domestic price sup-ports, while industrialists were grateful for the abolition of workers' participation in decision-making, the absence of conflicts with labor unions over wages, and the rising number of government contracts, particularly in the armaments industry. Much the same applied to vir-tually every profession, class, and type of organization. Almost every "member of the national community" benefited in some way, not only materially, but—what was perhaps more important—in terms of ideals and a sense of solidarity.

The latter lay at the heart of the National Socialists' success within the country. Unlike democracy, which had been perceived as austere and rationalistic, the dictatorship satisfied people's emotions. Skillful appeals to tradition played a major role in this success, on occasions such as Potsdam Day on April 21, 1933, when the governing coalition between revolutionary National Socialists and Prussian-conservative German Nationalists was celebrated by a manipulatory but effective invocation of the spirit of Frederick the Great, or when the annual harvest thanksgiving was celebrated on the Bückeberg in Westphalia with splendid tributes to old agricultural customs that helped bind the loyalties of the agrarian middle class to the new state.

The staging of political events, the transformation of slogans into magnificent theater, and the insertion of potent symbolism into everyday life—these were techniques the government had perfected as never before in German history. From the Olympic Games in Berlin in 1936 to the annual party rallies in Nuremberg, the National Socialist regime celebrated the grandeur of the nation and the indissoluble bands of community with precisely choreographed mass parades, ceremonies reminiscent of religious services, and magic rituals of redemption that affected the participants deeply. Not even the British ambassador Sir Nevile Henderson could resist their spell completely; he reported from Nuremberg that he found one performance "both solemn and beautiful," and the effect of the light show "was something like being inside a cathedral of ice."

The "cathedral of ice" created with dozens of antiaircraft spotlights revealed, more than any other symbol, the dual character of the Nazi appeal to the emotions: the last word in modern technology coupled with archaic ritual. This contrast was typical of the way the Third Reich presented itself, with autobahns, the Silver Arrow model Mercedes Benz, the first inexpensive radio receiver, the affordable Volkswagen, and the world's first jet-propelled plane, on the one hand, and Germanic sagas, castles of the Teutonic knights where the Nazi elite was educated, and solstice celebrations on the other. The newest inventions and invocation of the spirits of the dead flowed together.

The undeniable approval felt by the majority of the population for the Hitler regime was increased by its successes in foreign affairs, a

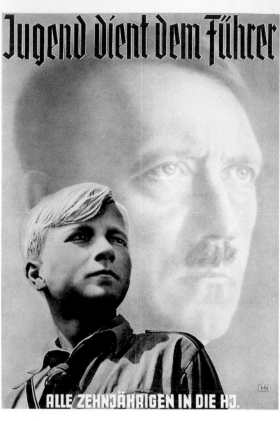

JUGEND DIENT DEM FÜHRER

ALLE ZEHNJÄHRIGEN IN DIE HJ.

Youth Serves the Führer
(poster, ca. 1939)

The Hitler Youth, which was proclaimed the official "state youth organization" in 1936, cleverly exploited the longings of older children and young people for acceptance in a group and romantic camp-fire experiences. In 1940 membership in the Hitler Youth or corresponding Association of German Girls became mandatory. Hitler explained the mission of the Hitler Youth at the party rally of 1935: "Boys will enter the *Jungvolk* ("Young Folk"), cadets will enter the Hitler Youth, then they will report for duty in the SA, the SS, and the other groups, and the SA and SS men will one day report for duty in the Work Corps, and in these organizations they will mature into soldiers of the people."

sharp contrast from the record of its unfortunate democratic predecessors. The general public failed to recognize the broader aims Hitler was pursuing with his foreign policy, however: From his first day as chancellor he wanted war, through which he intended not only to reverse the results of the Treaty of Versailles but to expand the borders of Germany and establish world dominance for the Aryan race. Only four days after his appointment he announced with complete candor to the commanders of the *Reichswehr* that his policy would be "conquest of new *Lebensraum* in the East and its ruthless Germanization"; unfortunately we know nothing about how the generals responded. In a tactically clever move Hitler signaled German willingness to seek rapprochement with foreign powers; this muted the hostile response to his seizure of power in the Western democracies, while all the time he was pushing forward preparations for war.

In a plebescite on January 13, 1935, the inhabitants of the Saar district voted to rejoin the *Reich*, and on June 18 a British-German agreement on the size of their respective naval fleets was signed; both these events tended to show Hitler in the light of a successful politician, while the western powers appeared willing to retreat. Rounding off this impression was Hitler's announcement on March 16 that compulsory military service would be reintroduced in Germany in conjunction with rearmament, in violation of the Treaty of Versailles. A year later the army, now renamed the *Wehrmacht,* occupied the Rhineland, and Britain and France offered no more than formal protests. That same year the Rome-Berlin Axis was created and the Anti-Comintern Pact signed with Japan, both of them alliances with an expressly anti-Soviet thrust.

Hitler failed to achieve the desired rapprochement with Britain, however, first of all because Joachim von Ribbentrop, the German ambassador in London and later foreign minister, was pursuing openly anti-English policies, and second because the German-Japanese alliance threatened British interests in the Far East. Relations cooled still further after Germany intervened in the Spanish Civil War, where it could test the preparedness of its air force, the *Luftwaffe.* At the same time the German Foreign Office noted with interest the degree to which the British seemed anxious to avoid being drawn into conflict on the Continent. Hitler had reason to assume he would have a largely free hand in carrying out his plans to expand Germany's borders.

By 1936 preparations for the coming war were in full swing. Hitler

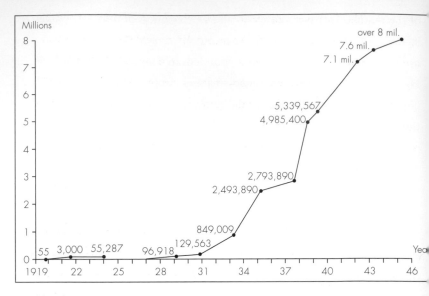

Millions

The NSDAP grew increasingly into a party of the people, not only in its composition but also in the number of its members. The sharp swings up and down reflect historical turning points: In 1923 the party declined after the failure of Hitler's putsch; membership began increasing slowly after 1928, as the social and economic crisis worsened, and rose steeply after the Nazis came to power in 1933. The annexation of Austria in 1938 spurred further growth, which continued in the phase of German victories up to 1942 and even beyond. By 1945 one out of five adult Germans was a member of the party.

wrote a memorandum creating a four-year plan, saying that the German economy must be ready for war at the end of that period. Economic planning and production were subordinated to this goal. Yet in a meeting with the foreign minister and commanders of the armed forces on November 5, 1937, a record of which is contained in the "Hossbach Protocol," Hitler's plans for expansion in Europe ran into resistance. The foreign minister, Baron Konstantin von Neurath, pointed to the international risks, and Baron Werner von Fritsch, commander-in-chief of the army, doubted that Germany's economic and military capabilities would allow it to undertake extensive military operations. A year later both critics were replaced by more accommodating men.

On March 12, 1938, the German *Wehrmacht* marched into Austria, after assurances had been received that Britain and Italy would not intervene. The German population reacted with jubilation to the annexation of Austria, and so did the majority of Austrians. The separation of 1866 had been overcome; Great Germany, the goal that both the liberals in the German National Assembly of 1848 and the Social Democrats of the 1919 National Assembly in Weimar had supported, was now a reality. The nightmarish character of this reality was perceived at first only by a minority of Austrian Jews, liberals, committed Catholics, and socialists who had failed to leave the country in time; they were swiftly rounded up in unannounced raids and arrested.

The success of the *Anschluß* showed Hitler that he had little to fear from the Western powers, and so only two weeks later, on March 28, he made the decision to annex Czechoslovakia as well. Two days after that he sent orders to the *Wehrmacht* to prepare to crush Czechoslovakia; the date of the invasion was set for October 1, 1938. Once again Western resistance was weak and limited to diplomatic protests. In a meeting in Munich on September 29, Britain, France, and Italy accepted German annexation of the Sudetenland—a ring-shaped territory comprising virtually the entire Czech-German border region, which had a large German-speaking population—in order to avoid war. A British-German nonaggression pact signed the next day by British Prime Minister Neville Chamberlain and Hitler strengthened the general conviction in the Western countries that Hitler would be content with a compromise and accept an offer of "colonial appeasement," meaning restoration to Germany of its former colonies.

It was the furthest thing from Hitler's mind. At the same time he was discussing peace with Chamberlain, the "Z plan" was being developed to build up a fleet to attack England. On March 15, 1939, the *Wehrmacht* occupied the "rump Czech state," demonstrating the worthlessness of diplomatic agreements between the Western democracies and the Hitler dictatorship. Only now did Britain rouse itself to take counter-measures by guaranteeing Polish independence and beyond that attempting to revive the old prewar British–Russian

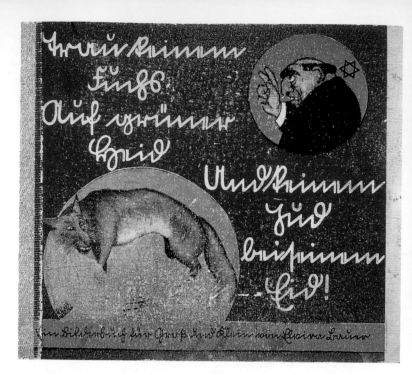

Anti-Semitic Children's Book
(Elvira Bauer, Nuremberg, Stürmer Verlag, 1936)

National Socialist anti-Semitism was more global than earlier forms; religious hostility toward Jews at least admitted the possibility of conversion, and cultural hostility the possibility of assimilation. Hitler's anti-Semitism, by contrast, stigmatized an entire group on the basis of unalterable characteristics: Anyone whose forebears had practiced Judaism remained inescapably a Jew, and the object of Nazis' paranoid delusions. Hitler imagined that Jews were at work everywhere undermining the foundations of society, and he considered Jews responsible for every feature of the modern world that made him feel anxious. For this reason, he declared, Jews had to be "separated from the human community." The Nazi publication *Der Stürmer* ("The Storm Trooper") sponsored a particularly brutal and primitive form of anti-Semitic propaganda; its publishers in Nuremberg brought out an illustrated book for children entitled *Trau keinem Fuchs auf grüner Heid und keinem Jud bei seinem Eid!* ("Trust no fox on the green heath and no Jew on his oath").

alliance. However, Hitler got the jump on them. Foreign Minister Ribbentrop and Stalin signed an agreement creating a Nazi–Soviet nonaggression pact on August 23. In a secret protocol Hitler and Stalin divided eastern Europe into two spheres of influence; the line of demarcation ran through the middle of Poland. Hitler believed he had

ERINNERUNG AN PARIS 1940

KLEINER FÜHRER DURCH PARIS

FÜR DEUTSCHE SOLDATEN

Brief Guide to Paris for German Soldiers
(Paris, 1940)

On June 22, 1940, the German *blitzkrieg* against France was ended by an armistice, signed like the other Franco-German armistice 22 years earlier in the forest of Compiègne. Northern France and the Benelux countries were placed under German military administration, and the unoccupied portion of France was governed by a pro-German administration under Marshal Pétain. The city of Paris, now under German military command, proved so attractive to German soldiers that strict regulations had to be issued to limit visits by members of the *Wehrmacht*.

almost reached his goal. He could not conceive of the possibility that the Western powers would prevent him from carving up Poland again. According to the report of the Carl Jacob Burckhardt, High Commissioner of the League of Nations in Danzig, in a meeting on August 11, 1939, Hitler spoke to him openly about his purpose in all this: All he wanted was to subject Russia. But if the West was too blinded to support him, he would make terms with Russia, defeat the West, and attack the Soviet Union afterward.

On September 1, 1939, German troops marched into Poland, and

seventeen days later the Red Army crossed the Polish border in the east. In contrast to 1914, the mood of the German public, and even of the *Reichstag* delegates in their Nazi Party uniforms, was somber; few of them believed that this military adventure would end well. Contrary to Hitler's expectations, the Western powers did not shrink back but declared war on Germany instead. The Second World War had begun, intentionally provoked by Hitler's desire for conquest, triggered by Stalin's complicity, and aided by the West's failure to resist German aggression until it was too late. Despite all the atrocities and war crimes committed in the following years by all participants, it is necessary to keep in mind that decisive responsibility for the outbreak of war lay with German leadership, and to a much lesser degree with Soviet leaders, while the Western powers engaged in justified self-defense.

German victory over Poland, aided by the Soviet invasion, was achieved in only five weeks. Germany and the Soviet Union divided Poland along the Bug River, and while the SS and Gestapo and the Soviet NKVD (the People's Commissariat for Internal Affairs) established control in their respective territories, the Reich turned its military might against western Europe. Beginning on April 9, 1940, German troops began occupying Denmark and Norway, anticipating British and French plans to send troops to their defense; this secured Germany's northern flank from attack and gave the Germans direct access to the Atlantic. An attack on the Netherlands, Belgium, and France followed on May 10. To the surprise of military experts, including the leaders of the *Wehrmacht*, the western campaign proved a triumph for Hitler's strategy. This success not only placed him at the peak of his popularity in Germany but also silenced opposition within the army officers' corps. He had gained unlimited authority in military affairs, and whatever resistance to the regime still existed within Germany became disheartened.

The next goal of the war was conquest of Great Britain. Hitler continued to hope that the British would fall into line, and it was with reluctance that he gave the order to begin the Battle of Britain, which did not end in the triumph for the German *Luftwaffe* that its commander-in-chief, Hermann Göring, had promised his Führer. Yet Hitler's main goal remained the war against the Soviet Union, as he declared to the leaders of the *Wehrmacht* on July 31, 1940. Unable to defeat the British, who refused even to consider capitulating, Hitler altered his strategic plans. Although he had first intended to subdue Britain before pursuing the war against the Soviet Union, now he explained that it would be necessary to defeat the Soviet Union first; only then would he wrest the "dagger pointed at the Continent"

from the British and force them to accept peace. It was the same fatal mistake Napoleon had committed in 1812, when he hoped to defeat Britain in Moscow. The strategic situation was made more complicated by Mussolini's independent campaign against Greece; this bogged down within a short time, forcing the Germans to come to the Italians' aid and deploy a significant part of their forces in the Mediterranean.

On November 12, 1940, Foreign Minister Molotov came to Berlin to raise further Soviet territorial demands extending from Finland to Turkey. This confirmed to Hitler the necessity for carrying out his long-planned attack on the Soviet Union; he now felt he could not afford to lose more time, and on December 18 he issued "Instruction No. 21" launching preparations for Operation Barbarossa, the campaign against the Soviet Union. Hitler expected the United States to enter the war by 1942 and wanted to have completed his expansionist military operations by then. After the success of the campaigns in Poland and France he believed he could defeat Russia within a few weeks. Then, as master of a colonial empire stretching to the "Eastern Wall," a line of defense that would run from Archangelsk to the Caspian Sea, he intended to seal off his huge realm from Anglo-American attack through bastions in the Middle East and northwest Africa. He would make continental Europe a self-sufficient German empire too

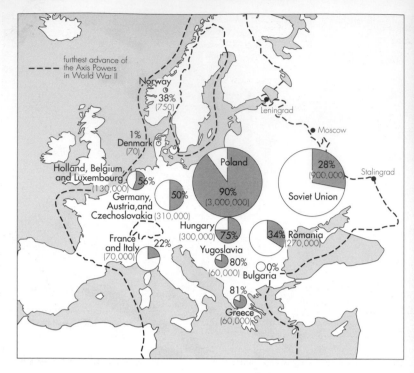

furthest advance of
the Axis Powers
in World War II

Norway
38%
(750)

Leningrad

Moscow

Denmark 1%
(70)

Poland
90%
(3,000,000)

Holland, Belgium,
and Luxembourg 56%
(130,000)

Germany,
Austria, and
Czechoslovakia (310,000) 50%

Soviet Union
28%
(900,000)

Stalingrad

Hungary
(300,000) 75%

France
and Italy 22%
(70,000)

Yugoslavia
80%
(60,000)

34% Romania
(270,000)

0% Bulgaria

81%
Greece
(60,000)

Jews Killed in Europe

(expressed in absolute numbers and as a
percentage of the total Jewish population for
each country)

large to blockade, and then undertake what Andreas Hillgruber has
called the "World *Blitzkrieg*" against the United States. As Germany's
ally, Japan was allocated a special role in this plan, which for the time
being required giving priority to strategic necessities over German
racial prejudices.

Operation Barbarossa commenced on June 22, 1941. Even though
the Red Army had already taken up offensive positions, it was caught
off guard, and whole army corps surrendered. Huge gains at the start
convinced both German military leaders and Hitler that they could
achieve victory within a short time. They began to shift the balance of
armaments production from the army to the navy, to prepare for the
coming campaign against Britain and America. But in the autumn of
1941 the pace of the German advance toward the east slowed, and it

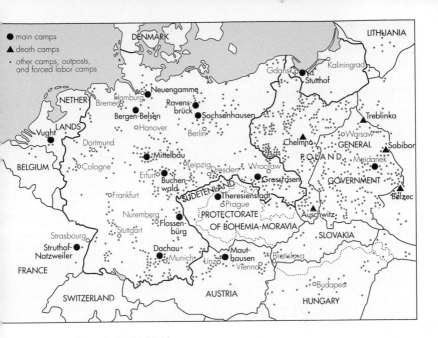

- ● main camps
- ▲ death camps
- · other camps, outposts, and forced labor camps

LITHUANIA

DENMARK

NETHER-
LANDS

BELGIUM

FRANCE

SWITZERLAND

Neuengamme
Hamburg
Bremen
Ravens-
brück
Bergen-Belsen
Sachsenhausen
Hanover
Berlin
Vught
Dortmund
Mittelbau
Cologne
Leipzig
Dresden
Wrocław
Erfurt
Buchen-
wald
Frankfurt
Theresienstadt
Prague
Nuremberg
Flossen-
bürg
Stuttgart
Strasbourg
Struthof-
Natzweiler
Dachau
Munich
Linz
Maut-
hausen
Vienna
Bratislava
Budapest

Gdansk
Stutthof
Kaliningrad
Treblinka
Warsaw
GENERAL
Sobibor
Chelmno
POLAND
Majdanek
GOVERNMENT
Belzec
SUDETENLAND
Grossrosen
PROTECTORATE
OF BOHEMIA-MORAVIA
Auschwitz
SLOVAKIA

AUSTRIA
HUNGARY

Concentration Camps in the Third Reich

finally ground to a halt as winter set in. Once again Hitler's strategic plans had gone awry.

On December 11, only four days after Japan attacked Pearl Harbor, the Führer declared war on the United States, even though his lead tank columns had just been stopped before reaching Moscow. The main rationale behind this move was to keep the Japanese in the war and prevent them from concluding a separate peace with the Americans. At first the impact of the American entry into the war was negligible, and during the first half of 1942 hopes of victory began to rise again at Hitler's headquarters. In southern Russia and Africa the advances of the German armies appeared unstoppable, and the Japanese took Singapore. By mid-1942 German troops had taken the heights of the Caucasus Mountains and were within a few miles of Alexandria, while Allied losses from German submarine attacks reached their peak. German power had achieved its greatest extent.

For occupied Europe this meant rule by the *Wehrmacht* and the SS.

In western Europe, military occupation followed the classic pattern to a large extent, although the Gestapo and Security Service *(Sicherheitsdienst)*—Heydrich's intelligence organization—committed brutal attacks against the civilian population, contrary to international law, in their pursuit of partisans and also in actions to round up Jews and gypsies. In the east the SS left the population in no doubt at all about what it could expect in the event of a German victory. Poland offered an opportunity to convert racist ideology into deeds. The Polish upper classes were systematically killed and millions of Jews deported from their homes to make room for ethnic Germans from eastern Europe. Migration on a huge scale was set in motion, preceding that of 1945. Similar events took place in the occupied portions of the Soviet Union. Behind the German lines, the *Wehrmacht* not only resorted to tactics prohibited by international conventions far more often than it did in the west; it also had the support of the Security Service. The latter executed Soviet political officials (commissars) without any pretense of formalities and systematically hunted down Jews. Russian prisoners of war were crammed into camps where conditions were designed to give the vast majority no chance of survival.

For the German population in these years the war did not bring widespread hunger, as had been the case in the First World War. Until 1944 no serious food shortages existed, for the occupied countries were ruthlessly stripped of their own resources. But the war intensified the tendencies of the totalitarian state, bringing with it a militarization of public life, increasing organization of the formerly private sphere, and social leveling. When rationing was introduced, the government understood how to exploit envy and class differences for its own purposes. There were appeals to solidarity within the "community of the people"; party and state organizations were created that included virtually every citizen in the end; block wardens kept an eye on their neighborhoods, and neighbors were encouraged to spy on one another. When the Allied air raids began, people were forced to spend time together in bomb shelters. All these factors tended to wear down class distinctions, and the population grew more homogeneous, as millions of people listened to the same slogans from the radio, stood in line for rationed goods, and took in the insipid entertainment offered on the radio and in movie theaters as a distraction from the war. What remained for individuals was retreat into the private sphere, while they avoided contact with the outside world as much as possible and concentrated on the most urgent task: finding ways to survive.

Meanwhile, the regime was making plans for the future. A massive project to rebuild the capital of the Reich was undertaken in the midst of the war, in preparation for the final victory: A gigantic world capital city, Germania, would arise on the site of the old Berlin. Construction of a broad-gauge railway network was begun in Europe that was to stretch to the Urals and make the previous railroads look like toys. SS architects created plans for gargantuan monuments to the dead that would also serve as "border fortresses" in Africa and on the Dnepr River.

The regime's main plans, however, concentrated on systematic elimination of its declared enemy, the Jews of Europe. Hitler had already announced on January 30, 1939, that a world war would result in "the destruction of the Jewish race in Europe." His war was not a battle for hegemony of the type Europe had known from time immemorial; it was a racial war. Hitler believed only select, homogeneous peoples were capable of establishing a lasting empire, and that the Aryan race was hindered in its pursuit of one through the divisive and corrupting nature of its age-old adversary, the Jews. The Weimar Republic and Western democracies, he was convinced, had in large measure succumbed to this "rot" (Zersetzung), which broke down healthy racial communities the way bacteria attacked a healthy body. The Soviet Union had the first government supposedly permeated by Jewish influence, representing a source of infection for the rest of the

Group of Three
(Felix Nussbaum, 1944)

During the German occupation of Belgium, friends helped the artist Felix Nussbaum (1904–1944) and his family to hide. In this painting he has depicted himself as an orthodox Jew, with a prayer shawl and yarmulke; he stands before a map on which the course of the Russian front has been traced, with a hand raised as if to ward off a threat. The boy in the foreground is studying the symbols of persecution, the newspaper of the occupation and the yellow star Jews were forced to wear; the woman between them is a figure of mute suffering. The Nussbaums' hiding place was reported, and they were deported to Auschwitz on July 31, 1944, in the last transport of prisoners to reach the camp. They were killed shortly before the camp administrators stopped gassing prisoners in October 1944.

world. In Hitler's sick logic it followed inescapably that the Jews must be removed from the healthy German racial community, the "body of the people," and that the Germans must seek *Lebensraum* in the wide expanses of eastern Europe, space to which their superiority entitled them. There they would play the role of masters, while the Slavs, another allegedly inferior race, would take the part of colonial slaves. The world war had to be fought, according to this demented logic, in order to exterminate the Jews.

The German leadership thus did not see revision of the outcome of the First World War as its primary goal in this war, as many of Hitler's conservative political allies believed and as a number of people still believe today. Nor was the goal political dominance in the sense of classic European foreign policy, conquest of territory representing additional economic resources and larger markets, or release of internal tensions in military undertakings. None of the rationales for war known in the history of Europe up to that point applies to German actions in World War II. Instead the goal was, in Hitler's own words, "initiation of the final stage of battle against the mortal enemy of Jewish-Bolshevism" in the Eurasian dominions of National Socialism.

The whole war effort prior to the campaign against the Soviet Union had therefore amounted to nothing more than tactical preparations. The attack on Poland was designed to create a staging area for the *Wehrmacht*'s march to the east; the invasion of France was intended to eliminate the danger of attack from the rear, as were Hitler's efforts to reach accommodation with Great Britain by dividing up the world. As soon as Poland was conquered, the Germans had begun rounding up millions of Jews and confining them to ghettos in the major Polish cities, just as they had earlier compelled Jews within their own country to wear identifying badges. But all these measures were merely preliminary, a preparation for the next step undertaken in direct conjunction with the war on the Soviet Union: the deliberate and remorseless extermination of the Jews as a prerequisite for the establishment of German world domination.

The Nazis had already acquired some experience in mass killings; the euthanasia program had gone into operation in October 1939, in the course of which some 80,000 people with mental disabilities had been shot, gassed, or given fatal injections. The procedure was now to be extended to the Jews. It is thought that Hitler gave the order for the "final solution" to the "Jewish question" in the summer of 1941. The exact timing is a matter of controversy, for Hitler tended to pass on criminal directives orally, avoiding their inclusion in written records that could later betray him.

After about six months of technical and administrative preparations, the heads of the agencies involved met at a villa by the shores of a lake in Berlin, the *Wannsee,* on January 20, 1942, to make the final arrangements. Organized mass murder had already been under way for some time, however. Security Service units *(SD-Einsatzgruppen)* in Russia had been carrying out mass executions by firing squads since the Germans had conquered the territory, and the first euthanasia experts arrived at the Chelmno concentration camp in the fall of 1941 to provide "special treatment" to 100,000 Jews deemed incapable of forced labor. Murder began at the Belzec camp in October 1941, and gassing at Auschwitz in January 1942.

The entire organization of the mass-murder industry was based on camouflage and deception from the start; after the Catholic Church had protested against the euthanasia program, the regime committed its most heinous crimes in secret. Nevertheless, the genocide against European Jews would not have been possible without the direct or indirect participation of numerous government agencies, organizations, and departments, that is to say, a large number of people. Even if the extent of the extermination of the Jews, and the details of its operation, did not become known during the war, there were enough references to it and information about it to make the existence of the extermination campaign a matter of public knowledge within Germany. The deportations took place in full public view; the transport of Jews to the east was known, and hundreds of thousands of soldiers on home leave from the Russian front talked about mass shootings. At the very least the general population had to have some suspicions of what was occurring, but habitual defense mechanisms and fallacious justifications proved stronger than consciousness of guilt and revulsion.

12

The End of the Third Reich and a New Beginning (1942–1949)

To most German and many foreign observers, the era from 1933 to 1942 appeared as one long, unbroken ascent of German power under Hitler's leadership. Germany's star rose and then exploded like a supernova; now its energy was consumed, and it would collapse into a cold, shrunken, black lump. By midwinter of 1942–43 the military commanders of the Third Reich had shifted to a purely defensive strategy. In actual fact the turning point of the war had come in December 1941, when the German armies bogged down short of Moscow, although the participants did not realize it at the time. But after the German Sixth Army capitulated in Stalingrad on February 2, 1943, it became clear even to the German population at home that the chances of victory were receding rapidly, and from then on one defeat followed another.

The concept of "Fortress Europe" devised next by the German

The Murderers Are Among Us
(film poster, 1946)

Wolfgang Staudte directed the first German film made after the war, produced by DEFA (German Film Company) and distributed under Soviet license. It addressed the question of how war criminals should be dealt with, in both moral and practical terms. In reality 5,025 people were tried for war crimes and crimes against humanity in the three western zones, including those sentenced by the International Military Tribunal in Nuremberg, and 486 people were executed. In the Soviet zone of occupation about 45,000 trials are estimated to have taken place, although many of them were not conducted within the framework of the rule of law. About 60,000 people were found guilty of Nazi crimes in other countries.

leadership came much too late, although it remains an open question whether it could ever have succeeded. Nazi propaganda in Europe now attempted to rally volunteers from all parts of the Continent for the struggle against the Soviet Union, but without great success. The peoples of Europe, and in particular the non-Russian ethnic minorities within the Soviet Union who originally hoped German troops would liberate them, had long since realized that the rule of their new masters was no whit less oppressive and cruel than that of Stalin's minions. The German army also failed to keep the war a coalition-based effort. One by one the allies of the Third Reich dropped away, either withdrawing from the war or changing sides and joining the Reich's opponents. This forced Hitler to extend his occupation to more and more countries, such as Italy in 1943 or Hungary in March 1944.

And "Fortress Europe" had no roof. The British began their carpet bombing of cities and industrial complexes in 1942. A year later the British and American air forces controlled the skies over Germany. After the destruction of Rostock from the air in 1942, German propaganda spoke of "terror attacks," a term that accurately reflected the intentions of the Allied strategists, for the primary aim of the bombing raids was not to reduce Germany's military potential but to strike terror into the population and leave it demoralized. They had limited success in this, but the material consequences of the bombing were devastating. More than half a million civilians lost their lives in the attacks; approximately four million houses and apartments were destroyed, and the civilian populations of the major cities had to be evacuated. Cathedrals, palaces, and old town centers went up in flames, and with them a considerable portion of Germany's cultural heritage. The face of daily life in Germany changed drastically.

What did the Allies want? As the fleets of bombers reduced German cities to rubble, thereby paying the Germans back—disproportionately, indeed many times over—for the destruction their bombers had caused in the western campaign and the Battle of Britain, the Allies held a series of conferences, at which they gradually developed a concept for a postwar order in Europe. Their first object, in Winston Churchill's words, was "to prevent Germany, and particularly Prussia, breaking out upon us for the third time." In January 1943, Franklin D. Roosevelt and Churchill reached an agreement that Germany must surrender unconditionally. At the Teheran Conference in November 1943 the Big Three, including Stalin as well as Roosevelt and Churchill, decided to shift Poland westward to the Oder River, giving the Soviet Union more territory to the east, and to give the northern part of East Prussia to the Soviet Union as well. A few weeks later the demarcation lines of the future zones of occupation in Germany were decided upon. Finally, in February 1945 the main powers of the anti-Hitler coalition reached an agreement at Yalta, which was released to the public, to divide Germany and Austria into occupation zones, make Berlin and its immediate surroundings a special territory, and include France as a fourth power of occupation. In parallel to the partition of Germany into occupation zones, all of central and eastern Europe was divided into spheres of interest, although the Allies were careful not to use that phrase. The end of World War II would bring with it the end of the old Europe; in the future Europe's main role would be as a buffer zone between global powers.

The path to the Yalta accords was marked by repeated and serious disputes between the Western powers and the Soviet Union, but in view of the threat still posed by Germany, the Western Allies made concession after concession to the Soviet dictator for the sake of victory. Old, historically grounded fears of a possible entente between Russia and Germany still haunted the West, and the Hitler–Stalin pact made on the eve of the war had showed it was not out of the question. Such fears had very little to do with Hitler's actual wishes; the German dictator indeed hoped for the break-up of the enemy coalition, but for different reasons; up to the very last days before com-

An Aerial View of Dresden after
the Bombing
(photograph, 1946)

cette fois jusqu'à BERLIN

All the Way to Berlin This Time
(American poster published in France, summer of 1944)

For the Allies, World War II represented a continuation of the struggle of World War I and the earlier wars against Germany or Prussia; National Socialism was viewed as the logical culmination of the "Prussian spirit" and the "German character," and for that reason it was necessary to march "all the way to Berlin this time," and stay there. The aim was not to liberate Germany but to occupy it permanently as an enemy nation. The Joint Chiefs of Staff Directive 1067 issued to the forces of occupation, which remained in effect until 1947, described the Allies' main goal as preventing Germany from ever again becoming a threat to world peace.

mitting suicide in his bunker in Berlin, he clung to the delusion that he would be able to defeat the Soviet Union with the aid of the British.

Within the Reich, the pressure exerted by the regime increased proportionally with the military defeats. To counteract the resignation that began to spread through the German population after the defeat at Stalingrad, Goebbels delivered a speech at the Berlin Sports Palace on February 18, 1943, in which he tried to whip the public up to a frenzy of fanaticism and determination to hold out, whatever the cost. At its climax he shouted the question, "Do you want total war?" and the hand-picked audience responded with frenetic cheers of affirmation. Not only the propaganda effort but also repressive terror was stepped up. "Operation Thunderstorm," for example, which took place on August 22, 1944, was directed against approximately 5,000 former politicians and political officials of the Weimar Republic, among them Konrad Adenauer and Kurt Schumacher, who were arrested and sent to concentration camps. A new category of "National Socialist leadership officers" was created within the army, analogous to the political commissars of the Red Army, to root out the last remaining pockets of coolness toward the regime's ideology in the military. The precedence of party officials over traditional military ranks was also signaled to the civilian population by giving *Gauleiter* (NSDAP leaders of forty-two administrative districts) the title of Commissars for the Defense of the Reich. The preparations for total war culminated in the formation of the German *Volkssturm* (People's Storm) in October 1944; this was a citizen's militia comprising all males between the ages of sixteen and sixty capable of bearing arms.

Yet the regime felt threatened from within as well as from without, although there was never any strong unified resistance against National Socialist rule in Germany. This makes it difficult to determine in retrospect what constituted resistance at the time, where it began, and what forms it took. The boundaries between private nonconformism, oppositional attitudes, active resistance, and direct conspiracy were fluid. Not everyone who refused to join a party organization can be counted as a member of the resistance, while many party members found their way into the opposition, and some of them no doubt joined the party for this reason. People's behavior under the conditions of a dictatorship can rarely be seen in terms of black and white.

From the beginning Communists participated in an active struggle against the regime, although they ceased their activities temporarily at the time of the Hitler–Stalin pact. Their leaders included Arvid Harnack and his circle, known as the *Rote Kapelle* (Red Chapel), and Lieutenant Harro Schulze-Boysen, who were uncovered and executed in August 1942. Resistance by Social Democrats was fragmented, like the party organization itself during the years of exile, and therefore less effective overall. Yet many risked their lives, were caught, and were executed, among them Julius Leber and Adolf Reichwein.

Such is the nature of totalitarian regimes, however, that they cannot be brought down by ordinary citizens but only by those within the power structure itself. In this instance some high-ranking officials and military officers, most of them motived by conservative ethical principles and Christian morals, formed a group led by Carl Goerdeler, the former mayor of Leipzig, Ambassador Ulrich von Hassell, and former Army Chief of Staff Ludwig Beck. They were later joined by members of the Kreisau Circle, a group of Christian socialists led by Count Helmuth James von Moltke and Count Peter Yorck von Wartenburg. The plans these groups devised for the future of Germany strike some observers as highly conservative—even reactionary—attempts to restore the old order, especially if viewed in the light of the basic values represented in the present-day German constitution. The conspirators stood closer to the traditions of the Bismarck state than the Weimar democracy, and since this also applied to their foreign policy goals, they appeared to the Allies as hardly less dangerous than the current regime in Germany.

This was a problematic misunderstanding, for it led to a situation in which the only German opposition capable of effective action could not count on Allied support. What is crucial to any assessment of these men, however, is not their political program but their readiness to pay any price that might ensue from taking action against Hitler and his regime, and to do so not out of considerations of expediency but on ethical grounds. As Hans-Henning von Tresckow, one of the leaders of the military opposition, put it: "The assassination attempt must take place, *coûte que coûte* [let it cost what it will] . . . for what matters is no longer the practical aim; what matters is that in the eyes of the world and of history the German resistance movement has dared to risk the decisive blow. Compared to that, everything else is unimportant."

The attempted assassination on July 20, 1944, failed; Hitler was

The Greater Sacrifice
(Adolf Reich, 1943)

The painting shows a winter scene in the Ludwigstrasse in Munich, in front of the war memorial known as the *Siegestor* ("victory gate"). On the left two members of the Hitler Youth are collecting money for the Winter Relief Campaign. The two women have turned to look at a soldier with an amputated leg, while in the background a war widow pushes a baby carriage. The picture's message is ambiguous; on the one hand it provides an illustration of Hitler's words, "If anyone is in doubt about whether he should donate again, let him look around. He will see someone who has made a far greater sacrifice." On the other hand the depiction of the population's suffering is almost subversive, and in fact the painter was accused of displaying a "defeatist attitude."

only slightly injured by the bomb Colonel Claus von Stauffenberg had hidden in the Wolf's Lair, Hitler's headquarters in East Prussia, and the conspirators did not succeed in seizing control of the key positions in the power structure before news arrived that the dictator had survived. The regime took a terrible and bloody revenge not only on the conspirators themselves but also on many of their relatives who had known nothing of the plot. It had been Prussian conservatives who helped bring Hitler to power, and now it was again Prussian conservatives who tried to correct the fatal error that members of their own class had committed. They were exterminated with inhuman savagery, tortured and killed with methods of fiendish cruelty, and only the war's end not long afterward prevented more family members' deaths along with 158 direct participants.

The fact that Prussian aristocrats joined together with their previous political antagonists—workers, socialists, and trade union activists—as well as members of the middle class to fight National Socialism to the utmost offered all political and social groups in Germany after the war a common standard, one that establishes respect for human dignity as the first principle of every polity. This ultimate sense of community, which embraces the political goals of all strata and classes of society in the Federal Republic of Germany, is the legacy of the men of the 20th of July movement.

Prior to this assassination attempt, the Western Allies had opened a third front in the war with their landing in Normandy on June 6, 1944. A war on several fronts at once, which clearly overtaxed the resources of the Reich, had thus become a reality, making German defeat inevitable. Unlike Ludendorff, however, who realized and accepted that defeat was unavoidable at the end of October 1918 and thus preserved the substance of the country and the government, Hitler was determined to fight to the bitter end, even if the price was Germany's complete annihilation. According to his insane reasoning, in the event of a defeat, the German people would have shown themselves to be weaker than their enemies and would therefore deserve to perish. As Hitler's *Wunderwaffen* (miracle weapons), the V-1 and V-2 rockets, were giving rise to nebulous hopes of German victory on the western front, and as the Soviet war machine was rolling over the exhausted German army between the Memel River and the Carpathian Mountains in the east, pushing a gigantic and growing stream of refugees before it that reached the borders of Germany—as these events were taking place, Hitler and his confederates declared war on their own people in the form of summary trials and executions, orders to hold out to the death, and orders to destroy German resources: "We will leave a wasteland for the Americans, British, and Russians." Fortunately there were enough mayors and *Wehrmacht* commanders who risked their lives—and frequently lost them—to prevent such orders from being carried out. Thus the occupation of Germany by Allied troops was an act of liberation not only for the inmates of the concentration camps but also for the German people in general, even though, in view of the fate they suffered personally after the surrender, some were unable to accept this at the end of the war.

This was because the German military defeat—which was sealed with an unconditional surrender of the *Wehrmacht* at Reims on May 7, 1945, that went into effect on May 8—also represented the end of Germany as a nation state. This is the "profound paradox" described by the emigré historian Hans Rothfels: "German patriots had to wish for the day of capitulation to arrive, no matter how few illusions they might have about what lay ahead."

What lay ahead was living with the consequences of the war that had now ended. In Germany it had cost about three times as many lives as the First World War; approximately 5.5 million people had died—an alarming figure, yet all the same not as high as the losses on the other side. In Poland alone there were 6 million dead, in the Soviet Union 20 million. Of the 5.7 million Russian prisoners of war in German camps, fewer than 2 million had survived. Many Germans had nowhere to live because so many buildings had been destroyed in the bombings, especially in the large cities in the western part of the country and Berlin; people were living in ruins and cellars. There were shortages of the most basic goods and clothing, but the greatest lack was food; some times were better than others, and the situation differed from region to region, but on average the amount of food available per person varied between one-third and two-thirds of the amount necessary to stave off a continual feeling of hunger. The consequences were both widespread epidemics and a soaring crime rate; the line between legal and illegal behavior blurred when it was a question of day-to-day survival.

Added to all this was the total upheaval in daily life caused by dislocation, as Germans fled before the advancing Soviet army, as they were forcibly expelled from the occupied Polish territories and most other parts of eastern Europe, and as Germany itself was partitioned. At the end of the war and in the years immediately following, there were 12 million refugees, displaced persons, and expellees, not counting the 2 million who died in the course of this largest migration in European history. The area of German settlement had shrunk to its size in the late Middle Ages; the five-hundred-year history of German settlement in eastern Europe was eradicated; communal structures in the remaining regions were shattered or in a state of turmoil, and traditional social milieus collapsed. Equally serious was the amount of moral destruction wrought by the violent dictatorship, the war, and a full knowledge of the horrors of the mass murders committed in the extermination camps, which were only now penetrating Germans' collective awareness in unfiltered form.

Whether Germany even still existed as a nation state was an open question, but one to which most Germans were heartily indifferent. Surviving to the next day was what counted. The political and legal vacuum was ended on June 5, 1945, by an official proclamation of the four victorious powers that they had assumed supreme authority in Germany and would exercise it jointly. This Berlin Declaration—which was published in the three languages of the occupying powers and in German, so that the population could understand what it said—officially established the measures the Allies had already decided upon at their wartime conferences. It replaced the German government with an Allied Control Council consisting of the commanders-in-chief of the four powers, with headquarters in Berlin, the capital of the former Reich. The Council was responsible for matters concerning Germany as a whole, while each of the four powers could

Achtung! Schlesier!

Ich suche meine Angehörigen:
Herrn *Theodor Kameko* (Vater)
Frau *Jda Kameko* (Mutter)
Fräulein *Olga Kameko* (Schwester)
zuletzt wohnhaft in Zobten, Bez. Breslau, Strehlenerstr. 29
sowie Fräulein *Elfriede Hoffmann* und Mutter
aus Frankenthal bei Neumarkt.
Wer weiß etwas?
Nachrichten erbittet:

Walter Kameko
LEIPZIG W 31
Jahnstr. 45 I. bei Hille.

Attention, Silesians! Who Has Informatio
(handwritten notice, ca. 1945)

This is one of many notices posted by peo‐
ple searching for news of relatives with
whom they had lost touch. In the summer
1945 the roads were filled with more mi‐
grants, refugees, and displaced persons t
ever before in German history. People fro
the cities, whose homes had been destroy
in the bombing, poured into the countrysi
looking for housing and food. The great
streams of refugees fleeing before the Rec
Army were followed by thousands of Ger‐
mans expelled from Poland and Czechos
vakia. Hundreds of thousands of soldiers
were trying to return home and escape in
ternment in prisoner-of-war camps. In add
tion, 700,000 survivors of the concentrat
camps had been released, along with ab
4.2 million people from all over Europe v
had been performing forced labor. Ninety
percent of the railroad lines were unusabl
at the end of the war. All the families torn
apart by war, imprisonment, and deporta
faced a highly uncertain future.

rule and administrate its own zone of
occupation as it saw fit. The special
status of Berlin, the capital city of the
Reich, was recognized by declaring it a
separate zone with four sectors, to be
administered jointly by the Allied mili‐
tary commanders in the city.

More particular measures were decided at a conference called by
the Big Three members of the Allied coalition—the United States,
Great Britain, and the Soviet Union—on July 17, 1945, in Potsdam,
outside Berlin. Meeting at Cecilienhof Palace, President Truman,
Prime Minister Churchill, and Premier Stalin established the Oder
and Neisse rivers as a provisional border; the German territories east
of the line would be administered by Poland, and the Soviet zone of
occupation would begin to the west of it. They further legalized the
expulsion of Germans from the areas east of the Oder-Neisse line and
from Czechoslovakia and Hungary, a process that was already well un‐
der way.

As far as the treatment of Germany itself was concerned, they
agreed that "German militarism and Nazism" must be eliminated, so
that Germany could never again threaten its neighbors or world
peace. To ensure these aims, they determined that Germany should

be completely disarmed and demilitarized, all industries relating to arms production dismantled, all National Socialists removed from public office, and political life reestablished on a democratic basis. The Potsdam Agreement specifically stated that Germany was to be "treated as a single economic unit." But as each power was directed to fulfill its own reparations claims from its zone of occupation, this principle was undermined from the start. In addition, the use of terms such as "political life on a democratic basis," which meant entirely different things in East and West, led in the ensuing period to the four powers interpreting the Potsdam Agreement in widely divergent manners, as best suited their own interests.

On November 20, 1945, the chief German perpetrators of war crimes and crimes against humanity went on trial before an Allied military tribunal in Nuremberg, the site of the National Socialist Party rallies. Even though the legal basis on which the trials were conducted was controversial and remains so today, one should keep in mind that most of the men in the dock would have been found guilty of violating traditional German criminal statutes. Furthermore, this kind of trial ensured that the crimes committed by Germans during the war and in the extermination camps received the widest possible publicity, with no attempt to cover them up. In the long run, the most salutary effect of the Nuremberg trials was their elimination of any possibility that Germans could take refuge in legends of betrayal and a "stab in the back," as had happened after World War I.

Everyone was confronted with questions about responsibility for the past that extended into the private sphere. As specified in the Potsdam Agreement, every German adult was required to undergo the "de-Nazification" process, although this naturally took different forms in the various occupation zones. The most rigorous procedure took place in the American zone, as the Americans displayed the greatest zeal in spreading democracy and democratic ideology. Yet judging actions and attitudes on the basis of a questionnaire, even one containing 131 separate questions, inevitably led to errors and mistaken conclusions in some cases. The judgments handed down by the de-Nazification courts often seemed arbitrary, eliciting protests even from committed opponents of fascism, and the large number of cases on the docket resulted in a decision to deal with the minor ones first. Then as time passed and the Cold War intensified, interest in pursuing war criminals declined, so that it was often those with the most incriminating pasts who got off scot-free. That this did not help the democratization process among the German people goes without saying, and the same applies to the Allies' reparations policy, which often took the form of dismantling machinery and industrial installations for shipment to one of the Allied countries. To an embattled population enduring very difficult economic times, this looked like willful destruction of jobs, and the people reacted with bitterness.

On the other hand, political life rebounded quickly, even if only on the local level at the start. Most of the German politicians who served as mayors and district administrators—as Allied appointees to begin with and from 1946–47 on legitimized as the winners of elections—were recruited mainly from the ranks of former officials of the Weimar Republic. In the early postwar period they joined together, founding new parties and refounding old ones for the separate occupation zones. They included the German Social Democratic Party (SPD), which reconstituted itself in Hanover under the leadership of Kurt Schumacher (1895–1952), and the Free Democratic Party (FDP), which drew its members from the former liberal parties of the Weimar era, the DDP and DVP, and flourished mostly in the southwest in the early years, led by Theodor Heuss (1884–1963) and Reinhold Maier (1881–1971).

The Christian Democratic Union (CDU) was, by contrast, a completely new party, a collective movement of Christian and middle-class voters. United by their experience in resisting Nazism, its leaders hoped to overcome the religious divisions of the old prewar party system along denominational lines, and its membership covered the political spectrum from Christian labor unions to liberals and moder-

Unification Conference of the Social Democratic and Communist Parties
(photo-montage poster, April 21–22, 1946)

After the war ended, Otto Grotewohl and the other leaders of the SPD in Berlin considered it a historical necessary to work closely with the German Communist Party to achieve "unity among the working class." KPD leaders Wilhelm Pieck and Walter Ulbricht hung back, however, in the belief they had the support of the majority of the population and did not need the cooperation of the Social Democrats. After the Communists suffered catastrophic defeats in elections in Hungary and Austria in November 1945, the Soviet Union pressed the two German parties to merge. The Socialist Unity Party (SED) was officially founded at a "unification conference" held on April 21–22, 1946. Thousands of German Social Democrats who refused to participate were arrested and sent to the concentration camps—which the Soviet forces of occupation had taken over and now operated for their own purposes—where the majority of them died.

ate conservatives. From its early days it was dominated by a group from the Rhineland and Westphalia headed by Konrad Adenauer, the mayor of Cologne. Their aspirations to leadership were challenged by Jacob Kaiser and the Berlin CDU, and most other parties experienced similar rivalries. Strong tensions existed between the SPD headquarters in Hanover and the Berlin SPD leadership under Otto Grotewohl, while the Berlin-based German Liberal-Democratic

Party (LDPD) under Wilhelm Külz, former minister of the interior in the Weimar government, vied for leadership of the liberals with the FDP.

These rivalries arose in part from the still potent symbolic role of Berlin as the capital of the Reich and in part from a desire to keep pace with the rapid developments in the eastern zone, where the Soviets had encouraged the formation of political party organizations very early on. There the occupying power was of course primarily interested in furthering the German Communist Party (KPD), whose leader Walter Ulbricht (1893–1973) had returned to Berlin from Moscow a few days before the end of the war. Ulbricht's original intention was to create a civilian political leadership that would in theory, at least, represent something like a pan-German government and would raise no one-sided demands for introducing socialist or Communist-style rule.

However, this concept of a popular-front government failed. The occupying Soviets' hopes were disappointed, for the KPD attracted far fewer members than the SPD and middle-of-the-road "bourgeois" parties, and the Soviets soon altered their policies regarding political parties. In October 1945 the KPD began demanding a merger with the SPD, and the central committee of the SPD in Berlin under Otto Grotewohl came under strong pressure from the Soviets to agree. Social Democratic leaders who resisted disappeared under mysterious circumstances, never to be seen again; others were not released until much later from camps in Siberia or from Buchenwald, the concentration camp in the Soviet zone that the Soviets adapted to fit the new regime. Only one vote was taken on the merging of the two parties; it was held among SPD members in West Berlin, 82 percent of whom rejected the Soviet demands. Despite this, the Soviets forced the union of the KPD and SPD in their zone at a "unification party conference" on April 22, 1946. The resulting organization, the German Socialist Unity Party (*Sozialistische Einheitspartei Deutsch-*

lands, SED), rapidly grew into a Leninist cadre party subordinate to the Soviet Union.

The split between the three western zones and the Soviet zone of occupation became evident on other levels as well. One part of the confrontation consisted of accusations from both sides that the other was responsible for the partition of Germany—a pointless dispute at bottom, since the growing gap between the western and Soviet zones was an inevitable consequence of the international tensions between the powers themselves. In reality this antagonism had begun in 1917 and had merely been subordinated for a period to the need to combat the common enemy in the form of Hitler. It was further exacerbated by Soviet policy in eastern Europe, where the Soviet Union used its military might to consolidate its strategic geographical position and surround itself with a belt of satellite states. The Soviets signaled no limits to their expansionist aims; direct conflicts between Soviet and Anglo-American interests arose in Iran, Turkey, and Greece, resulting in a worldwide confrontation between the Soviet bloc and the Western powers.

Nowhere else did the Cold War have such a direct effect as in occupied Germany. When the United States demanded in July 1946 that the four zones of occupation be unified economically, as stipulated in the Potsdam Agreement, in order to improve the supply of goods to the population, the Soviet Union refused, calling it a measure aimed at furthering American economic imperialism. Conversely, Washington interpreted Soviet policy on Germany as an attempt to seize the whole country for the Soviet sphere of influence. Thus the American leadership decided to push ahead with unification of the western zones, even if it increased the danger of a long-term partition of Germany as a whole. This turning point in American—and British—policy was announced in a speech delivered by Secretary of State James F. Byrnes in Stuttgart on September 6, 1946, in which he urged the Germans to found a noncommunistic democratic state without delay.

· ALL OUR COLOURS TO THE MAST ·

On January 1, 1947, the American and British zones were linked to form an economic "Bizone." (The Bizone did not become the Trizone, the economic precursor of the Federal Republic of Germany, until April 8, 1949, when the French zone joined.) To stave off the threat of partition, the Bavarian state government invited the leaders of all the German state governments to a conference in Munich scheduled for June 6, 1947, but the talks collapsed before they had even started over disputes about what was to be put on the agenda.

However, such problems directly concerned only a few politicians. Ordinary Germans had worries of quite a different kind. The most pressing problems were the collapse of the economy and the struggle to find enough food from day to day. The wartime economy had put large amounts of money in circulation, but there were very few goods to buy. As a result, a black market flourished, in which most Germans

In the winter of 1946–47 the European economy was in desolate condition; simultaneously the Communists were consolidating their position in eastern Europe, Communists were participating in the governing coalition in France, Communists were poised to take control in Italy, and Greece had plunged into civil war again. Faced with this situation, the United States altered its European policy to one of containment. On June 5, 1947, Secretary of State George Marshall announced the assistance plan that was named after him, in which a defeated Germany was to be included. German inclusion was in fact a key element of the Marshall Plan. Under pressure from the Soviet Union, the countries of eastern Europe refused to participate. The poster advertises the plan's European Reconstruction Program, which cost 12.5 billion dollars.

participated in order to survive. Virtually everything was available, either for cash or barter. Cigarettes played an important role as a substitute currency; anyone with American cigarettes could trade them for unlimited amounts of bread and butter. People with no access to them had to rely on trips to the countryside to stock up on provisions, on handouts from friends who were better off, or on American charity organizations, such as C.A.R.E., whose packages began flooding the country in 1946 and saved hundreds of thousands of people from starvation.

The American government viewed the economic misery prevailing in more or less dire form throughout Europe with some alarm. At the State Department, officials feared it could aid the rise of Communism. To counteract this possibility, George C. Marshall, the new Secretary of State, offered an aid program consisting of loans, food supplies, and raw materials to all the nations of Europe. The Soviet Union rejected it emphatically at once for all the countries in its bloc, but the Marshall Plan proved extremely helpful for the economic recovery of western Europe, including the western zones of Germany. For these German zones to be included in the plan, however, fundamental changes were required, in order to normalize the ratio between available goods and the amount of money in circulation.

Thus on June 20–21, 1948, currency reform was carried out in the western zones, and simultaneously Ludwig Erhard (1891–1977), economic director of the Bizone, announced independent measures ending most production and price controls. Overnight the black market disappeared, and as the shelves began to fill with the wares people had been holding back, the administrators of the Soviet zone introduced their own currency reform, which was supposed to be extended to the whole of Berlin. Instead, however, the Western powers introduced the new *Deutsche Mark* (DM) in their sectors of the city. The Soviets responded on June 24, 1948, with a total blockade of Berlin.

In the view of British Foreign Minister Ernest Bevin, "The abandonment of Berlin would have serious, if not disastrous, consequences in Western Germany and throughout Western Europe." The Western powers based their Berlin policy on this premise, and to Moscow's surprise they responded with the largest airlift ever seen up to that time. In an unparalleled effort of manpower and organization, the Western Allies flew almost 200,000 missions into the city during the eleven months the blockade lasted; planes landed every two to three minutes at one of the three West Berlin airports, carrying a total of about 1.5 million tons of food, coal, and building materials. During this period the division of the city was accomplished. The municipal government of Berlin, which had been chosen in citywide free elections, was driven out of its offices in the Berlin City Hall by a Communist putsch in the fall of 1948, and took up new quarters in Schöneberg, a district in West Berlin. While this government in West Berlin led by Ernst Reuter (SPD) successfully resisted the pressure arising from the blockade, the Soviets installed their own set of officials in the east, headed by Friedrich Ebert (SED), son of the former president. The political division of Berlin was now complete.

The human and political drama surrounding events in Berlin drew the public's attention away from developments in Germany as a whole, where a parallel partition was also going forward. On July 1, 1948, the military governors of the three Western occupying powers formally presented to the heads *(Ministerpräsidenten)* of the West German states the Frankfurt Documents, which called for the convening of a National Assembly to write a constitution, and announced that a statute would be prepared by the powers of occupation to govern relations with a future German government. As so often in German history, it would once again be the states *(Länder)* that founded a national government. However, the minister-presidents refused to create a permanent West German nation; their creation would be provisional, until such time as a full German state became possible, and there would accordingly also be no constitution but only a "Basic Law."

Once this basis had been agreed upon, representatives of the minister-presidents met at Herrenchiemsee Palace in Bavaria and drafted a basic law that was then presented to a Parliamentary Council composed of delegates from the state legislatures. The council assembled on September 1, 1948, in a zoological museum in Bonn, under the beady glass eyes of two stuffed giraffes; later it met in a nearby teachers' training college to debate passage of the Basic Law, with Konrad Adenauer, leader of the Christian Democratic Party, in the chair. It went into effect on May 23, 1949, after formal approval by the three Western military governors.

Few contemporaries were aware that the founding of the Federal Republic of Germany represented one of the final steps in what was to be a long-term partition of the country. Adenauer himself urged the council to move along and get the final vote over with on May 8, 1949, reminding the delegates, "We're not adopting the Ten Commandments here, just a law that will be in force for an interim period." The Federal Republic thereby called into existence correspondingly saw itself as a provisional "trusteeship," a partial step toward the founding of a German nation state. The same held true of the constitution formally accepted by the German People's Council—dominated by the Socialist Unity Party—in East Berlin on October 22, 1948, although in theory it was valid for all of Germany. In this early phase of its existence the German Democratic Republic, the state formed on the basis of this constitution on October 7, 1949, also declared creation of a full German nation state to be one of its permanent goals.

TOURO

Fernexp

DER
ELEGANTE
FERIENZUG
MIT LIEGEBETT
FÜR JEDEN
GAST

Prospekte in Ihrem Reisebür

13

A Divided Nation

(1949–1990)

Two German states in the anterooms of world politics: This development put a decidedly different face on the "German question." Instead of one Germany in the heart of Europe, after 1949 there were two, located on the precarious borders of two global power blocs and as such the objects of particular favor and attention, from the United States in one case and the Soviet Union in the other. While this was particularly true of the two German states during the Cold War, it applied more or less to all the countries of Europe. Silence had descended on the Concert of Europe. In each camp the pressure from the opposite camp drew nations together, reducing the inclination to develop their own exclusive policies.

This trend was strengthened by the dawning of the nuclear age; national sovereignty acquired a new definition after the atom bomb was dropped on Hiroshima on August 6, 1945, and the Soviets success-

---

Touropa Holiday Express
(advertising poster for the German Federal Railroads, 1954)

After World War II ended, West Germans craved good food and nice homes. In the mid-1950s, the "gluttony wave" and the "home furnishings wave" were followed by a travel boom, as people sought to escape their drab, bombed-out country and enjoy the sunny climate of southern Europe. In groups organized by large travel agencies, Germans in the hundreds of thousands swarmed to the beaches of Mallorca or to Rimini; the sight of so many of them lying in rows turning pink prompted Italians to nickname the upper Adriatic coast the "Teuton Barbecue." Travel on this scale eclipsed the wildest dreams of the Nazis' "strength through enjoyment" movement.

fully exploded their first atom bomb in August 1949. After that only the nuclear powers appeared to possess real freedom of action when a crisis threatened; the sovereignty of European countries was derivative at best, guaranteed by one or the other of the two superpowers, which spread its nuclear umbrella over its own sphere of interest and dictated the political, ideological, and economic conditions that would prevail there. The traditional right of nation states to self-determination was overlaid by the politics of bipolarity, which governed the military, ideological, and economic domains. Stalin stated this principle clearly in a discussion with Yugoslav Communists in the spring of 1945: "This war is not like the wars of the past; whoever controls a territory will impose his own social system on it, as far as his army can reach. It cannot be otherwise."

The division of Europe was thus a precondition for the world peace that was born out of the Second World War. Only if both sides recognized the existing frontiers and spheres of power could the unstable balance between the superpowers be maintained. A divided Germany was an essential structural support in this edifice, and Berlin a keystone; had the architecture ever collapsed, it would have set off a third world war. For this reason Germany was paradoxically unified at the same time it was divided. On the one hand it was carved into two states that belonged to opposing blocs, but on the other the four big powers that had won the Second World War attached great importance to their sovereign authority for Germany as a whole. For this reason the Soviet troops of occupation retained the name Group of Soviet Forces in Germany into the 1980s, much to the displeasure of the government of the German Democratic Republic (GDR). In all questions of German policy including the stationing of troops on German soil, the Big Four thus had the last word, and the sovereignty of both German states necessarily remained limited in consequence.

The more things change, the more they remain the same. As the great powers maneuvered, Germany was the field on which they assembled their troops and where the war would be fought if it came to one, but also the diplomatic parquet on which strategic deals were struck to keep interests in balance and prevent war. This had been Germany's role in the center of Europe since the close of the Thirty Years' War; now it continued in a new variation.

On September 21, 1949, the three High Commissioners of the Western forces of occupation ordered the chancellor of the Federal Republic of Germany (FRG) to appear before them, so that they could solemnly present the "Occupation Statute" to the head of the new republic's government. It set down the supreme authority of the occupying powers, which took precedence over Bonn's Basic Law. To make these circumstances absolutely clear, the three representatives of the Allies wanted to stand on a red carpet during the ceremony, while the German delegation would be assigned a position to one side of the carpet. Konrad Adenauer had been chosen federal chancellor by the newly elected first German *Bundestag* (Federal Parliament) with the slimmest possible majority only a few days before. His cabinet included politicians from the Christian Democratic Union, the Free Democratic Party, and the German Party, a conservative agrarian party from the region around Hanover that was later absorbed by the CDU; the Social Democratic Party, under the leadership of Kurt Schumacher, was relegated to the benches of the opposition for the time being. The new federal chancellor, fresh from his democratic legitimation through this election, had not the slightest intention of letting the high commissioners treat him like an inferior, and he stepped right up onto the forbidden carpet, too. The Allies responded to Adenauer's gesture with tight smiles; the new federal chancellor had made it clear he intended to use every inch of the leeway available to him.

Where foreign policy was concerned, Adenauer knew very well that this leeway was narrowly circumscribed. In his first speech to the *Bundestag* on September 20, 1949, in which he stated the policies of his government, he emphasized that his primary aim was to integrate the Federal Republic, now powerless and represented in international affairs by the victorious powers, into the "western European world" as soon as possible, and to achieve sovereignty, military security, and freedom of action. He announced further that he intended to link the partial state of the FRG once and for all with the West, both culturally and philosophically, to prevent Germany from ever again pursuing a swing policy between East and West or rapprochement with the Soviet Union. The firm ties to the West envisaged by Adenauer also aimed at overcoming the divisions between France and Germany and making Germany a reliable and predictable political partner. The first chancellor of the Federal Republic was convinced that only from such a secure position would reunification become conceivable as a solution to the German question.

The course of world politics favored Adenauer's aims. The Cold War turned into a hot war when Communist North Korea attacked the southern part of the country on June 25, 1950. It seemed to the leaders of the Western world as if the Kremlin were embarking on a global offensive that could lead to a third world war. The permanent demilitarization of Germany had been one of the most important Allied war goals. Now it appeared obsolete, especially since an army had existed de facto for some time in East Germany, camouflaged under the name Barracks-based People's Police *(Kasernierte Volkspolizei)*. Could anyone know whether it was developing plans for an attack along the same lines as North Korea? The solution seemed to be a European Defense Community (EDC), an international military organization with integrated troop contingents from France, Italy, the Benelux countries, and also the FRG. In May 1950 the Bonn government had already begun confidential discussions on building up a West German army. The negotiations over creating the EDC were long and hard fought; they met with resistance in all the participating countries, and Adenauer made the situation even more difficult by insisting on a treaty that would allow Germany to participate on an equal basis with the other countries.

Nor was everyone within Germany itself willing to go along with a policy of unconditional integration into the West. In all the major parties, from the governing CDU to the opposition SPD, there were politicians who favored breaking the ties to the Western bloc and seeking to create a unified, neutral Germany between the two super-powers of the Cold War, even if this could only be achieved at the price of limited sovereignty. In the spring of 1952 this hope appeared almost within grasp: Stalin sent several notes to the Western Allies and the government of the Federal Republic in which he proposed unifying the two partial German states into a neutral whole to be placed under the control of the Big Four, with strictly limited armed forces; it would be a democracy based solely on "democratic and peace-loving parties"—whatever that might mean from a Soviet per-spective. The Western powers rejected Stalin's proposal, and the gov-ernment of the Federal Republic concurred unconditionally in this rejection, convinced that integrating West Germany into the Western bloc was more important than uniting both parts in a weak whole wa-vering between East and West. But even if Bonn had taken a different view, it would not have altered the majority decision in Washington, London, and Paris.

Was this a missed opportunity for German unity? The discussion has continued up to the present day, and it will not end until the So-viet archives are opened and the real intentions of the Soviet Union are revealed. It is probable that the Allied decision was based on accu-rate assumptions, however; the Soviet campaign occurred in the deci-sive months before the Federal Republic joined the Western security and economic communities, and almost everything suggests Stalin's aim was to prevent its integration into the Western pacts and the for-mation of an EDC at the last minute. The policymakers of the Fed-eral Republic did not fail to seize an opportunity to achieve German

unity by making the entire country neutral; they never in fact had that option.

The EDC treaty was signed on May 26, 1952, but broke down two years later when the French National Assembly refused to ratify it; the majority of the delegates saw it as encroaching too far on French sovereignty. However, by then it was too late to undo the integration of West Germany into the Western alliance. On May 5, 1955, the Treaties of Paris went into effect, the most important of which regulated the Federal Republic's entry into the North Atlantic Treaty Organization (NATO). (NATO had been created on April 4, 1949, as a military alliance between Canada, Great Britain, France, Iceland,

Divided into 3? Never!

(enamel on tin, "Curatorium for an Indivisible Germany," ca. 1960)

Whereas the GDR and the Soviet Union regarded the status of the two German states as equal and the Oder-Neisse line as the permanent border, in the West German view Germany theoretically continued to exist "within the frontiers of December 31, 1937," in other words, within the area established by the Treaty of Versailles and the plebescites in Schleswig, Upper Silesia, and the Saar. This was the definition of German territory recognized by the Allies in London on November 14, 1944, and reflected in the Potsdam Agreement as well as in Article 116 of the Basic Law, pending "final settlement in a peace treaty." All the same, the West German government avoided using the term "frontiers of 1937" after the Eastern treaties went into effect in 1972; and since the inner-German basic treaty of the same year, the call for reunification on these terms, as laid down in the preamble of the Basic Law, has been regarded as superseded.

Norway, Denmark, Italy, Portugal, and the Benelux countries under U.S. leadership, with the signatories agreeing "that an armed attack against one or more of them in Europe or North America shall be considered an attack against them all," and that they would provide mutual military assistance in such an event. Greece and Turkey had joined in 1952.)

From the German perspective in 1955, membership in NATO meant not only security but also a return to sovereignty, which was granted by the Western powers in the *Deutschlandvertrag* (Germany Treaty) as a revised version of one of the Paris agreements came to be known in German. It was limited sovereignty, however, since the victors of World War II still reserved special rights in all questions of policy regarding Germany, as well as the right to station their troops on German soil. In addition, the FRG pledged not to manufacture a series of strategic weapons systems, including nuclear weapons. From the Allied perspective the accession of the Federal Republic to NATO looked somewhat different; according to Lord Ismay, the NATO Secretary General, the purpose of the alliance was "to keep the Americans in, the Russians out, and the Germans down."

This was the lesson drawn from the history of the twentieth century: If Germany, the unpredictable power in the heart of Europe, was to be tamed and made reliable, it could not be excluded from the community of nations and humiliated; that had been the decisive flaw

Learning from the Soviet People Means Learning to Be Victorious
(poster, Leipzig, 1951)

The Western policy of integrating Germany into its international pacts was pushed ahead after the Korean War broke out. The GDR responded to this in its propaganda efforts with the image of two ships: On the left the leaky pirate ship of the West, with the Marshall Plan, NATO, and Western bloc inscribed on its sail, and Churchill, de Gaulle, Franco, and the French Foreign Minister Schuman on board, desperately bailing; Adenauer, in a Nazi uniform, has already fallen overboard. Bearing down on this pitiful craft is a mighty Soviet ship flying the flag of peace and carrying representative heroes of the Soviet-bloc countries.

No—Therefore CDU
(campaign poster for the parliamentary elections of 1949)

The threat of Soviet Communism was experienced as very real in Germany, given the oppression and loss of political and human rights prevailing in the Soviet zone and Soviet expansion in eastern Europe. Such fears contributed significantly to the Federal Republic's integration into western Europe, and it was therefore tempting to exploit them for partisan political purposes, even though this seriously damaged the relationship between the governing coalition and the opposition parties.

in the peace order of 1919. Instead it was crucial to bind Germany—for the time being that meant West Germany—so firmly to the Western community that these ties could not be undone, even if political conditions should change. This applied not only to military pacts but equally to the economic and political spheres. Western Europe banded together as a result of the catastrophes Europeans had experienced in this century, and from a recognition that by forging economic, military, and political links countries would be forced to abandon isolated national policies.

When Winston Churchill called for the creation of a "United States of Europe" in a speech in Zurich on September 19, 1946, and said it should be based on a partnership between France and Germany—a shocking idea at the time—he did not envision Great Britain as a member. This was thoroughly in keeping with the spirit of classic British "balance of power" policy, which sought to keep the restless Continent across the Channel quiet with a system of pacts, so that Britain could safely devote itself to its far-flung interests overseas. But the collapse of the British and French colonial empires during the 1950s made it clear that the era of European world domination was gone for good; Europe had been thrown back on its own resources and could have some say in the alliance with the United States only if it gathered and concentrated its remaining might. The first step taken to link Europe together economically was the founding of the European Coal and Steel Community (ECSC) in 1951, which placed production of both commodities in France, Germany, Italy, the Netherlands, Belgium, and Luxemburg under a single oversight body. It was followed by the union of these same countries, known as The Six, in the European Economic Community (EEC) and the European Atomic Energy Community (EURATOM) on March 25, 1957. The most recent developments in this process have been the creation of the European Union (EU), with its vast superstructure of commissions, councils, general directorships, and bureaucrats, and the European Parliament in Strasbourg.

For the present-day observer the world of the original founding is long gone, and with it the florid, hopeful rhetoric that accompanied the first steps toward European unification. In retrospect the bombastic oratory seems just as improbable as the willingness of all the first participants to relinquish some of their national independence, as if it were a matter of course. The extent to which the world had changed became apparent when Chancellor Adenauer and French President Charles de Gaulle (1890–1970) conducted a joint review of French and German troops after signing the treaty on Franco-German cooperation on January 22, 1963; the review was held on the fields of Champagne, where so much blood had flowed in battles between the two countries. From the bitterest of enemies to the closest of allies—after centuries of fateful entanglements, this represented a profound turning point in European history.

The fact that the Western community of nations was willing to include the Federal Republic after World War II had far-reaching consequences. From the start, American support for the Adenauer government lent considerable prestige to the new democracy within Germany itself. For the first time in German history, being a democrat was equivalent with success. Who can say how the first German democracy, the Weimar Republic, would have fared if a man such as Ebert, Stresemann, or even Brüning had enjoyed the goodwill of the Allies, as Konrad Adenauer did after World War II? The development of the West German democracy owes its success in part to this factor, although it was certainly aided by the "economic miracle."

At the outset the prognosis for an economic boom was not good. In the winter of 1949–50 unemployment reached heights reminiscent of the worst years of the Weimar Republic, and food rationing, which had been introduced in 1939, did not end until March 1950. Then, however, the outbreak of the Korean War brought a worldwide economic upswing that spurred considerable growth in the West German economy. After years of deprivation, Germans had an all but insatiable appetite for consumer goods, and German industries, battered by war damage and Allied dismantling, invested large sums in new production facilities. The Marshall Plan provided the necessary capital and set the course toward increased economic ties with the West. Then during the Korean War, when the United States and western European nations—Germany's chief foreign competitors—had to devote much of their production capacities to arms manufacture, German exports were able to penetrate world markets. Finally, German labor unions' willingness to hold down wage demands in the first few years of the Federal Republic's existence paid off. Although wages increased at a slightly lower rate than the gross national product, the pay of the average worker nonetheless grew by 5 percent annually. After the greatest defeat in their history, Germans experienced the greatest economic upturn in their history.

The West German government used its economic leverage to introduce social policy reforms little short of revolutionary. The Federal War Victims Relief Act *(Bundesversorgungsgesetz)*, passed in 1950, provided assistance to three million people, and the Equalization of Burdens Act of 1952 initiated an unprecedented redistribution of wealth within the population, in order to indemnify those who had lost their property and savings as a result of the war, expulsion, and expropriation in the East.

The Federal Displaced Persons Act, Workplace Labor Relations Act, Federal Compensation Act, pension reform, immediate payment of wages in case of illness, child care allowances—the basis of the laws creating the social welfare state as Germans know it today—stem from the Adenauer era, a period when people believed that unlimited economic growth was possible and that the country would remain able to afford such programs indefinitely.

The inner stability of German democracy is closely related to the "economic miracle" and social policies of the 1950s. The total West German population numbered 47 million; this included 10 million expellees and displaced persons from the German regions in the East, Czechoslovakia, and Hungary whom the Federal Republic had absorbed, just as it would later absorb a further three million refugees from the GDR. Extremist political parties existed on both the right and left, but their chances of attracting significant numbers of voters were small, since Germany's prosperity had given such an enormous boost to the process of democratization. "Bonn isn't Weimar"—this was the phrase used to explain the almost inexplicable, namely the transformation of an entire people within the span of fifty years. All the passions, the fanaticism, and convulsions of the Weimar Republic that caused 22 million people to cast their votes for the Communist and National Socialist Parties in the March elections of 1933 seemed to have been swallowed up, the way the earth absorbs rain.

They had been replaced by the republic in Bonn, which was un-emotional, rational, sober—quite boring, in fact—and a marvel of stability. Two slogans with which the Christian Democratic Party of Konrad Adenauer and his successful Economics Minister, Ludwig Er-hard (1891–1977), won election after election were "Affluence for Everybody" and "No Experiments." Most citizens had had their fill of politics—the sociologists dubbed them a "skeptical generation"—and instead devoted themselves to their private lives and hard-earned pleasures, investing in homes, Volkswagen "bugs," and vacations in Mallorca. The old patriarch in the Palais Schaumburg (the official residence of the federal chancellor) could look after the nation.

The great majority of prominent figures in West German cultural life, from the literary Group 47 to the opinion-makers at the weeklies *Der Spiegel* and *Die Zeit,* felt alienated from a government that ap-peared to them stolid, materialistic, and backward-looking. This was nothing new; the cultural avant-gardes of both the Weimar Republic and the kaiser era had viewed themselves as opposition movements in a similar manner, and a fundamental antagonism between an "intellec-tual elite" and a "power elite" seems to be a defining characteristic of the modern period in Europe generally. What *is* surprising in retro-spect is how insubstantial and derivative most of the cultural output of the Federal Republic appears in comparison with that of the Wei-mar era. The few exceptional figures, among them the poet Paul Celan and the novelist Günter Grass, tended to be writers whose roots lay farther to the east.

The other German state, the German Democratic Republic, had little to offer that could match the attractiveness of this robust and

WEGWEISER
durch den
AUS-LASTEN-GLEICH

Kriegssachschaden
Sparerschaden

Ostschaden

Vertreibungsschaden

Sowjetzonenflüchtlinge

Grenzen des Deutschen Reiches 1937 ▬

Guide to the Equalization of Burdens Act
(pamphlet, Bayreuth, 1955)

The Equalization of Burdens Act passed by the *Bundestag* on May 16, 1952, over the opposition of the Social Democrats and West German Communist Party, resulted in the greatest redistribution of wealth in German history. Every West German with a total net worth of more than 5,000 DM at the time of the 1949 currency reform was taxed at 5 percent of the total sum, payable in 30 yearly installments. The yield—by 1983 it amounted to approximately 126 billion marks—was paid out to compensate refugees and expellees for the losses they had suffered, as well as citizens whose property had been destroyed in the war. These funds helped thousands of people make a new start in the West after the war and become integrated into West German society.

Map key: Black = War damage, loss of savings; Light gray = losses in the East; Light gray and white = losses through expulsion; Dark gray = refugees from the Soviet zone successful model. The GDR was the westernmost outpost of the Soviet sphere of influence and as such was regarded by Stalin and his successors as a strategic pillar of their system. Its creation in 1949 was consequently more than just a reaction to the founding of the FRG. The GDR's first head of state was the Communist Wilhelm Pieck (1876–1960) and the head of government was the former Social Democrat Otto Grotewohl (1894–1964), both later members of the SED. However, the man with real power—if one discounts the "friends" in the Soviet Union—was First Deputy Minister-President Walter Ulbricht (1893–1973), who step-by-step took over all key positions in both the party and the state.

The legitimation of the GDR was weak from the beginning. Although the government was able to reawaken a great deal of dormant idealism through its promise to establish socialism, this resulted in neither free elections nor economic success. The Soviet model was visible in all areas of public and political life. The SED, headed by the Politburo of the Central Committee, exercised control over the government, society, and the centrally planned economy. The Ministry for State Security, created in 1950 on the model of Moscow, was organized along military lines and strove to nip all opposition in the bud by establishing a network of spies throughout the country. "Enemies of the state" were arrested on nebulous charges and occasionally without any charges at all. The militarization of public life went beyond what was necessary to run the National People's Army; it was a form of political *Gleichschaltung* of the whole population, serving to create and enforce uniformity, as did the rituals of an ever-expanding cult of the state. Although people in the GDR worked very hard, the standard of living and quality of products remained considerably below Western standards. Production levels in nationally owned companies and agriculture between the Elbe and Oder rivers sank to far below prewar levels, yet despite this the economy of the GDR was considered by far the most successful within the Council for Mutual

Economic Assistance (COMECON), the Eastern counterpart of the European Economic Community.

At the second party conference of the SED in July 1952 it was announced that socialism would have to be built under the conditions of the "intensifying class struggle" that Marxist doctrine declared was inevitable. The penitentiaries filled with the victims of arbitrary judicial verdicts; agriculture was collectivized, the middle class effectively destroyed, and a one-sided build-up of heavy industry accompanied by drastic price increases and a 10 percent increase in production norms for industrial workers. Ulbricht's radical course appeared risky to the Soviets, and in June 1953 the coercive measures were suddenly rescinded on Moscow's instructions.

The "leaders of the working class" thought of everything except the workers, whose increased norms were not reduced. The first to go on strike on June 17, 1953, were construction workers on large building sites along the Stalin-Allee, intended to become a showcase for socialism. The strike swiftly spread to other industries in the GDR. It began mainly with demands for better economic and social conditions, but soon the mood shifted to one of general hostility toward the SED regime. Demands were raised for West German political parties to be allowed in the GDR, and for free and secret elections. The strike turned into a national protest movement, and the regime was able to stay in power only by calling for Soviet tanks, which crushed the rebellion. For all the bitterness it left behind, the uprising was not a complete failure. The population and the regime had tested one another, learning the other's strengths and weaknesses; the SED leadership now knew what its limits were and how important it would be to satisfy the population's needs for basic material goods if the party dictatorship were to survive. The entire world had witnessed that Communist rule in the GDR would vanish in a puff of smoke if not backed up by Soviet tanks rolling through the streets in times of crisis.

It was now also clear that the GDR had no chance to prevail in a direct competition with the Federal Republic for legitimation. When

Handing Out Party Membership Cards
(Hans Mrozcinski, 1953)

By 1952 the SED had established itself so firmly in East Germany that Walter Ulbricht was able to announce at the Second Party Conference that the building of socialism was proceeding "according to plan." In practice this translated not into the introduction of new ideas but into adaptation to the antiquated system of Soviet Stalinism. The conference passed a motion requiring "even more thorough" study of Stalin's writings. In addition to the cult of Stalin, the SED leadership concentrated on creating cadres, promoting criticism and self-criticism, and control from above by Party organizations as the most effective means of cementing their hold on power.

it furthermore became evident that the Federal Republic's ties to Western security organizations were irreversible, the Soviet Union shifted its stance in 1955, advancing a new theory that the "German question" had been permanently solved through the creation of two German states with different sociopolitical systems. This made reunification of Germany through integration into the West impossible. Policy in the GDR underwent a corresponding transformation: Clearly recognizing its inability to keep pace in political and economic competition with the FRG, the GDR rejected the goal of reunification under the existing prospects. In these circumstances it was only logical that later, after 1974, the GDR went on to proclaim itself a "socialist nation" in a "socialist German state," thereby categorically denying the existence of a national community that included West Germany—at least as long as socialism had not established itself there, too.

In reality, however, the bright lights of West Berlin exercised an almost magical attraction for the people of the German Democratic Republic, with the result that the stream of refugees across the border grew larger and larger, reaching a total of 1.65 million by 1961, a figure equivalent to the entire population of East Berlin. Over the long term the Soviet Union could not go on permitting so many people to "vote with their feet," in Lenin's phrase. Even more dangerous than the loss of people and productive capacity was the loss of face suffered daily by "socialism as it actually exists." In October 1958 Nikita Khrushchev, the new ruler in the Kremlin, demanded that the Western Allies withdraw from Berlin and relinquish control over the access routes through the GDR; Berlin would become a "free city." After his election President Kennedy responded by formulating the three essentials for Berlin from the American point of view: freedom for the population, the continued presence of Western troops, and free access by air, water, rail, and the autobahns. The war of nerves over the city escalated until on the night of August 13, 1961, East German soldiers and paramilitary forces dug trenches and erected barbed-wire fences around the free sector of Berlin. During the next few weeks a solid wall of cement through the center of the city was added to these barriers. From then on anyone trying to flee to West Berlin risked being shot by the border guards.

Quite apart from its lethal and intimidating effects, the Berlin Wall created clarity. Its construction represented a one-sided violation of the city's status, which the Western Allies could not have prevented except by risking war. The Cuban missile crisis, which brought the world to the brink of nuclear war in 1962, made the situation even clearer: The price of peace was an understanding on each side that the other's sphere of influence was inviolable. The world powers' agenda was now detente instead of confrontation. By insisting on reunification and its status as sole representative of all Germans, the Federal Republic, until then the United States' most loyal ally against the Soviet Union, was becoming a mounting obstacle in the great powers' search for equilibrium. The Hallstein Doctrine, which called for the Federal Republic to break off diplomatic relations with every country that sent diplomats to East Berlin, proved a dead end. Especially in the Arab world, where leaders calculated that support from the Soviet Union could be worth more to them than anything Bonn could give, the inclination grew to recognize the GDR and accept a rupture with the FRG as part of the bargain.

Within the country signs were pointing toward change as well. In October 1963 Chancellor Konrad Adenauer—affectionately known as *der Alte,* "the old man"—resigned, bringing the first postwar era to a close. His successor, Ludwig Erhard, the popular "father of the economic miracle," and his party, the CDU, won the parliamentary elections on September 19, 1965, in conjunction with its Bavarian sister party, the Christian Social Union, falling only four seats short of an absolute majority. However, the Free Democratic Party (FDP), their partner in the governing coalition, lost a quarter of its seats, while the opposition SPD under its charismatic leader Willy Brandt (1913–1992) posted significant gains. Furthermore, Erhard did not succeed in turning his success at the polls into lasting policies. Part of his strategy for victory had been to promise voters massive increases in government entitlement programs, but now government expenditures began rising at a faster rate than the gross national product. An economic recession added to the budget difficulties, and Erhard, who had once made vigorous consumption his campaign slogan, was now forced to preach moderation—in vain. His government finally lost its majority because the FDP refused to share responsibility for the growing budget deficit and left the coalition on October 27, 1966.

The Grand Coalition between the CDU/CSU and SPD that followed under Chancellor Kurt Georg Kiesinger (1904–1994) represented a transition. While the government's economic policies met with success—the recession ended, and new tax regulations helped to strengthen and prolong the economic upturn—the partners were too heterogeneous for the coalition to last. In the area of German and eastern European policy, both the SPD and FDP were prepared to follow the signals toward detente coming from Moscow, Washington, and Paris and to recognize the current "realities," namely the division of the Continent and with it the partition of Germany. This meant reaching some kind of settlement for "regulated co-existence" with the German Democratic Republic. The Kiesinger government in fact took some steps in this direction by discarding the Hallstein Doctrine and establishing diplomatic relations with Romania and Yugoslavia, and also by entering into direct talks with Moscow. In addition, the West German cabinet decided in May 1967 to accept and respond to communications from the GDR government. This new realism went too far for numerous CDU/CSU politicians, particularly the leadership of the CSU. Kiesinger managed to hold his cabinet together by achieving a consensus to ignore the problems for the time being.

At this point not only policy on eastern Europe and Germany seemed stranded, but the ship of state as a whole. A fundamental shift in the political and cultural climate of West Germany had begun in the early 1960s. The rising generation regarded the values of its parents as obsolete and suspect, in a repetition of the generational conflict that typically occurs in German history every fifty years, be it the *Vormärz* movement of the 1840s, the *fin de siècle,* or the Weimar era. Once again a young generation found itself unable to endure the attitudes of its elders, while the elders saw themselves as rational and enlightened, stripped of illusions but with a willingness to compromise, and prepared to accept the limitations on what could be achieved. Young Germans delivered a scathing critique of the society in which they were growing up, heaping scorn on the pragmatism of the Adenauer era, the conservative-restorative foundations of the early postwar republic—which allowed many officials, judges, and diplomats from the Nazi era to continue their careers untouched—the cultural stagnation accompanying the growth of prosperity, the defamation of leftist and radical ideas, which had been going on for decades, and the frenzied consumerism of a generation seeking to compensate for the psychological and material deprivations it had endured during the war and immediate postwar years.

Just as a delayed shock reaction to the industrialization of Europe had set in at the start of the twentieth century and led to radical new views on how life should be lived, so too it appeared in the early 1960s as if it took a later generation fully to absorb the horrors and crimes of the National Socialist era. A deep surge of moral outrage surfaced in West German society among thoughtful people; intellectuals, university students, opinion-makers, teachers, professors, and journalists were overcome by a need to make up for the failure of their mothers and fathers to resist, and to demonstrate their abhorrence of what Germans had done. Only so, they felt, could they avoid being implicated in the crushing burden of guilt for the most recent chapter of German history.

A wave of protest swept across Germany, borne on a tide of antifascist moral indignation and set in motion when a student participating in a demonstration against a state visit to West Germany by the Shah of Iran was shot and killed by a West Berlin policeman on June 2, 1967. The protesters wanted to tear down the "fossilized structures" of society, expose the institutions of liberal German democracy as bastions of "everyday fascism," unmask the Establishment and replace it with an enlightened "counter-elite." For several years the "extra-parliamentary opposition" (*Außerparliamentarische Opposition,* or *APO*) mounted protests approaching civil insurrections at universities and elsewhere; Marx and Lenin, long relegated to the status of outworn, cynically manipulated idols in eastern Europe, experienced a second brief heyday in the liberal West. The sparks of rebellion failed to ignite, however, because the workers—the pillars of a new socialist society according to Marxist hopes—now had a great deal more to lose than their chains, and because the dream of a cultural revolution in the Federal Republic on the model of Maoist China was nothing more than a grotesque fancy, completely out of touch with the realities of daily life. The APO quickly splintered into countless small political sects, some of which were absorbed by the peace movement of the late 1970s and others by the terrorist underground.

The fundamental mood of the country had altered, however, as became apparent in the *Bundestag* elections on September 28, 1969. The SPD, which presented itself as the party of change in contrast to the ruling CDU, won more than 40 percent of the vote for the first time in its history, and its leader, Willy Brandt, reached an agreement with Walter Scheel, head of the FDP, to form a governing coalition.

The era of this coalition, which lasted from 1969 to 1982 under chancellors Willy Brandt and Helmut Schmidt, can be regarded as a kind of counterpart to the Adenauer era. Adenauer's goal of integration with the West was followed by Brandt's Eastern policy, which aimed at reducing tensions and normalizing relations between West Germany and the Soviet bloc states of eastern Europe. His ultimate aim was to secure peace by creating a mesh of pacts recognizing the partition of Germany, in which the Federal Republic would be firmly embedded. Domestically Brandt countered Adenauer's program of "No Experiments" with his own call to "Risk More Democracy" in reforms and greater cultural openness. While some decisions in the areas of education and family policy seemed questionable and overly

Alle
reden vom
Wetter.

Wir nicht.

SDS SOZIALISTISCHER DEUTSCHER STUDENTENBUND

ideological, the overall policy was a resounding success, creating a dialogue between the Bonn government and its liberal and leftist critics, who had responded to Adenauer's efforts to "restore the old order" with coolness. Now they became a dominant intellectual force in the altered climate of opinion of the 1970s. Adenauer and Brandt belong together in the history of West Germany; Brandt built on Adenauer's beginnings, and they represent two sides of the same coin.

The new Eastern policies did not originate with the Germans, however, but rather with the superpowers. President Nixon and Soviet Foreign Minister Andrei Gromyko had declared that the tensions surrounding Berlin should be reduced through talks, and on March 26, 1970, representatives of the Four Powers met in the headquarters of the Allied Control Council in Berlin to negotiate a Berlin accord. It was finally concluded on September 3, 1971, and led to considerable easing of the situation in West Berlin, an island surrounded by the GDR. Had a CDU-led government been in office in West Germany, it could hardly have ignored this new phase of detente, but Brandt's government had far fewer reservations in following the lead of the more powerful Western Allies and agreeing to nonaggression pacts with Moscow and Warsaw. Just as Adenauer had earlier accepted the wishes of the Western Allies for German integration with the West, because he was convinced it was for the best, so now Brandt vigorously pursued rapprochement with the Soviet bloc states and the GDR, not only because this was in accord with the wishes of his American allies, but because he himself believed it was urgently necessary.

The debate in the *Bundestag* over these "Eastern treaties" reached its climax on March 22, 1972, a shining hour in German parliamentary history comparable to the National Assembly's epic legislative duels of 1848–49 in St. Paul's Church. For the first time in decades legislators grappled with the questions of what Germany really was, and what its future should be. Speakers from the governing parties praised the opportunities that "normalization" between East and West would create for Germany, while speakers from the opposition CDU stressed the dangers. The focus of the discussion lay not on matters such as the exchange of ambassadors and what form West German relations with eastern Europe would take but on the future of Germany within Europe: Did German reunification "within the borders of 1937" take precedence, as the Christian Democratic opposition insisted? The treaties certainly made that possibility appear more remote. Or should priority be given to peace and detente throughout Europe, as the governing coalition argued, even if the price had to be abandonment of German hopes for reunification? Was Germany's goal still to become a unified nation again, or did that now belong to the past?

As the legislators talked of several possible futures for Germany, several interpretations of the past naturally emerged. Four very different understandings of German history dominated the debate. Richard von Weizsäcker, speaking for the opposition, argued that all German policy must be directed at recreating the German nation state as Bismarck had founded it in 1871. Alluding to Ernest Renan's famous definition of a nation ("a vast solidarity, constituted by knowledge of the sacrifices that we have made in the past and of those we are willing to make in the future"), Weizsäcker described Germany as "the quintessence of a shared past and future, of language and culture, of consciousness and will, of government and territory. With all its flaws, with all its errors arising from the spirit of the times, and yet with a common will and consciousness, this nation of ours was given its stamp in the year 1871. It is from this, and from this alone, that we today have a sense that we are Germans. It has not yet been replaced by anything else."

Weizsäcker was vehemently contradicted by speakers from all camps. A speaker from the SPD pointed to the difference between a state and a nation, observing that a great majority of the nation had been oppressed by Bismarck's state. Those wishing to shape the future with reference to Germany's past, he continued, should rather seek to carry on the struggle for freedom represented by the Peasants' Wars, the Enlightenment, the workers' movement, and the resistance against Hitler.

Several delegates from southern Germany who took the floor saw themselves in an entirely different historical context. In their view, Germany was actually nothing but an assemblage of various states, regions, and cities—Prussia, Bavaria, Württemberg, Saxe-Coburg-Gotha, and many others—which came together to form a nation state only very late in their history, and then only for a short time. And finally, the Social Democrat Carlo Schmid referred to the German nation state as a historical form of community that had once existed but was now virtually obsolete, no more than a preliminary step on the way to the nation of Europe.

Writers' Congress in Stuttgart
(press photograph, 1970)

No previous federal chancellor had ever been seen in the company of writers and poets, as Willy Brandt is here at a conference attended by the authors Günter Grass, Heinrich Böll, and Bernt Engelmann. In the early 1970s the sense of moral mission felt by a small literary elite and the new political climate overlapped and appeared to be leading toward a new unity among political and intellectual leaders. For many observers the key figure in this constellation was Willy Brandt.

For the time being he appeared to have the last word. The Eastern treaties were followed by the inner-German Treaty on the Basis of Relations (*Grundlagenvertrag*) of December 21, 1972; proceeding from the assumption that two German states existed, it established "neighborly relations" between them and declared the existing borders inviolable. Soon thereafter both German states were admitted to the United Nations with equal rights. Both sides had emphasized their differing views on "fundamental questions, including the national question," in the treaty, but in practical terms a lasting solution to the German question appeared to have been found.

It had not. While politicians, scholars, and journalists vied with one another—in a rare consensus—to describe the existence of more than one German state in Europe and the border between them as the historical norm, as the price that had to be paid for the hubris of the National Socialist era, and last but not least as an unavoidable sacrifice for world peace, people continued to die at the Wall, and to bleed to death after being shot by guards or wounded by automatic firing devices or mines along the borders. Those wanting to exercise their right to travel outside the country freely—guaranteed in the United Nations Convention on Human Rights which the GDR had just ratified—could expect harassment, official discrimination against all their relatives, and prison sentences. After East Germany had signed the inner-German basic treaty and the Final Act of the Helsinki Conference on Security and Cooperation in Europe, an opposition existed within the GDR prepared to demand respect for human rights and the right to travel freely; the existence of this opposition disturbed the new pragmatic harmony between the two Germanys. "Change through rapprochement" was the formula that Egon Bahr, Willy Brandt's adviser on German policy, had developed as early as 1963; it implied that Communist regimes could not be eliminated, only changed. Thus in relations with the GDR, Bahr believed, it was important to stabilize the SED regime. Only then would the GDR government feel confident and secure enough to grant the population greater freedom.

There was certainly something to be said for the inclination to neglect fundamental principles of liberty and democracy in the pursuit of a somewhat Machiavellian *realpolitik* in dealings with the GDR. At all events it enabled the West German government to buy the release of tens of thousands of political prisoners from East German jails and negotiate some easing of restrictions in travel across the border. Even Willy Brandt's sensational resignation on May 6, 1974, brought about by an incredibly stupid espionage operation of the GDR Ministry for State Security within the chancellor's staff, did not alter official inner-German relations. Nor did the changeover on September 17,

1982, when the SPD–FDP coalition broke down and Helmut Kohl (CDU) became chancellor at the head of a CDU–FDP coalition, have any effect on the German question or the way it was viewed by West German government officials or newspaper editors. In 1987 Erich Honecker, head of the East German government and general secretary of the SED, made an official visit to the Federal Republic. The press photographs published around the world showing Kohl and Honecker, with deadpan expressions, jointly reviewing an honor guard of the *Bundeswehr,* signaled that relations in central Europe were now on a normal and stable footing.

It is the case in politics and history that nothing lasts longer than a provisional solution, while nothing is more fragile than a situation designed to last. German unity was already well on the way to becoming a reality when the chancellor and chairman of the Council of Ministers were shaking hands. Where the road began is not entirely clear, but it must have been somewhere in the forests of White Russia. It was there that American spy satellites first registered the appearance of ultramodern Soviet intermediate-range mobile missiles in 1976. The unsettling aspect of this discovery was the fact that these missiles threatened Europe and western Asia but not the United States.

Helmut Schmidt, federal chancellor at the time and unlike his predecessor not a visionary but a hard-headed pragmatist, was among the first Western politicians to grasp the implications: These weapons made it possible to attack Europe by circumventing the American nuclear umbrella. They created the eventuality of a war in Europe that would not threaten the North American continent; as a result Europe could be strategically decoupled from the United States and became vulnerable to both political and military blackmail. Soviet leader Leonid Brezhnev appeared to be pursuing a dual strategy, in which the Soviet Union was building up a new threat to strategic balance behind a curtain of friendly diplomatic overtures. The Soviet invasion of Afghanistan in December 1979 increased suspicions in the West. NATO responded with a "double track" decision to station corresponding in-

Nuclear Power? No Thanks!

(poster of the Citizens' Initiative of the Rhine-Main-Neckar Region, Frankfurt/Main, 1980)

During the 1970s and '80s Europe underwent a profound shift in values. The earlier cult of technology and economic progress gave way to deep pessimism about the future of civilization. This shift was nowhere more apparent than in West Germany, where citizens' initiatives sprang up everywhere opposing nuclear power plants, expansion of airports, construction of new autobahns, and government censuses. Germans, who had appeared to be models of obedience toward authority, now set about astonishing the rest of the world with their antigovernment militancy.

termediate-range missiles in western Europe, and thereby open a European nuclear umbrella under the larger American one.

A public-opinion debate over implementation of the NATO decision erupted in Europe; it was particularly ferocious in Germany. A peace movement formed that vehemently opposed the stationing of Western missiles in Germany and mobilized hundreds of thousands of pacifistically minded citizens. When some factions of the governing parties lent this opposition their support, the realist Helmut Schmidt could no longer feel sure he had the backing of his own party; this played a major role in his departure as chancellor and replacement by Helmut Kohl, leader of the CDU. It is one of Kohl's achievements as chancellor that he pushed through deployment of the new missiles over considerable public opposition; equally, the peace movement deserves credit for making sure that no one could accuse Germany of being bellicose and aggressive. Both actions, the upgrading of missile systems and demonstration of a firm resolve for peace, in fact went hand in hand and sent an unmistakable signal to Moscow.

In addition, after Ronald Reagan was elected president of the United States, the Western superpower altered its policy toward the Soviet Union. Not content to continue the poker game with the Russians over intermediate-range missiles, the new administration proposed another round of rearmament, involving installation of a missile-defense system that would make the United States immune to nuclear attack. It was Reagan's express intention to force the Soviet Union to arm itself to death, and in European intellectual circles it was customary to express outrage over this and ridicule the former actor in the White House. However, Reagan's policy of confrontation met with success that no one had anticipated. The Soviet Union staked everything on this one issue and forced arms production to the limit, sending the country into a spiraling economic collapse. The war in Afghanistan, which dragged on and imposed further enormous costs, was the final straw.

Mikhail Gorbachev, the new—and by Soviet standards relatively young—head of the Communist Party who seized power in the USSR in 1985, had the courage and far-sightedness to draw the logical conclusion from the disaster. The whole world learned two Russian words, *perestroika,* "restructuring," and *glasnost,* "openness." The aim was renewal of the Soviet Union and its principles of leadership, and the creation of an efficient economy, a modern state, and policies more oriented toward the needs of the people, to rejuvenate the whole country by the close of the century. In many respects he was successful. But like so many reformers of the past, once he loosened the reins of absolute authoritarian rule in order to modernize the system, Gorbachev lost control over the pace of developments. Just like Jacques Necker in 1789, who wanted to reform government finances in France and helped set off the French Revolution instead, Gorbachev attempted to reform the Soviet Union but ended by blowing it to bits.

The altered climate in the Soviet Union made itself felt throughout eastern Europe. Opposition groups such as Charta 77 in Czechoslovakia or Solidarity in Poland emerged into the open and discovered that their governments had grown hesitant to use the old repressive measures. Elsewhere, as in Hungary, the Communists in power—or at least some of them—discovered they had liberal, pluralistic inclinations and began copying Gorbachev's reforms. The satellite countries of eastern Europe pulled away from the Soviet Union one after another, with Poland taking the lead. The rapidity of these developments was connected with the medium in which they occurred: For the first time a revolution took place not mainly in the streets but on television. The coverage of demonstrations in Prague looked just like the images from Dresden or Warsaw, but this was because people in Prague had seen the pictures of the Dresden demonstrations on their television sets, just as people in Dresden had previously seen the broadcasts from Warsaw.

Events provided the material; images created the objects they depicted; the revolution proceeded through television; and everything else simply occurred as a result. This is why the upheavals progressed with such extraordinary speed, and why—in great contrast to earlier revolutions—there was no bloodshed at all. The demonstrators occupied not the centers of power but prime time.

For a few months it appeared as if the GDR might withstand the tide, an island in the storm, despite the seething discontent in the population. Erich Honecker and his ruling cadre were not the only ones convinced of this. Honecker, blind to all the signs that the Soviet Union was collapsing, believed weaklings and traitors were at work in Moscow. But West Germans also observed the mounting unrest among the inhabitants of the GDR with more concern than hope. Hardly anyone could imagine that the Soviet Union would let its western outpost go, and many recalled the pictures of the June 1953 uprising in East Berlin. People were aware, too, that Egon Krenz, a leading member of the East German politburo, had just been in China and congratulated leaders there on the massacre of demonstrators in Tiananmen Square. Something similar might have been in the offing in Leipzig or Berlin.

Those who feared the SED leaders were capable of it would not have misjudged them; the misjudgment lay in the speculations about Soviet interests. Gorbachev realized perfectly well that with its very German, pig-headed dogmatism the SED was digging its own grave. Furthermore, connections between the Soviet Union and the "Western Group of Soviet Forces" in the GDR had been interrupted since Poland had broken out of formation. The Soviet leadership had no choice but to pull back and consolidate its front lines. The Soviet Union was preparing to withdraw into its inner sanctum, to try to come to grips with its own destructive internal contradictions; it would release the countries on its western perimeter to Europe, on the assumption that, rich as it was, the West would come to the rescue of the eastern European economies and would also give the Soviet Union credit for the mode of its withdrawal.

When in the fall of 1989 the cry went up from demonstrators in the hundreds of thousands, "We are the people"—to be transformed soon thereafter into "We are one people"—unnerved security officials turned to the Soviet ambassador in the GDR to demand military backing in suppressing the protests. The unthinkable happened. The Russians turned them down, and that spelled the end for

SED rule. The death-blow to the regime came from its Hungarian comrades, who opened their western border to the swelling tide of fleeing East Germans. What options remained to the men around Honecker? On the evening of November 9, 1989, they opened the crossing points in the Berlin Wall. The unification of the two German states was inevitable, and was accomplished within less than a year.

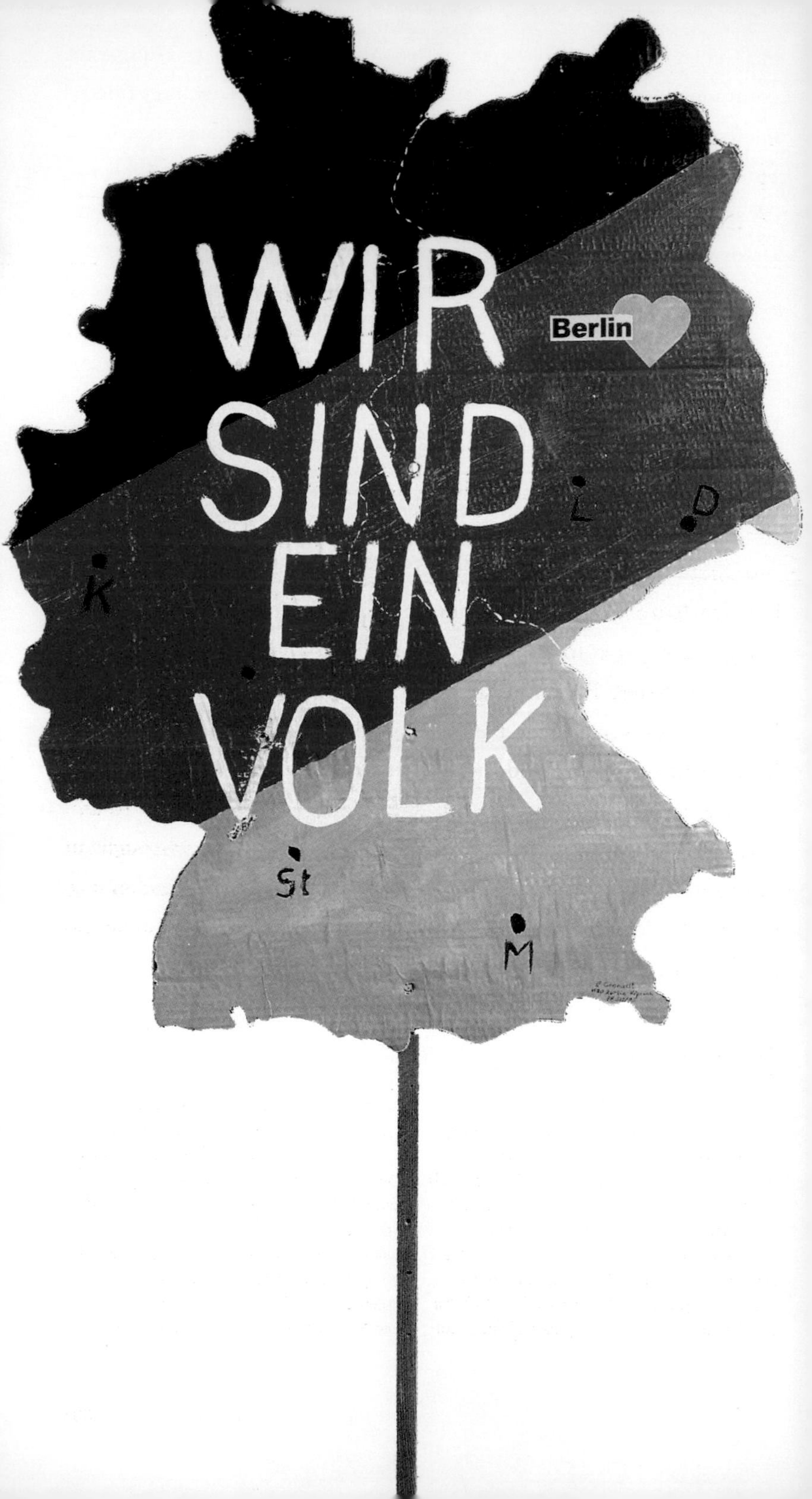
WIR
SIND
EIN
VOLK
Berlin
K
L
D
St
M

14

Epilogue: What Is the German's Fatherland?

Since the Wall has come down, anyone familiar with Berlin who takes a walk from the *Reichstag* to the old Prussian legislature must be prepared for a strange sight. There used to be a narrow but clearly marked path to follow. It was very simple—you just went straight along next to the Wall. Now the Wall is gone, and as you walk from the Pariser Platz through the Potsdamer Platz to the Leipziger Platz, you are surrounded by a surrealistic dream landscape: a wasteland on all sides, here and there the odd building still standing amid ruins and rubble, and under your feet the old tunnels leading to and from Hitler's bunker. The armada of construction cranes brought in to raise a new city center in the sandy soil of the Mark Brandenburg only reinforces the impression of a vast gaping space; there is as yet no beaten path, no sign pointing the way.

We Are One People
(hand-painted cardboard sign, fall 1989)

In early November 1989 people took to the streets in the hundreds of thousands in Leipzig, Dresden, and East Berlin. The early shouts of "No violence!" were soon drowned out by calls of "We are the people!" The latter slogan still addressed the aims of reform within the German Democratic Republic and abolition of the SED dictatorship, but after the border to the West was opened on November 9, 1989, the call shifted to "We are one people!" The great majority of the East German population no longer wished for an "altered" GDR but for unity instead. Many of them favored unification in the hopes that it would quickly bring their standard of living up to Western levels, while others feared that if they did not act swiftly, changes in the Soviet Union might slam shut the existing window of opportunity. The pressures created by East Germans' expectations hastened the reunification process considerably.

The new open space in the center of Berlin has certain similarities with the intellectual landscape to which Germans have found themselves suddenly transported. Only now do we realize how snug and comfortable life was in our postwar world, which seemed so stable. Our intellectual debates on the past and future of Germany and Europe took place in a political constellation where the only real change came from the Third World. In the northern half of the globe the two superpowers held one another in check like two scorpions trapped in a bottle, each immobilized by the presence of the other. And in between them lay the two Germanys, paralyzed twice over, first because they were stuck on the front lines of the Cold War, and second because they were historically responsible for the situation having arisen at all. Germany had been the reason the postwar order took the shape it did.

This location offered special perspectives on the German past and the future. The history of the German nation state had ended in shock and shame. For one group, the future lay in an idealistic dream of Europe that often bore little resemblance to the actual European Community, and for another group it lay in a romantic idyll of regions and homelands. A patriotism based on the constitution of the Federal Republic, which might replace the traditional ties to the nation, remained a cold entity in the heads of a few thoughtful people. For forty years, throughout all the disputes over the German past, widespread agreement existed on one point: The Germans' nation state was a model that had been tested by history and rejected as unworkable.

This has changed radically—and also so abruptly and so unexpectedly that we have only just begun to digest the implications. With the transformation of Europe, the Germans—of all people—have now been given a second chance to found a nation state. Although for decades the official policy was to insist on reunification as a goal, the rhetoric was bombastic and hollow; no one had mapped out a new German government and few people really wanted one, with the result that the Germans have found themselves in an open field, much like the people walking above Hitler's bunker in the center of Berlin. One obvious approach in such an unforeseen situation is to take the experience of history as a guide. The historical parallel suggests itself immediately, in terms both of the fluidity of Europe's future and the renewed unification of German lands in the center of the Continent. The return of the nineteenth century, it would seem, is the order of the day, or to put it more precisely, a repeat of the constellation that existed immediately after the collapse of the Napoleonic empire, before the balance of power in Europe was fixed anew by the Congress of Vienna.

Back then the idea of a German nation grew out of a confrontation with French nationalism and spread through the German-speaking territories of central Europe; in the heady atmosphere of the Wars of Liberation it became a palpable reality, something people could experience directly, and from there to the wish for a modern nation state such as the French and British possessed was only a step. This kind of state failed to materialize, however; again and again it seemed within grasp, only to recede as Prussia and Austria battled for hegemony, as the principalities and their rulers jealously clung to their privileges, and as the other nations of Europe did their best to head it off.

And over and above this there remained the problem referred to as the "German question": How would this Germany be constituted, where would its borders be drawn, what role would it play in Europe, with what tasks would it be entrusted? No clarity existed on any of these points. "Small Germany," an alliance of territorial princes founded with the aid of Prussian bayonets in 1871, was achieved almost by accident, primarily as a result of temporary disharmony in the Concert of Europe, when the two great powers on the perimeter, Britain and Russia, remained hostile in the aftermath of the Crimean War. No one could seriously claim that the path to German unity was foreordained.

Have we today come full circle? Do we find ourselves once again with the collapse of a system of dual hegemony behind us, and before us the uncertain prospect of a new and prominent role for Germans in a reordered Europe? Has a constellation arisen once more in which Germany's national ambitions can be fulfilled only at the expense of its European neighbors? And is it once again the nation's thinkers, the philosophers and above all the historians, who are preparing to justify such a solo flight on the basis of the past, creating myths to foster a fatal new belief in a special German role? Is German history a cycle of endless repetition?

If this were so, then those people would be right who are now inclined to project the hopes, frustrations, failed attempts, and cataclysms of the past century of German history into the future, and who derive their bleak prognoses from the catastrophic course of the first German nation state. We know it well, the old fear of the abiding German penchant for exaggerated, aggressive nationalism, an apparently unalterable feature of the national character.

But this fear is unfounded. The times in which Germans followed a separate path or thought they had a special role to play are over. A number of powerful historical continuities have come to an abrupt end—not for the first time in German history—eliminating the conditions that darkened German political culture and gave rise to the destructive, neurotically intensified nationalism of the nineteenth century and first half of our own.

The present in Germany differs from the past in at least four fundamental respects:

1. For the first time in history, the German nation state is "fulfilled in the present," as Ernest Renan said with reference to France. Nietzsche once observed, "The Germans are from the day before yesterday and the day after tomorrow—as yet they have no today." This was so in his day because from the time the idea of a nation state was born at the beginning of the nineteenth century, the nation and the state were always two different things. The early nationalists dreamed that they might recreate the medieval empire, a vast territory including Bohemia and northern Italy, but led by Germans. Later, many people re-

garded Bismarck's Small German state as only a down payment on a Great German empire, which they would own in the fullness of time. The Weimar Republic was torn apart in a struggle to undo the Treaty of Versailles and restore the pre-1919 eastern border, while the partial nation that was the Federal Republic declared it a political imperative to reestablish the frontiers of 1937.

In other words, the form of the state at any given moment was never enough; it was always just a provisional solution, a way station en route to a utopia that could be attained either through force or not at all. This was why the expression of German nationalism and the search for identity took their particular neurotic forms. That phase of German history is now over. As of October 3, 1990, the Federal Republic of Germany is the only conceivable form that a state for the German nation could take; it has no legitimate competition whatever in the minds of its citizens. For the first time, the question once posed by Ernst Moritz Arndt—"What is the German's fatherland?"—now has an unambiguous and lasting answer.

2. For the first time in their history Germans can have a full measure of both unity and freedom. Throughout the modern period this never appeared possible; it always seemed that if they could achieve unity, then they could have only a crippled form of freedom, or vice versa. According to the Treaty on German Unity of 1990, the preamble of the Basic Law will be altered, and the sentence that calls on the people to complete the unity and freedom of Germany will be replaced by one that reads, "This Basic Law is hereby valid for the entire German people."

This means that the old discussion over whether the identity of Germans is determined by national tradition or commitment to a constitution—a discussion that has lasted from the *Vormärz* to the recent *Historikerstreit* (historians' debate)—has been resolved. From now on the German nation state will be the structure created by the democratic institutions of the Basic Law. The two have become identical.

3. For the first time in their history the Germans have formed a union not over the opposition of their neighbors but with their consent. The newly reunified Germany is no longer perceived as a threat to the peace of Europe. Certainly people will remember the dark eras of the past, and some fears prompted by the concentration of population and economic might in the center of the Continent are understandable. Nevertheless, Germany is accepted as a necessary part of the European system, even as a future major power.

The reason is clear: Germany has been integrated into several economic, military, and political treaty organizations, and this integration cannot be reversed. A further conclusion is obvious: It is in the interests of both Germany and Europe to promote European unification, so that a constellation never again arises in which Germany's power can became an unpredictable force in the community of nations.

4. For the first time in its history the German nation state is irrevocably tied to the West. The revolution in the GDR demonstrated to the entire world that the people of East Germany desired to share not only in the West's economic order but also its political culture. This is new; until now the political culture of Germany was characterized by its divisions. The country lay on both sides of the Roman *limes,* the limits of the Roman Empire, and on both sides of two further historical dividing lines, the Main and Elbe rivers. It belonged both to the Latinized West with its Renaissance and Enlightenment traditions, and to the more recent German-Slavic East.

The political achievements of the modern era—popular sovereignty, parliamentary government, human rights—belonged to the West, but the West also came to Germany as an enemy, in the form of Napoleon. This had profound consequences, for Germany developed its national identity precisely in its struggle against the "Corsican monster," against France and the West. As a result, a tendency existed for vehement antagonism toward the West to surface in all German crises when patriotic feelings were aroused, along with a corresponding rejection, as might be expected, of Western political culture with all its attendant institutions and norms.

Two recent success stories, German integration into the Western alliances following World War II and the "economic miracle," have in fact made Germany a part of the West. This is evinced not only by the substantial stability of its democratic institutions but also the unself-consciousness with which Germans have adopted Western culture, particularly the Anglo-American variety, down to its most trivial aspects. Today those groups in Germany who reject the institutions and culture of Western parliamentary democracy, cherishing dreams of an alternative political, cultural, or economic path, represent a minority without the slightest prospects of political success.

All of these facts support the assumption that the present situation is entirely new to German history, thus not only permitting but in fact requiring us to reflect anew on what the term "nation" means in the context of German and European history and for the future. It has become clearer in retrospect that postwar West Germans as a rule misjudged the value of the modern nation state as it emerged in the late eighteenth century from the American and French revolutions. This is hardly surprising, given that the experiment of the first German nation state from Bismarck to Hitler had gone so catastrophically wrong. But it is also true that West Germans' pride in having put the nation state behind them—an achievement they felt placed them some distance ahead of their neighbors on the road to a united Europe—had a certain similarity to sour grapes.

Now Germans have it back again, the nation state, even though establishing it in people's minds will demand a great deal of time and patience. But it is precisely here that the necessity for such a state becomes evident, for it is only through national solidarity, through people's sense of nationhood, that it will be possible to make some headway in the foreseeable future against the deep internal dislocations Germany has experienced. Does not a glance at Germany's neighbors to the north and west prove that from the nineteenth century onward the nation state, and only the nation state, has proved a stable repository for lasting democratic institutions? The valedictions to the nation state were premature. As long as no corresponding institutions legitimated by democratic elections are available on a European level, there is no alternative to it in sight, and even after a European government is created, a number of governmental tasks will still have to be performed at the national level. The nation states of the West have altered in the course of the past 150 years, losing some of their sovereignty and autonomy as well as their claim on the sole loyalty of their citizens. But while the nation state has lost in importance, it has by no means become superfluous.

The second founding of a whole German state has taken place under far more auspicious circumstances than the first; it justifies optimism that this time Germany's ties to Europe will hold it steady and allow it to settle gradually into a normal position among the countries of the West. This does not guarantee that no economic or political crises lie in store, which could expose serious internal divisions and occasion sharp debate. But the signs are increasing that such debates will be less agonizing and extreme than in the past, and in particular that antidemocratic forces can reckon on far less support than in previous crises.

Now that the most important causes of disturbance and unhealthiness in central European culture and politics have either disappeared or declined in influence, the prospect exists not only for stable democratic institutions but also for a calmer and more civil tone in the discussion of public issues, in a Germany that is a Western nation like any other. The "German question," long the cause of so much disquiet among Germans and other nations alike, has been answered: We now know what Germany is, and what it can and should be.

Suggested Reading

Middle Ages

Blumenthal, Uta-Renata. *The Investiture Controversy: Church and Monarchy from the Ninth to the Twelfth Century.* Philadelphia, 1988.

Dollinger, Philipp. *The German Hansa.* Stanford, 1970.

Ennen, Edith. *The Medieval Town.* Amsterdam, 1979.

Fuhrmann, Horst. *Germany in the High Middle Ages, ca. 1050–1200.* Cambridge, 1986.

Geary, Patrick J. *Before France and Germany: The Creation and Transformation of the Merovingian World.* New York, 1988.

Haverkamp, Alfred. *Medieval Germany, 1056–1273.* 3d ed. Oxford, 1992.

Leuschner, Joachim. *Germany in the Late Middle Ages.* Amsterdam, 1980.

Leyser, Karl J. *Rule and Conflict in an Early Medieval Society: Ottonian Saxony.* Bloomington, 1979.

Reuter, Timothy. *Germany in the Early Middle Ages, c. 800–1056.* London, 1991.

Riché, Pierre. *Daily Life in the World of Charlemagne.* Philadelphia, 1988.

Rösener, Werner. *Peasants in the Middle Ages.* Urbana, 1992.

Early Modern History

Blackall, Eric A. *The Emergence of German as a Literary Language, 1700–1775.* 2nd ed. Ithaca, 1978.

Blanning, T. C. W. *Joseph II and Enlightened Despotism.* London, 1970.

Boyle, Nicholas. *Goethe: The Poet and His Age. Vol. 1: The Poetry of Desire, 1749–1790.* Oxford, 1991.

Bruford, Walter H. *Culture and Society in Classical Weimar, 1775–1806.* Cambridge, 1975.

Carsten, F. L. *The Origins of Prussia.* Greenwood, 1981.

Cole, Helena, Jane Caplan, and Hanna Schissler, eds. *The History of Women in Germany from Medieval Times to the Present: Bibliography of English-Language Publications.* Washington, DC, 1990.

Dickens, A. G. *The German Nation and Martin Luther.* New York, 1974.

Evans, R. J. W. *The Making of the Habsburg Monarchy, 1550–1700: An Interpretation.* Oxford, 1984.

Frevert, Ute. *Women in German History: From Bourgeois Emancipation to Sexual Liberation.* New York, 1989.

Fulbrook, Mary. *Piety and Policy: Religion and the Rise of Absolutism in England, Württemberg, and Prussia.* Cambridge, 1983.

Gagliardo, John G. *Germany under the Old Regime, 1600–1790.* London, 1991.

————— *Reich and Nation: The Holy Roman Empire as Idea and Reality, 1763–1806.* Bloomington, 1980.

Gulyga, Arsenii. *Immanuel Kant: His Life and Thought.* Boston, 1987.

Hsia, R. Po-chia. *Social Discipline in the Reformation: Central Europe, 1550–1750.* London, 1992.

Hughes, Michael. *Early Modern Germany, 1477–1806.* Philadelphia, 1992.

McClelland, Charles E. *State, Society, and University in Germany, 1700–1914.* Cambridge, 1980.

Reill, Peter Hanns. *The German Enlightenment and the Rise of Historicism.* Berkeley, 1975.

Robisheaux, Thomas. *Rural Society and the Search for Order in Early Modern Germany.* Cambridge, 1989.

Rosenberg, Hans. *Bureaucracy, Aristocracy, and Autocracy: The Prussian Experience, 1660–1815.* Boston, 1966.

Scribner, R. W. *The German Reformation.* Atlantic Highlands, NJ, 1986.

Sheehan, James J. *German History, 1770–1866.* New York, 1989.

Vierhaus, Rudolf. *Germany in the Age of Absolutism, 1648–1763.* New York, 1988.

Nineteenth Century

Berdahl, Robert M. *The Politics of the Prussian Nobility: The Development of a Conservative Ideology, 1770–1848.* Princeton, 1988.

Blackbourn, David, and Geoff Eley. *The Peculiarities of German History: Bourgeois Society and Politics in Nineteenth-Century Germany.* Oxford, 1984.

Blanning, T. C. W. *The French Revolution in Germany: Occupation and Resistance in the Rhineland, 1792–1802*. Oxford, 1983.

Breuilly, John, ed. *The State of Germany: The National Idea in the Making, Unmaking, and Remaking of a Modern Nation-State*. London, 1992.

Carr, William. *A History of Germany, 1815–1990*. 4th ed. London, 1991.

Chickering, Roger. *We Men Who Feel Most German: A Cultural Study of the Pan-German League, 1886–1914*. Boston, 1984.

Craig, Gordon A. *The Germans*. 1982. New York, 1991.

———— *Germany, 1866–1945*. New York, 1978.

Eley, Geoff. *Reshaping the German Right: Radical Nationalism and Political Change after Bismarck*. Ann Arbor, 1991.

Epstein, Klaus. *The Genesis of German Conservatism*. Princeton, 1975.

Hardach, Karl. *The Political Economy of Germany in the Twentieth Century*. Berkeley, 1980.

Hohendahl, Peter Uwe. *Building a National Literature: The Case of Germany, 1830–1870*. Ithaca, 1989.

James, Harold. *A German Identity, 1770–1990*. New York, 1989.

Kitchen, Martin. *The Political Economy of Germany, 1815–1914*. London, 1978.

Mosse, George L. *The Nationalization of the Masses: Political Symbolism and Mass Movements in Germany from the Napoleonic Wars through the Third Reich*. Ithaca, 1991.

Pflanze, Otto. *Bismarck and the Development of Germany*. 3 vols. 2nd ed. Princeton, 1990.

Schorske, Carl E. *German Social Democracy, 1905–1917: The Development of the Great Schism*. Cambridge, MA, 1983.

Schulze, Hagen. *The Course of German Nationalism: From Frederick the Great to Bismarck, 1763–1867*. Cambridge, 1991.

Sheehan, James J. *German History, 1770–1866*. New York, 1989.

Sperber, Jonathan. *Rhineland Radicals: The Democratic Movement and the Revolution of 1848–1849*. Princeton, 1991.

Wehler, Hans-Ulrich. *The German Empire, 1871–1918*. 1985. Leamington Spa, 1989.

Ziolkowski, Theodore. *German Romanticism and Its Institutions*. Princeton, 1990.

Twentieth Century

Breitman, Richard. *German Socialism and Weimar Democracy*. Chapel Hill, 1981.

Carsten, F. L. *The Reichswehr and Politics, 1918–1933*. Berkeley, 1973.

Fritzsche, Peter. *Rehearsals for Fascism: Populism and Political Mobilization in Weimar Germany*. New York, 1990.

Fulbrook, Mary. *The Divided Nation: A History of Germany, 1918–1990*. New York, 1992.

Gay, Peter. *Weimar Culture: The Outsider as Insider*. Westport, 1981.

James, Harold. *The German Slump: Politics and Economics, 1924–1936*. Oxford, 1986.

Jarausch, Konrad H. *The Enigmatic Chancellor: Bethmann Hollweg and the Hubris of Imperial Germany*. New Haven, 1973.

Jones, Larry Eugene. *German Liberalism and the Dissolution of the Weimar Party System, 1918–1933*. Chapel Hill, 1988.

Kolb, Eberhard. *The Weimar Republic*. London, 1988.

Laqueur, Walter. *Weimar: A Cultural History, 1918–1933*. New York, 1980.

Mosse, George L. *The Crisis of German Ideology: Intellectual Origins of the Third Reich*. New York, 1981.

Ringer, Fritz K. *The Decline of the German Mandarins: The German Academic Community, 1890–1933*. Hanover, 1990.

Stern, Fritz. *The Politics of Cultural Despair: A Study in the Rise of the Germanic Ideology*. Berkeley, 1974.

National Socialism

Barkai, Avraham. *From Boycott to Annihilation: The Economic Struggle of German Jews, 1933–1943*. Hanover, 1989.

Bartov, Omer. *Hitler's Army: Soldiers, Nazis, and War in the Third Reich*. New York, 1991.

Bracher, Karl Dietrich. *The German Dictatorship: The Origins, Structure, and Effects of National Socialism*. Harmondsworth, 1980.

Broszat, Martin. *Hitler and the Collapse of Weimar Germany*. Leamington Spa, 1987.

Browning, Christopher R. *Ordinary Men: Reserve Police Battalion 101 and the Final Solution in Poland*. New York, 1992.

Hoffmann, Peter. *The History of the German Resistance, 1933–1945*. 1977. Cambridge, MA, 1979.

Jäckel, Eberhard. *Hitler's Worldview: A Blueprint for Power*. Cambridge, MA, 1981.

Kater, Michael H. *The Nazi Party: A Social Profile of Members and Leaders, 1919–1945*. Cambridge, MA, 1985.

Kershaw, Ian. *The "Hitler Myth": Image and Reality in the Third Reich.* Oxford, 1987.

Schleunes, Karl A. *The Twisted Road to Auschwitz: Nazi Policy toward German Jews, 1933–1939.* Urbana, 1990.

Turner, Henry A. *Hitler's Thirty Days to Power.* 1933. New York, 1996.

Weinberg, Gerhard L. *The Foreign Policy of Hitler's Germany. Vol. 2: Starting World War II, 1937–1939.* Chicago, 1980.

———— *The Foreign Policy of Hitler's Germany. Vol. I: Diplomatic Revolution in Europe, 1933–36.* Chicago, 1983.

After 1945

Bark, Dennis L., and David R. Gress. *A History of West Germany. Vol. I: From Shadow to Substance, 1945–1963. Vol.2: Democracy and Its Discontents, 1963–1991.* Oxford, 1989.

Braun, Hans-Joachim. *The German Economy in the Twentieth Century.* London, 1990.

Childs, David. *The GDR: Moscow's German Ally.* 2nd ed. Boston, 1988.

Fulbrook, Mary. *Anatomy of a Dictatorship: Inside the GDR, 1949–1989.* Oxford, 1995.

Gedmin, Jeffrey. *The Hidden Land: Gorbachev and the Collapse of East Germany.* Washington, DC, 1992.

Gimbel, John. *The American Occupation of Germany: Politics and the Military, 1945–1949.* Stanford, 1968.

Merrit, Anna J., and Richard L. Merrit, comp. *Politics, Economics, and Society in the Two Germanies, 1945–75: A Bibliography of English-Language Works.* Urbana, 1978.

Pond, Elizabeth. *After the Wall: American Policy toward Germany.* New York, 1990.

Turner, Henry Ashby, Jr. *Germany from Partition to Reunification.* Rev. ed. New Haven, 1992.

Credits

Works of Art and Photographs

All reproductions courtesy of the German Historical Museum (Deutsches Historisches Museum) in Berlin, with these exceptions: stained glass window with portrait of Charlemagne from the Strasbourg Cathedral, courtesy of Musée de l'Œuvre Notre-Dame, Strasbourg; portrait of Otto III, courtesy of the Bavarian State Library (Bayerische Staatsbibliothek), Munich; fresco in Church of the Four Crowned Saints, Rome, courtesy of Bildarchiv Foto Marburg; engraving of Frederick Barbarossa, courtesy of Municipal Museum of Munich (Münchner Stadtmuseum); manuscript illustration of Hansa ships, courtesy of Archive for Art and History (Archiv für Kunst und Geschichte), Berlin.

Maps

"Denominational Divisions in Germany and Central Europe in 1555," after F.-J. Schütz, *Geschichte: Dauer und Wandel von der Antike bis zum Zeitalter des Absolutismus* (Frankfurt), p. 284; "Development of Railroads in Central Europe up to 1866," after H. Lutz, *Zwischen Habsburg und Preußen,* p. 329; "Jews Killed in Europe," after H.-U. Thamer, *Verführung und Gewalt,* p. 707; "Concentration Camps in the Third Reich," after H.-U. Thamer, *Verführung und Gewalt,* p. 690. All maps drawn by Kartographie Huber, Munich.

Tables and Charts

"The Founding of Cities and Towns in Central Europe: Development from 1150 to 1950," after H. Stoob, *Forschungen zum Städtewesen in Europa,* vol. 1 (Cologne: 1970), p. 21; "The Population of Germany West of the Elbe River from 600 to 1800," after F.-W. Henning, *Das vorindustrielle Deutschland* (Paderborn, 1974), p. 19; "Percentage of the Estates in the Total Population of Germany and Europe in 1500 and 1800," after H. Möller, *Fürstenstaat oder Bürgernation: Deutschland 1764 bis 1815* (Berlin, 1989), p. 100; "Average Diet from 1800 to 1850," after F.-W. Henning, *Die Industrialisierung in Deutschland 1800 bis 1914* (Paderborn, 1973), p. 53; "Number of Bookstores in Cities of the German Confederation," after H. Lutz, *Zwischen Habsburg und Preußen: Deutschland 1815–1866* (Berlin, 1985), p. 156; "Numbers of German Emigrants from 1820 to 1913," after Ploetz, *Raum und Bevölkerung in der Weltgeschichte,* part III (Würzburg, 1958), pp. 162, 226; "Urban Population Growth in the Nineteenth Century," after W. Woytinsky, *Die Welt in Zahlen,* vol. 1 (Berlin, 1925), pp. 132–133; "Production of Coal and Pig Iron, 1800–1913," from E. J. Hobsbawm, *Industrie und Empire: Britische Wirtschaftsgeschichte ab 1750* (Frankfurt, 1969), p. 169; "The Price of Bread, 1919–1924," from R. Berg, *Grundkurs deutsche Geschichte: Ein Lehr-und Arbeitsbuch für die Kollegstufe in Bayern,* vol. 2, 2nd ed. (Frankfurt, 1988), p. 58; "Net National Product per Inhabitant of the German Empire and the Federal Republic of Germany, 1850–1975," from H. Schulze, *Weimar: Deutschland 1917–1933* (Berlin, 1982), p. 42; "Growth of Nazi Party Membership, 1919–1945," from H.-U. Thamer, *Verführung und Gewalt: Deutschland 1933–1945* (Berlin, 1986), p. 576.

Index